HANDBOOK
of
Silicone
Rubber
FABRICATION

HANDBOOK
of
Silicone Rubber
FABRICATION

Wilfred Lynch
Consulting Engineer

VNR **VAN NOSTRAND REINHOLD COMPANY**
NEW YORK   CINCINNATI   ATLANTA   DALLAS   SAN FRANCISCO
LONDON   TORONTO   MELBOURNE

Van Nostrand Reinhold Company Regional Offices:
New York Cincinnati Atlanta Dallas San Francisco

Van Nostrand Reinhold Company International Offices:
London Toronto Melbourne

Library of Congress Catalog Card Number: 77-10986
ISBN: 0-442-24962-4

Manufactured in the United States of America

Published by Van Nostrand Reinhold Company
450 West 33rd Street, New York. N.Y. 10001

Published simultaneously in Canada by Van Nostrand Reinhold Ltd.

15 14 13 12 11 10 9 8 7 6 5 4 3 2 1

Library of Congress Cataloging in Publication Data

Lynch, Wilfred.
   Handbook of silicone rubber fabrication.

   Includes bibliographical references and index.
   1. Silicone rubber. I. Title.
TS1927. S55L95   678′.72   77-10986
ISBN 0-442-24962-4

This book is dedicated

To J. Harry DuBois and Sven K. Moxness for
their leadership and inspiration.

PREFACE

The fabrication of silicone rubber has grown rapidly in volume and importance during the roughly thirty years since its commercial development began. Materials and methods have changed considerably. This book has been directed toward the need for a source of general information on fabrication methods commonly used in the silicones industry today.

Writing about the broad field of fabrication requires help from many sources. It is impossible to acknowledge all of these. However, special mention should go to James E. Mohrhauser, President of Moxness Products, Inc., for allowing me access to much of the process equipment and records of his company and to David Sanders, President of Medical Engineering Corporation, for his cooperation, without which the time spent on this book would have been impossible. I would also like to thank the following people: Richard N. Thomson of Precision Rubbers, Leicestershire, England; Dr. Frederick H. Sexsmith of Hughson Chemicals, Erie, Pa.; Robert D. Walker and Charles E. Kind of Moxness Products of Racine, Wisconsin; E. M. Jeram, Silicones Department, General Electric, Waterford, New York; David K. Ratliff of Amphenol Connector, Broadview, Illinois; Henry M. Gajewski and J. Donohue of Travenol Laboratories, Inc., Morton Grove, Illinois; and many others who were willing to take the time to supply illustrations and data. The numerous illustrations should appeal to students and professionals not directly involved in fabrication as well as experts in the field. Many of the photographs were taken by Paul G. Flagg of Racine, Wisconsin, and most of the diagrams were produced by Rubin Hoffman of Clintonville, Wisconsin.

WILFRED LYNCH

CONTENTS

INTRODUCTION

The main thrust of this book is to describe the methods currently in use for the fabrication of silicone rubber and to tie these in with some of the more commercially important and interesting applications. Consequently, silicone chemistry is covered in a rather elementary fashion.

There are a number of excellent texts covering the chemistry of silicones[1] available to the reader who would like to study this subject in depth. Also, much of the important literature concerning silicones appears in the patents, and these are referred to at appropriate points in the text.

To conform to the gradual move to metrics in the U.S., metric equivalents are given throughout the text. The equivalents are often rounded out numbers, especially where ranges are given. Handy conversion tables are also included for those using the book as an engineering reference.

"Silicones" is the popular term used to describe a whole family of organo-silicon compounds based on a backbone or molecular chain of alternate silicon and oxygen atoms. Depending on the length of the chain and the organic groups attached to the silicon atoms, these compounds range all the way from water thin through heavy oil-like fluids to greases, gels, rubbers, and solid resins.

Silicones do not occur in nature. They are derived from silica or quartz, the most common mineral in the earth's crust. Although it was over one hundred years ago that pioneer chemists such as Friedl and Crafts[2] and Wöhler[3] experimented in this area, it was not until the middle 1940s that the silicones were introduced on a limited scale as commercial products. In the short interval of thirty years the silicones have found applications in almost every major industry and have become well over a billion dollar industry. The unique characteristics of these materials include their outstanding resistance to aging and weathering, their retention of desirable physical characteristics over a wide temperature range (700F° or 390C°), and their unusual surface properties, particularly water repellency.

During the 1930s, Dr. J. Franklin Hyde, while working for the Corning Glass Works, had developed the first practical silicone compound, a resin for use as an electrical insulating varnish. Because of their heat resistance, the silicones appeared to be the ideal material to be used in conjunction with woven glass tapes which the Corning Glass Works had introduced for electrical applications.

There was considerable organic chemistry involved in the production of silicones. Because of the lack of experience in this field, the Corning Glass Works joined hands with the Dow Chemical Company to form a joint venture to produce silicone products called the Dow Corning Corporation. In 1944 Dow Corning started to produce silicone fluids and dielectric greases solely for military use. The fluids, because of their relatively constant viscosity over a wide temperature range, were used as damping fluids in sensitive aircraft instruments. They were also used as anti-foam agents in the lubricating oils of aircraft engines. The greases were used as a moisture-proof sealing compound in the spark plug wells of aircraft engines, retaining their electrical insulating properties and consistency whether at hottest engine temperatures or at sub-zero.

During the 1930s, research on silicone chemistry was also being carried out in the research laboratories of the General Electric Company and it was there that Dr. Eugene G. Rochow[4] discovered the "Direct Process" for the production of chlorosilanes which was to lead to the economical production of silicones. This was followed by the first patent application for silicone rubber by M. C. Agens,[5] also of General Electric. The first silicone rubbers sacrificed physical strength and elongation to achieve resistance to extreme temperatures. Many developments have produced a wide range of formulations since that time and silicone rubbers have become the most versatile of all the elastomers.

The first step in the production of the silicones involves the reduction of silica (SiO_2) to silicon (Si) in an electric arc furnace. The silicon is then converted to methylchlorosilanes by a direct process reaction with methyl chloride in the presence of copper as a catalyst.

$$CH_3Cl + Si \longrightarrow \begin{cases} (CH_3)_3 SiCl & \text{small amounts} \\ (CH_3)_2 SiCl_2 & \text{+ of other} \\ CH_3 SiCl_3 & \text{products} \end{cases}$$

The chlorosilanes react with water. Trimethyl chlorosilane is mono-functional, it reacts with water to form a dimer:

$$(CH_3)_3 SiCl + H_2O \longrightarrow (CH_3)_3 SiOH + HCl$$
trimethylsilanol

$$(CH_3)_3 SiO{:}H + HO{:}Si(CH_3)_3 \longrightarrow CH_3-\underset{\underset{CH_3}{|}}{\overset{\overset{CH_3}{|}}{Si}}-O-\underset{\underset{CH_3}{|}}{\overset{\overset{CH_3}{|}}{Si}}-CH_3 + H_2O$$

It can also react with the surface of various materials such as fabrics, imparting water repellancy and other properties. However, in the control of silicone polymer molecular weight, it is used as an end blocking unit.

Dimethyl chlorosilane is difunctional and reacts with water to form siloxane polymers:

$$(CH_3)_2 SiCl_2 + 2H_2O \longrightarrow (CH_3)_2 Si(OH)_2 + 2HCl$$

$$HO-\underset{\underset{CH_3}{|}}{\overset{\overset{CH_3}{|}}{Si}}-O{:}H + HO{:}-\underset{\underset{CH_3}{|}}{\overset{\overset{CH_3}{|}}{Si}}-O{:}H + HO{:}-\underset{\underset{CH_3}{|}}{\overset{\overset{CH_3}{|}}{Si}}-OH \longrightarrow$$

$$\left[-\underset{\underset{CH_3}{|}}{\overset{\overset{CH_3}{|}}{Si}}-O-\underset{\underset{CH_3}{|}}{\overset{\overset{CH_3}{|}}{Si}}-O-\underset{\underset{CH_3}{|}}{\overset{\overset{CH_3}{|}}{Si}}-O \right]_n + H_2O$$

Polymerization continues until stopped by the addition of end blocking trimethyl units:

$$\begin{array}{ccccc}
CH_3 & CH_3 & & CH_3 \\
| & | & & | \\
-Si-O-Si-O\!:\!H + HO\!:\!-Si-CH_3 & \longrightarrow \\
| & | & & | \\
CH_3 & CH_3 & & CH_3
\end{array}$$

$$\begin{array}{ccc}
CH_3 & CH_3 & CH_3 \\
| & | & | \\
-Si-O-Si-O-Si-CH_3 + H_2O \\
| & | & | \\
CH_3 & CH_3 & CH_3
\end{array}$$

The lower molecular weight polymers are fluids. The higher molecular weight polymers are gums from which the viscoelastic rubbers are made through cross-linking mechanisms.

Methyltrichlorosilane is trifunctional and reacts with water to form oxygen cross-linked polymers which may be used as the basis for rigid resins.

$$2CH_3 SiCl_3 + 3H_2 O \longrightarrow 2CH_3 Si(OH)_3 + 3HCl$$

$$\begin{array}{cccc}
& CH_3 & & OH \\
& | & & | \\
HO-\ &Si-O\!:\!H\ HO\!:\!-\ &Si-OH \\
& | & & | \\
& O\,H & & OH \\
& O\!:\!H & & \\
& | & & \longrightarrow \\
OH-\ &Si-OH & \\
& | & \\
& CH_3 &
\end{array}$$

$$\begin{array}{ccccc}
CH_3 & CH_3 & CH_3 & CH_3 & O \\
| & | & | & | & | \\
-Si-O-Si-O-Si-O-Si-O-Si-O \\
| & | & | & | & | \\
CH_3 & O & CH_3 & O & CH_3 \\
CH_3 & | & CH_3 & | & CH_3 \\
| & | & | & | & | \\
-Si-O-Si-O-Si-O-Si-O-Si- \\
| & | & | & | & | \\
& CH_3 & O & CH_3 & \\
& CH_3 & | & CH_3 & \\
| & | & | & | & \\
-Si-O-Si-O-Si-O-Si- \\
| & | & | & | & \\
& & O & CH_3 &
\end{array}$$

The silicon-oxygen linkage in the silicone polymer chain

$$
\begin{array}{cccc}
\text{CH}_3 & \text{CH}_3 & \text{CH}_3 & \text{CH}_3 \\
| & | & | & | \\
-\!\text{Si}\!-\!\text{O}\!-\!\text{Si}\!-\!\text{O}\!-\!\text{Si}\!-\!\text{O}\!-\!\text{Si}\!-\!\text{O} \\
| & | & | & | \\
\text{CH}_3 & \text{CH}_3 & \text{CH}_3 & \text{CH}_3
\end{array}
$$

is the same strong Si—O—Si bond occurring in quartz, sand, and glass and which contributes the outstanding high temperature properties of the silicones and their resistance to oxidation by ozone, corona, and weathering. On the other hand, organic polymer chains such as occur in

$$
\begin{array}{ccccccc}
\text{H} & & \text{H} & \text{H} & \text{H} & & \text{H} \\
| & & | & | & | & & | \\
-\!\text{C}\!-\!\text{C}\!=\!\text{C}\!-\!\text{C}\!-\!\text{C}\!-\!\text{C}\!=\!\text{C}\!-\!\text{C} \\
| & | & & | & | & | \\
\text{H} & \text{CH}_3 & & \text{H} & \text{H} & \text{CH}_3
\end{array}
$$

organic rubber, often have double carbon bonds which are quickly cleaved by ozone, ultraviolet light, heat and other environmental conditions.

While methyl siloxane is the basis of silicone polymers, it has been found that by substituting other organic groups in very small ratios ($\frac{1}{10}$ of 1%) compared with the methyl groups, along the methyl siloxane polymer chain, desirable variations in properties may be obtained. The addition of phenyl groups improves the low temperature properties of silicones (to $-150°F$, $-100°C$, and lower), their resistance to radiation, and in the case of the gum stocks, contributes greater clarity. Phenylchlorosilanes can be produced using chlorobenzene in the "direct process":

$$
C_6H_5Cl + Si \xrightarrow[\Delta]{Cu} (C_6H_5)_2 SiCl_2, \; C_6H_5 SiCl_3 \text{ etc.}
$$

The desired proportion of the reactive phenylchlorosilane is then introduced into the polymerization process described on p. xiii.

The addition of vinyl groups improves the vulcanization characteristics and the compression set resistance of the vulcanizate,

$$
\begin{array}{cccc}
& & \text{H} \quad \text{A} & \\
& & | & \\
\text{CH}_3 & \text{CH}_3 & \text{C}\!=\!\text{CH}_2 & \text{CH}_3 \\
| & | & | & | \\
-\!\text{Si}\!-\!\text{O}\!-\!\text{Si}\!-\!\text{O}\!-\!\text{Si}\!-\!\!-\!\text{O}\!-\!\text{Si}\!-\!\text{CH}_3 \\
| & | & | & | \\
\text{CH}_3 & \text{CH}_3 & \text{CH}_3 & \text{CH}_3
\end{array}
$$

The double bond is the site of crosslinking (at A) and/or chain extension reactivity (at B)

$$-\overset{\overset{\displaystyle CH_3}{|}}{Si}-O-\overset{\overset{\displaystyle CH_3}{|}}{Si}-O-\overset{\overset{\displaystyle CH_3}{|}}{\underset{\underset{\displaystyle CH_3}{|}}{Si}}-\overset{\overset{\displaystyle H}{|}}{\underset{\underset{\displaystyle B}{}}{C}}=CH_2$$

Where a combination of properties is desired, both phenyl and vinyl groups may be substituted for methyl groups along the siloxane chain.

Superior resistance to many solvents is obtained through substitution of trifluoropropyl groups $(CF_3 CH_2 CH_2-)$ for most of the methyl groups along the siloxane chain. The family of polymers produced is known as the fluorosilicones.

Silicone fluids, because of their importance, should be of general interest even to the rubber specialist. A brief discussion of their applications would seem to be appropriate. As fluids, silicones are applied in a broad range of commercially important products, mainly because of their unusual surface activity. Most common are the dimethyl silicone fluids. Much of the dimethyl silicone fluid finds its way into furniture and car polishes of the aerosol emulsion "spray and wipe" type, emulsion cream, solvent wax dispersion and paste wax, including paste wax polish-cleaners. The addition of only 2 to 3.5% of silicone fluid in aerosol "spray and wipe" type polish produces a gleaming surface with improved depth. This results from the silicone acting as a lubricant for the randomly deposited wax crystallites, permitting them to be laid down and oriented into continuous films without hard rubbing. The resultant film does not smear and liquid spillage is easily wiped off because of the water repellency of silicones. The lower the viscosity of the silicone fluid used, the easier the wiping off and the drier the film—but also the lower the gloss. The higher viscosities give better gloss but there is more tendency to smear. Exhaustive tests have been run to show that the addition of silicones to polishes enhances the gloss and gives added durability to the finish without any degradation of the original surface.[6] The patent literature covering polishes is quite extensive.[7]

Glycol substituted methyl silicones are super wetting agents and are used in glass polishes and hard surface cleaners.

The dimethyl fluids are widely used as defoamers. Because of their extremely low surface tension (averaging 20 dynes per centimeter), as little as 1.34 ounces per thousand gallons (10 grams per thousand liters) rapidly breaks down and disperses a mountain of foam. Foaming during the preparation of industrial chemicals, cosmetics, foods, and drugs can lead to lost time and materials, lowered equipment capacity, and probably lower product quality. Due to the very small quantities of silicones needed, their inertness and physiological safety,[8,9,10,11,12] there is no concern of contamination or detraction of product properties. These same defoamers are used to treat cows with cholic and humans suffering from gas distress.* The foam control characteristics of certain silicone fluids makes them an indispensable ingredient for the production of even-cell structure in plastic foams. The polyurethane cushioning used for mattresses, vehicle seats, chairs and packaging is a good example of this.

The low surface tension combined with the "non-stick" characteristic of silicone fluids, leads to their wide use as release agents in the molding of rubber and plastics and in foundry molding. The undiluted fluids are sometimes used for "break-in" purposes but in normal operations they are used as water emulsions or solvent solutions. Water emulsions are usually preferred because they are more economical, odorless, and nonflammable. Solutions may be prepared with a wide choice of solvents. All the solvent grade hydrocarbons, both aliphatic and aromatic, such as petroleum naphthas, Stoddard solvent, toluene, xylenes, gasoline, and kerosene can be used and are the least expensive choices. In addition, the halogenated hydrocarbons, including chloroform, carbon tetrachloride, and trichloroethylene, are suitable solvents. These solvents are expensive but are nonflammable and are used where fire hazards exist and rigid safety rules must be observed. All solvents must be considered toxic and should be used only in well-ventilated areas.

Standard silicone mold release agents, because of their persistence and non-stick characteristics, cannot be used where plastics or rubber parts are being produced which must be painted after molding. The paint would not wet the molded surface. Specialty silicone fluids which give the same good release but allow painting of the molded product are available** for this purpose. Silicone mold release agents are easily applied by spraying or brushing. They spread evenly and rapidly into even the finest detail because of the low surface tension.

---

*Antacids containing Simethicone. (Simethicone is a Trademark of Dow Corning Corp.)
**SF-1080 by Silicone Product Div., General Electric.

They will not decompose at temperatures used in plastics or rubber processing and therefore will not cause smoke, objectionable odors, or react with the molding material. Reduced build-up on the mold cavity surface means less down time for mold cleaning and less mold cleaning means reduced mold wear. Silicone mold releases are not recommended for use with silicone rubbers or resins.

In foundry practice, release fluids similar to those for plastics and rubber are used in the production of shell molds. Shell molds are thin, porous walled precision molds for the casting of small and medium size metal castings. They are made by coating a hot metal pattern with foundry sand to which a thermosetting resin binder has been added. The length of time the hot pattern is in contact with the resin sand mixture determines the thickness of the shell wall. The porosity of the shell allows the casting material to gas freely, leading to sounder castings, and the light weight of the shell molds compared to the old sand flash type improves the opportunities for automation of the process. The use of silicones leads to a clean, reliable release. They will not carbonize at molding temperatures or build-up on the pattern surfaces.

Special silicone coatings are available for the treatment of ingot molds used in pouring stainless and other specialty alloy steels. Not only is sticking of the ingot essentially eliminated, but the surface quality of the ingot is greatly improved: molten metal splashes drop back into the melt rather than adhering to the walls of the mold. When mold walls are free of oxide-coated metal splashes, a greatly improved ingot surface quality is produced. Inclusions, pits, folds, scale, and other ingot surface defects are greatly reduced. Any scale that forms is less adherent and more easily removed. Ingot quality improvement reduces metal grinding losses and shortens ingot preparation time. The improved ingot surface quality, in some grades, allows reduction of the billet to desired size in the initial soaking heat without interrupting rolling to cool, grind, and reheat the billet. There is a reduction in cost of both material and labor for ingot preparation and billet processing.

A very small quantity (1% or less) of 30,000 cps dimethyl silicone fluid, when added to thermoplastic resins such as nylon, acetal, polystyrene, ABS, and polypropylene prior to molding, becomes a built-in mold release—eliminating the nuisance of periodic spraying or wiping of the molds. Substantial savings in part removal time and reduction in injection cycle time due to improved melt flow have been reported.[13] Tensile strength of the silicone treated plastics generally falls off 5 to 10%, but elongation to break is usually higher, therefore parts can be ejected over more severe undercuts than usual. Surface friction, wear properties, and mar resistance are also improved.

The incorporation of very small amounts of silicone fluid in certain sticky organic rubbers can improve their release both from the mill rolls and the molds.

Many household products whose performance is improved by the addition of silicone fluids are packaged in aerosol containers. The presence of silicone in each case improves the performance of the aerosol valve, helping to keep it clear and lubricated. Some of the aerosol packaged products which gain from the addition of silicones are: spray starch, fabric size, leather and textile water repellents, lube sprays for antisqueak or winter antifreeze use on rubber auto door gaskets, oven protectants, high temperature paints, shoe polishes, vinyl cleaner, baking and frying pan release, metal protective coatings, etc.

The silicone fluids are also characterized by high dielectric strength which is maintained over a wide range of temperatures and frequencies. They have high flash points, low vapor pressures, and are non-oxidizing. They are used as liquid dielectrics in pulse transformers and capacitors and as dielectric coolants for klystrons, magnetrons, etc.

Many personal care products benefit from the incorporation of small amounts of silicone fluids. In hand lotions and creams they act as emollients and provide a non-sticky, luxurious feel. They protect against waterborn irritants, such as harsh detergents and other household cleaning specialties. Despite their water repellency, silicone films allow natural skin transpiration. The lower viscosity fluids contribute the best feel but offer the lowest protection. Higher viscosity fluids (1000 cps) are required for maximum protection. The best compromise between feel and protection appears to be obtained with about 350 cps dimethyl fluid.

Where alcohol solubility is required, a methyl phenyl fluid should be used. In products where mineral oils and silicone fluids are to be blended, a methyl alkyl fluid may be used. Suntan lotions incorporating silicones resist washing off by either bathing or perspiration.

The ultra-violet screening agent should be miscible with the silicone fluid.

In hair sprays the silicones make the resin film more elastic, improving the feel of the hair without affecting the curl retention. An effective moisture barrier is provided against humid weather and sheen is improved.

Shampoos and rinses incorporating silicones provide excellent hair conditioning properties and result in less snarling because of the lubricity of the silicones on the hair.

Silicone fluids are also used in insect repellents, anti-perspirants and after shave lotions. In shaving creams they lessen razor drag.

As a concrete treatment, silicone fluids may be used as an admixture. They impart greater strength and freeze-thaw durability. On concrete highways and bridge decks they aid in resisting the effects of road oils and chemicals.

As a masonry surface treatment, silicones can be diluted with mineral spirits and brushed on to extend the life, reduce efflorescence, and act as a primer for masonry paints. Silicone fluids added to paints improve the flow and surface structure, reduce bubble formation, keep pigments from separating, and improve weather resistance under extremes of temperature, chemicals in the air, etc.

In automotive applications a silicone fluid is used in fan clutches for high performance. Silicones can also give outstanding performance as brake fluid. Because silicone fluids are compressible by as much as 17% of their volume, they can be used as shock-spring combinations in special vehicles.

The silane coupling agents should be of more than passing interest to the rubber or plastics specialist. They promote adhesion of mineral fillers to rubber and plastic polymers, greatly increasing the reinforcing contribution of the filler, even after prolonged exposure to moisture. The silanes, which may be represented by the general formula $R^1 Si (OR)_3$, are characterized by dual functionality. R^1 represents an organo-functional group which will react with the polymer (amino, mercapto, methacryloxy, and vinyl epoxy are most common). OR represents a hydrolyzable alkoxy group at the other end of the silane molecule. Moisture, which is normally on the surface of mineral fillers, hydrolyzes alkoxy groups to form silanols that react with the surface of the mineral filler particles, thus a bond is formed between the filler and the polymer. The most effective results are achieved by the use of less than 1% of the filler weight of silane. The silane may be added to the filler prior to its compounding with the polymer or it may be added during compounding. While silane coupling agents are most widely used in the production of glass reinforced plastics, there is a growing demand for them in high quality non-black, mineral-filled rubbers.

The thermosetting silicone resins are another interesting member of the silicone family. Trifunctional siloxanes, such as described on p. xiv, may be crosslinked to form a rigid, glass-like cured resin. Difunctional groups may be incorporated to give varying degrees of flexibility to the resin. The low molecular weight uncross-linked trifunctional siloxanes are solid at room temperature but become quite fluid at temperatures above 200°F (95°C), which makes them the ideal resin constituent for easy flowing, low pressure molding compounds.

Silicone molding compounds are preferred encapsulation materials for delicate electronic components such as semiconductor modules. They are supplied in convenient to handle granular form. They can be transfer molded around delicate wire connections without breaking them. They will cure to a rigid section and can be removed from the mold in $1\frac{1}{2}$ to 5 min. Transfer pressures may be as low as 200 psi (14 kg/cm^2) and mold temperatures from 310°F (155°C). The combination of excellent electrical properties, high heat distortion temperature, flame, thermal, and moisture resistance of the silicone molding compounds help produce high quality electronic devices with high standards of reliability.

The silicone resins can also be used as binders in the production of precision molded ceramic parts. When mixed with mineral fillers, such as asbestos, glass fibers, silica, quartz, or metal oxides, with a resin level of 5 to 20%, the resin contributes good flow of the mixture for compression or transfer molding. After a mold cure of 5 min or more at 300 to 350°F, the molding may be removed from the mold and ready for firing. During firing, the resin is reduced to silica and becomes part of the ceramic molding. There is very little weight loss and the surface detail and finish are outstanding.

The addition of silicone resin in paints and varnishes has been very successful where extreme service conditions are encountered. On boat hulls, large diesel engine exhaust stacks, and all types of outdoor applications, silicone resin modified alkyd finishes have proven to be durable for many years, even when exposed to salt, moisture, ultraviolet radiation, and great fluctuations in temperature. They resist yellowing and are easy to apply.

The most intriguing family of silicones, however, are the rubbers. Their versatility both of process and application, makes them interesting to anyone fabricating or using rubber products and that, after all, is what this book is about.

Rubber may be loosely defined as a material possessing forcible recovery from long range extension. It is known that this property is dependent on the molecular structure of the material and is largely independent of its chemistry. Any chemical structure which forms long, flexible, coil-like chains, can, when cross linked to a specific degree, exhibit rubbery properties. Since silicones are quite different from all other materials, silicone rubbers exhibit a unique combination of properties leading to their use in many applications where organic rubbers cannot perform satisfactorily.

The American Society for Testing and Materials has classified silicone rubbers (ASTM D 1418) in the following manner:

The letters MQ designate rubber produced from the simple dimethyl silicone polymer. MQ is preceded by the letter V when vinyl side groups are present (p. xv), P when there are phenyl groups and F for fluorine containing groups.

The ASTM designations will be used where possible in the text to avoid the confusion of the many product numbers listed by the raw material suppliers. General-purpose stocks will be found listed as MQ or VMQ, extreme low temperature stocks as PMQ or PVMQ, and fuel, oil, and solvent resistant stocks as FVMQ. The practice of separately classifying compounds as heat vulcanizing or room temperature vulcanizing (RTV) is followed in this book for convenience. However, it becomes increasingly difficult to make such a distinction as new interjacent compounds are developed. Some so-called RTV's are being hot molded today with very fast cycles on volume applications.

References

1. Rochow, Eugene G., *Introduction to the Chemistry of Silicones*, 2nd Edit. John Wiley & Sons, New York, 1951, Meals, R. N. and Lewis, F. M., *Silicones*, Van Nostrand Reinhold, New York, Noll, Walter, *Chemistry and Technology of Silicones*, Academic Press, New York, 1968.
2. Lewis, F. M., "The Science and Technology of Silicone Rubber," *Rubber Chemistry and Technology*, Vol. XXXV, 5 (Dec. 1962).
3. Smith, *Analysis of Silicones*, John Wiley & Sons, 1974.
4. U.S. Patent 2,380,995.
5. U.S. Patent 2,448, 756.
6. Thimineur, R. J., "Silicones, a Key Ingredient in Aerosol Furniture Polishes," *Aerosol Age* (Sept. 1970).
7. U.S. Patents   2,523,281   2,584,413   2,614,049
                  2,626,870   2,812,263   3,341,338
                  3,393,078   3,497,365   3,551,168
                  3,544,498   3,576,779   3,600,414
                  3,645,946   3,702,769
8. Carson, S., Weinberg, M. S., and Oser, B. L., "Safety Evaluation of Dow Corning ® 360 Fluid and Antifoam A," *Proceedings of the Scientific Section of the Toilet Goods Association*, No. 45, 8–19 (May 1966).
9. Kern, S. F. and Anderson, R. C., "Observations on the Toxicity of Methyl Silicone," *J. Am. Pharm. Assoc.*, **38**,(10), 575–576 (Oct. 1949).
10. Rowe, V. K., Spencer, H. C. and Bass, S. L., "Toxicological Studies on Certain Commercial Silicones," *J. Ind. Hygiene and Toxicology*, (1948), **30**, (6) 332–352.
11. Lehman, A. J., *Bulletin of the Association of Food and Drug Officials of the U. S.*, Vol. XIV, (3), 89 (July 1950).
12. Lehman, A. J., *Bulletin of the Association of Food and Drug Officials of the U. S.*, Vol. XV, (3), 86 (July 1951).
13. *Modern Plastics*, p. 70 (Mar. 1975).

HANDBOOK
of
Silicone
Rubber
FABRICATION

1 | THE UNIQUE PROPERTIES OF SILICONE RUBBER

SERVICE TEMPERATURE

The most outstanding characteristic of silicone rubber is the retention of its many desirable properties over the very wide temperature range of $-150°$ to $600°F$ ($-100°$ to $315°C$). There are applications which take advantage of these temperature extremes, e.g., door seals and outer switch seals, which must remain flexible at the low temperatures of the upper atmosphere on aerospace vehicles, or oven door seals which must withstand broiling temperatures. However, the most attractive feature is that at moderate operating temperatures silicone rubber offers unlimited life.

Defining the useful life of a rubber as the period of time during which it retains an elongation of at least 50%, it has been estimated[1] that silicone rubber has a useful life of up to 20 years at $250°F$ ($120°C$), or up to five years at $300°F$ ($150°C$). But intermittent exposure to the service temperatures would considerably prolong the useful life. Under the hood, automotive equipment can experience temperatures of $300°F$ ($150°C$) and higher. The useful life of the best organic rubbers such as EPDM or polyacrylic would be measured in days rather than years at such temperatures.[2]

MECHANICAL PROPERTIES

Rubbers behave so much differently than rigid materials that some conventional engineering terms have different connotations. To the rubber engineer, for example, *resilience* is a measure of rebound in-

1

stead of the usual strain-energy per unit volume. A highly resilient rubber can store more mechanical energy than any other common material. A rubber with good resiliency, for example, would be ideal as a golf ball material but not as practical for use in a shock mount.

The *ultimate tensile strength* of silicone rubbers, which ranges from a few hundred to about 1500 psi (105 kg/cm²), is not as meaningful as the *modulus*, which in rubber parlance is the stress required to produce a particular elongation. It is a measure of the material's stiffness. It is not a constant and therefore is not the same as Young's modulus for rigid materials. It is also much lower than Young's modulus. The stress is expressed in pounds per square inch (psi) or kilograms per square centimeter (kg/cm²).

The *ultimate elongation* of silicone rubber varies greatly, depending on the particular stock, how it has been processed and postcured. Certain compounds can produce elongation values of over 1000%.

Some silicone rubber vulcanizates, particularly high strength stocks, will demonstrate a great change in *modulus* as they are subjected to repeated stress cycling. This is described as the "Mullins effect," after the first investigator of this phenomenon.[3] Apparently, filler-polymer attachments (probably hydrogen bonds) are ruptured during stress and remain ruptured as long as the rubber specimen is flexed. These weak attachments then re-form when the specimen is at rest for some time. The time during which the material regains its original stiffness will decrease at elevated temperatures.

The values in Table 1-1 were observed when a test specimen of 70 Duro, VMQ was subjected to repeated cycling of 200% in an Instron testing machine. The specimen was cycled at the rate of 20 in./min.

Note that at about 20 cycles the rubber modulus has "leveled out" at approximately two-thirds of its original value. The same test specimen was then baked in an air circulating oven at 400°F (205°C) for 1 hr and retested. The results shown in Table 1-2 indicate the degree of modulus recovery after such treatment and the relatively quick return to its service modulus.

This changing of modulus or stiffness during flexing can create problems for the designer and user of rubber products. This is especially true where the accurate calibration of stress is important in the function of the rubber part. Timing diaphragms, torsion mounts, roller pump headers, boots, and lever seals on sensitive switches are a

TABLE 1-1.

No. of Cycles	Tensile Stress		% of Original Value
	psi	kg/cm^2	
1	357	25.13	100
2	324	22.81	90.76
3	305	21.47	85.43
4	290	20.42	81.23
5	283	19.92	79.27
6	276	19.43	77.31
7	271	19.08	75.91
8	267	18.80	74.79
9	262	18.45	73.39
10	260	18.30	72.83
11	256	18.02	71.71
12	252	17.74	70.59
13	251	17.67	70.31
14	249	17.53	69.75
15	248	17.46	69.47
16	247	17.39	69.19
17	245	17.25	68.63
18	243	17.11	68.07
19	241	16.97	67.51
20	240	16.90	67.23
21	240	16.90	67.23
22	239	16.83	66.95
23	238	16.76	66.67
24	237	16.69	66.39
25	237	16.69	66.39

few examples of applications where changes in modulus are critical. Such products should be calibrated after a series of 20 to 30 cycles. Where this is not possible, a lower strength general-purpose type of formulation with good resilience may be indicated. A general-purpose VMQ stock subjected to the same cycling series gave the results shown in Table 1-3.

A graphic comparison of the high strength rubber from Table 1-1 is made with two popular general-purpose rubbers in Fig. 1-1.

Compression set may be defined as the amount, expressed as a percent, by which a standard test button fails to return to its original thickness after being subjected to a compressive stress for a prolonged period of time. The resistance to compression set of silicone rubber is excellent over its entire service temperature range.

TABLE 1-2.

No. of Cycles	Tensile Stress		% of Original Value
	psi	kg/cm^2	
1	297	20.91	83.19
2	280	19.71	78.43
3	273	19.22	76.47
4	267	18.80	74.79
5	265	18.66	74.23
6	260	18.30	72.83
7	258	18.16	72.27
8	257	18.09	71.99
9	256	18.02	71.71
10	253	17.81	70.87
11	250	17.60	70.03
12	250	17.60	70.03
13	249	17.53	69.75
14	248	17.46	69.47
15	245	17.25	68.63

Compression set values for silicone rubber are usually determined after 70 hr at 302°F (150°C). Some VMQ formulations have compression set values as low as 7 to 10%. Low compression set is an essential property in seals such as "O" rings, gaskets and grommets, and in rolls.

The practical *hardness* range of silicone rubber as measured with the *Shore A* instrument is 25 to 75. Some softer or harder compounds may be obtained with a considerable sacrifice of properties. This very broad range of hardness is achieved through the combination of molecular characteristics and inert fillers. Consequently, there is not the problem of leaching of softeners and other additives often experienced with the organic rubbers.

The *specific gravity* of silicone rubbers ranges from 1.1 to 1.6. The higher durometer compounds and the FVMQ types have the highest specific gravity.

Values for *coefficient of friction* range from <.25 to >.75. In some cases, the coefficient of friction may be reduced with a thin coating of "elastoplastic" silicone resin.* The surface of silicone rubber becomes very slippery when in contact with most fluids.

*R-4-3117 Conformal coating, Dow Corning Corp.

TABLE 1-3.

No. of Cycles	Tensile Stress		% of Original Value
	psi	kg/cm^2	
1	159	11.19	100
2	156	10.98	98.11
3	154	10.84	96.86
4	152	10.70	95.60
5	151	10.63	94.97
6	149	10.49	93.71
7	148	10.42	93.08
8	148	10.42	93.08
9	147	10.35	92.45
10	148	10.42	93.08
11	147	10.35	92.45
12	147	10.35	92.45
13	147	10.35	92.45
14	147	10.35	92.45
15	147	10.35	92.45
16	147	10.35	92.45
17	147	10.35	92.45
18	147	10.35	92.45
19	147	10.35	92.45
20	147	10.35	92.45
21	146	10.28	91.82
22	146	10.28	91.82
23	146	10.28	91.82
24	146	10.28	91.82
25	146	10.28	91.82

Data courtesy of Moxness Products, Subsidiary of Versa Technologies, Inc.

The *release characteristics* of silicone rubber are superior to any other rubber. They are used as coatings on release papers and parts of machinery or rolls handling sticky materials such as hot polyethylene, candy, adhesives, etc.

The control of *noise and vibration* is very important. It is known that excessive noise can be detrimental to health and the vibration which produces the noise damaging to equipment. Silicone rubber is ideal as a vibration damping material. It exhibits little change in transmissibility or resonant frequency over the temperature range -65°F (-54°C) to 300°F (149°C). Nor will its dynamic absorption characteristics change with aging. These unusual properties, coupled

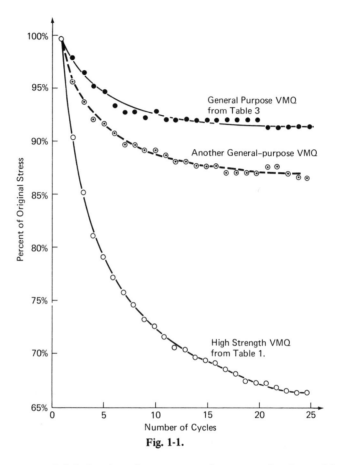

Fig. 1-1.

with its ease of fabrication into many forms, make it an ideal material for effective noise and vibration control.

ELECTRICAL PROPERTIES

There is no better flexible, electrical insulation than silicone rubber. It retains dielectric strength, power factor, and insulation resistance over its high and low temperature range where other flexible insulation becomes useless. The almost flat curve for the dielectric strength of a typical silicone rubber stock, over a wide temperature range, is illustrated in Fig. 1-2.

When exposed to a direct flame, silicone rubber insulation burns to a non-conducting ash, and, as long as it is not subject to extreme vi-

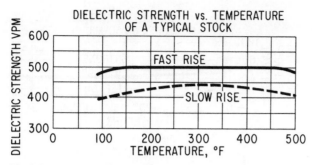

Fig. 1-2. (*Courtesy Silicone Products Dept., General Electric Co.*)

brations, will continue in operation for extended periods of time. On the other hand, organic insulating materials will fail in a matter of minutes upon exposure to a direct flame. This feature, combined with the additional current carrying capacity of silicone rubber insulated cable, leads to its specification on all combat type naval vessels and in aerospace applications where the lower weight and high reliability are attractive assets. The additional current carrying capacity of silicone rubber insulated conductors is due not only to its higher operational temperature but also to its much higher thermal conductivity. In other words, the conductor never does get as hot as it would under the same electrical load with organic types of insulation.

Silicone rubber also has extreme resistance to ozone and its corona resistance approaches that of mica. Because ozone and corona usually occur together, one often associates resistance to them as being related. Actually they are two different phenomena; polyethylene and tetrafluoroethylene, which are quite resistant to the chemical attack of ozone, will break down quickly due to mechanical cavitation when subjected to severe corona discharge. In its resistance to corona, silicone rubber is unsurpassed by any other flexible insulation.

The dielectric fatigue life of silicones is high. Organic polymers with higher initial dielectric strength exhibit a more rapid decrease when subjected to voltage stress over a prolonged period of time (see Fig. 1-3).

Figures 1-4, 1-5, and 1-6 illustrate the dielectric constant, power factor, and volume resistivity values of silicone rubber. Because of its inherent resistance to moisture, the electrical characteristics remain outstanding under moist service conditions. All values are deter-

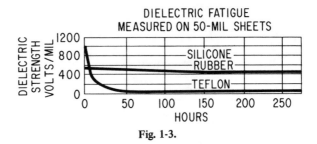

Fig. 1-3.

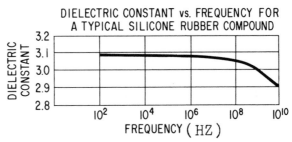

Fig. 1-4. The dielectric constant is a measure of an insulation's ability to store electrical energy. It is the ratio of the electrical capacity of a condenser using the elastomer in question as the dielectric to the capacity of a similar condenser using air as the dielectric.

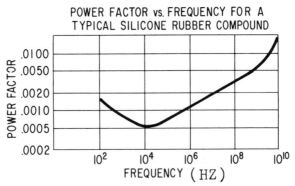

Fig. 1-5. The power factor of an insulating material is its tendency to generate heat in service. If a capacitor using an elastomer as the dielectric is charged and then immediately discharged there is an energy loss in the form of heat. If this step is repeated rapidly, the electrical loss results in heating of the dielectric. The ratio of this loss to the energy required to charge the capacitor is known as power factor. It is usually expressed as a decimal fraction or a percent of the charging energy. Figure 1-5 indicates that silicone rubber is a low loss material.

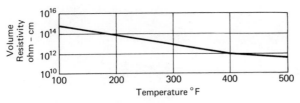

Fig. 1-6.

mined by ASTM methods. Electrical properties are essentially the same for all silicone polymers but variations can be caused by the fillers and additives used in compounding.

For the same reason that exposure to direct flame or temperatures as high as 2000°F does not leave a conductive ash, flashover does not leave a conductive track, therefore the arc resistance of silicone rubber is high.

A general comparison of flexible insulating materials is given in Table 1-4.

Other unique features of silicone rubber which make it an ideal electrical insulation material for extreme service conditions include:

1. Its ability to bond into a continuous, homogenous insulation jacket, (pp. 126 and 203) impervious to water,* oil, and conductive contaminants such as carbon black, metallic dust, etc.
2. Its resistance to vibration damage even at sub-zero temperatures.
3. Its superior resistance to damage by impinged abrasive action which quickly cuts through rigid mica insulation.
4. Its lack of attraction for rodents. Squirrels in particular often dine on exposed organic insulation, causing occasional power failures.

CHEMICAL RESISTANCE

Generally, silicone rubbers have good chemical, fuel, and oil resistance and are particularly useful at temperatures which preclude other chemical resistant elastomers with the possible exception of the fluoroelastomers, such as Viton[R]. Fluorosilicone rubbers (FVMQ) are more resistant than general purpose (MQ, VMQ) or ex-

---

*Certain moisture-resistant stocks are stable in electrical characteristics after 6 months immersion at 160°F (70°C) or after 125 days immersion in boiling water!

TABLE 1-4.

Property	Units	Silicone Rubber	Polytetra-fluoroethylene	SBR Rubber	Butyl Rubber	Oil-Base Rubber	Polyvinyl-chloride	Poly-ethylene
Temperature rating	°F	300–480	480	170	190	170	140–220	170
	°C	150–250	250	75	90	75	60–105	75
Mechanical water absorption	mg/sq in.	10	0.5	15	8	20–30	8–10	0.5
	mg/sq cm	1.6	.08	2.3	1.2	3.9	1.4	.08
Insulation resistance	Megohm constant	30,000	50,000	2000	30,000	21,000	2000	50,000
Dielectric Constant		3.0	2.1	5.0	3.5	5.0	5 to 8	2.3
Power factor	%	0.1	0.1	4.5	3.0	5.0	5 to 8	0.1
Dielectric strength		Excellent	Excellent	Very good	Very good	Excellent	Excellent	Excellent
Tensile strength	lb/sq in.	1200	2000	800	800	1200	1500	1500
	kg/sq cm	84	140	56	56	84	105	105
Elongation	%	400+	150	350	400	300	200	400
Heat aging 5 days @ 200C	% retention	Tensile 75 Elongation 60	Tensile 85 Elongation 75					
Cold bend @ −55C	—	Passes	Passes	Fails	Passes	Fails	Fails	Passes
Ozone and corona resistance	—	Excellent	Good	Fails	Good	Good	Very good	Good
Radiation resistance	ergs/gram (gamma radiation)	10^8	4×10^5	4×10^8	3×10^8	2×10^9	10^{10}	10^{10}
Flammability	—	Burns to non-conducting ash	Self-extinguishing	Burns	Burns	Burns	Self-extinguishing	Burns
Chemical resistance	—	Good	Excellent	Fair	Fair	Poor	Very good	Good
Processibility		Good	Poor	Good	Good	Good	Very good	Very good
Weathering		Excellent	Excellent	Poor	Excellent	Fair	Excellent	Must be pigmented

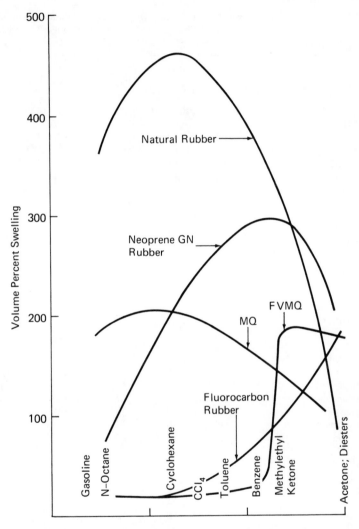

Fig. 1-7. FVMQ has excellent solvent resistance and MQ has good solvent resistance in comparison to the others. (Adapted from F. M. Lewis, The Science and Technology of Rubber. Silicone Products Dept., General Electric Co.)

TABLE 1-5. CHEMICAL RESISTANCE

| | | VMQ | | FVMQ | |
Material	Weight Change %	Volume Change %	Durometer Change Points	Volume Change %	Durometer Change Points
Acids					
Nitric conc.	+10	+10	−30	+5	0
Nitric 7%	<1	<1	−2	0	0
Sulfuric conc.		Disintegrates		Disintegrates	
Sulfuric 10%	<1	<1	−2	0	0
Acetic conc.	+2	+3	−4	+20	−
Acetic 5%	+4	+4	+8	−	−
Hydrochloric conc.	+1	+1	−6	+10	−5
Hydrochloric 10%	+2	+4	−4	0	−5
Hydrochloric 3%	<1	+1	−2	−	−
Bases					
Sodium hydroxide 20%	<1	<1	−2	0	−5
Hydroxide 1%	<1	<1	−4	0	0
Ammonium hydroxide conc.	+2	+2	−4	+5	−5
Ammonium hydroxide 10%	+3	+2	−6	0	0
Salts					
Sodium chloride 10%	<1	<1	−2	−	−
Sodium carbonate 2%	<1	<1	0	−	−
Solvents					
Ethyl alcohol	+5	+6	−10	+5	0
Acetone	+5	+15	−15	+180	−20
Toluene	+75	+120	−30	+20	−10
Gasoline, regular	+65	+130	−25	+20	−12
Gasoline, aviation	+60	+110	−30	+10	−5
Mineral spirits	+65	+110	−30	0	0
Carbon tetrachloride	+130	+110	−25	+20	−5
Hydraulic Fluids					
Hollingshead H-2	+4	+5	−10	−	−
Hollingshead H-2	+9	+12	−15	−	−
Skydrol	+4	+4	−8	+25[c]	−10
Skydrol[a]	+7	+8	−10	−	−
PRL3161	+5	+7	−8	−	−
PRL3161[a]	+9	+9	−15	−	−
Oils					
Castor oil	<1	<1	−4	−	−
Lard oil	<1	<1	−4	−	−
Linseed oil	<1	<1	−2	−	−
Mineral oil	+5	+6	−6	−	−

TABLE 1-5. (Continued)

Material	Weight Change %	VMQ		FVMQ	
		Volume Change %	Durometer Change Points	Volume Change %	Durometer Change Points
Oils (Cont.)					
ASTM #1 oil[b]	+3	+5	−6	0	−5
ASTM #3 oil[b]	+20	+31	−20	+5	−5
Silicone oil SF96 (100)[b]	+25	+35	−25	0	−5
Silicone oil 42,000 cstk.[b]	+9	+10	−12	0	−5
Other					
Water	<1	<1	<1	0	0
Hydrogen peroxide 3%	<1	<1	<1	0	0
Pyranol 1476	+4	+4	−8	−	−

[a] 70 hr @ 212°F 100°C.
[b] 70 hr @ 300°F 149°C.
[c] 7 days 128f (49°C).

VMQ data from General Electric Silicones Technical Data Book S-1E.

Data on FVMQ from Dow Corning Bulletin 17-052.

treme low temperature (PMQ, PVMQ) types. There are some exceptions to this. For example, after one week's immersion in acetone at 77°F (25°C), VMQ exhibits a volume swell of 15% vs. 180% for FVMQ. Other chemicals which are more damaging to the fluorosilicones include: ammonia, ammonium hydroxide, ethylene oxide, monoethanolamine, glacial acetic acid, ethyl and methylalcohol, and certain hydraulic fluids such as Skydrol.* Sometimes FVMQ stocks are blended with 5 to 30% of other silicone rubber stocks to achieve intermediate fluid resistance. This also serves the purpose of reducing the material cost.

The effect of solvents on silicone rubber is mainly that of swelling and softening. However, once the solvent has evaporated, the rubber usually regains most of its original properties. Where chemical or fluid resistance is of prime concern, the higher the durometer

---

*The most complete compilation of fluid resistance data available is to be found in the Dow Corning Corporation Bulletin 17-052.

TABLE 1-6. SILICONE RUBBER COMPARED WITH OTHER SYNTHETIC ORGANIC RUBBERS IN THEIR RESISTANCE TO SOME COMMON DELETERIOUS FLUIDS.

(Values are expressed as % volume swell after a 3-day immersion.)

	Temp.		MQ	FVMQ	Viton B	Hypalon	Thiokol	Neoprene	Nitrile	Acrylate
	°F	°C								
Organic										
Acetone	77	25	15	181	300	18	25	40	130	250
Benzene	77	25	175	27	12	275	100	290	100	350
70/30 Isooctane/toluene	77	25	200	22	2	110	10	75	22	40
Ethyl acetate	77	25	175	140	280	60	25	60	105	250
Methylene chloride	77	25	150	150	25	250	det.	150	300	300
Inorganic										
Hydrochloric acid (conc.)	77	25	5	8	1	5	det.	4	11	det.
Nitric acid (conc.)	77	25	-10	4	4	0	det.	det.	det.	det.
Sulfuric acid (conc.)	77	25	det.	det.	4	10	det.	det.	det.	det.
Sodium hydroxide (50%)	77	25	-1	1	0	0	2	2	0	det.
Steam	300	149	+2	-2	—	—	—	—	—	—
Functional										
ASTM Oil #3	400	149	49	4	3	—	-2	—	10	16
MIL-L-7808 Lubricant	400	204	31	13	10	—	—	—	—	—
OS-45 Hydraulic fluid	400	204	80	13	3	—	—	—	—	—

Adapted from the Vanderbilt Rubber Handbook 11th Edition, p. 200.

(amount of filler) and the tighter the cure, the better will be the performance of a particular formulation.

Typical chemical resistance of VMQ and FVMQ materials are shown in Table 1-5. Comparison of these silicone rubbers with other rubbers is shown in Table 1-6 and graphically in Fig. 1-7.

As is apparent from the data in Table 1-5, water has a negligible effect on silicone. Steam at up to 30 psi (2 kg/cm^2) has little effect also. It is necessary however, when silicone rubber is to be subjected to steam or hot water service, that all acidic residues of peroxide catalysts be removed through adequate high temperature post curing. Platinum catalyzed addition reaction stocks are best for this type of service. Moisture absorption by silicone rubber does not materially affect its properties. Nor is weathering a problem for silicone rubber. Sunlight, ozone, oxygen, bacteria, fungus, soil chemicals, etc. have little effect. Silicone rubber insulation tapes, used on both above ground and underground electrical connections, have been removed and examined by the author after approximately fifteen years of service and found to be in first-class condition.

INERTNESS

Well cured silicone rubber is odorless and tasteless. It does not cause staining or deterioration of other materials with which it comes in contact. Its inert nature is probably best illustrated by its complete lack of toxicity and very minimum of tissue reaction when implanted in animals.

TABLE 1-7. RADIATION RESISTANCE— SILICONE RUBBER.

Dosage (Rads)	VMQ		PMQ	
	Elongation (%)	Tensile Strength (psi)	Elongation (%)	Tensile Strength (psi)
None	200	1,200	600	1,200
5×10^6	130	1,000	450	1,100
5×10^7	50	900	225	900
1×10^8	20	600	75	850

Courtesy Silicone Products Dept., General Electric.

Radiation, through increased cross linking, increases the hardness of silicone rubber and reduces the elongation. It may increase tensile strength at first, but later it will drop off rapidly. The changes occur more rapidly at high radiation levels because of the heat produced. PMQ types are more resistant to radiation effects than VMQ types (see Table 1-7). The service life vs. the radiation dosage will be dependent on the degree of flexibility required for the application. In the case of wire and cable insulation, for example, with electrical properties little affected by radiation and very little elongation being required, very high dosage may be experienced without affecting service. Sterilization dosage (generally about 2.5 megarads) has a negligible effect on silicone rubber medical parts.

THERMAL PROPERTIES

The *thermal expansion coefficient* of silicone rubber is very high: The volumetric thermal expansion ranges from 3.3 to $5 \times 10^{-4}/°F$ (5.9 to $8 \times 10^{-4}/°C$), the linear from 1 to $1.7 \times 10^{-4}/°F$ (2 to $3 \times 10^{-4}/°C$) which is 2 to $2\frac{1}{2}$ times that of organic rubbers or as much as 20 times that of carbon steel!

The addition of fillers lowers the coefficient of expansion of the compound (see Fig. 1-8). This very high coefficient of expansion causes molded items to shrink appreciably when they cool from the temperature of mold vulcanization. This thermal contraction or mold shrinkage makes it difficult and expensive to mold silicone rubber to close dimensional tolerances. Very often the product designer, more familiar with tolerances for metal parts, specifies closer tolerances on a rubber part than is needed for the part to be functional. He forgets that rubber, by its very nature, does not have to be as precise as a metal part which cannot be stretched or deformed to make it fit. Where experience dictates that close tolerances are necessary, the thermal expansion characteristics of the particular compound should be checked experimentally, since there are so many compounding and molding factors which contribute to variations in shrinkage.

The *thermal conductivity* 'k' is an important property of silicone rubber. Two to three times as high as organic rubbers, it contributes

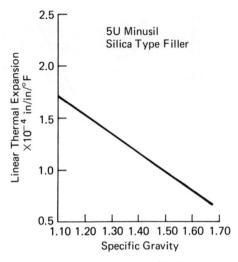

Fig. 1-8. Linear thermal expansion of cured and conditioned silicone rubber (temperature range 75 to 250°F). (*Courtesy Silicone Products Dept., General Electric.*)

to faster cures because it affects the time required to heat the interior of a rubber product to the vulcanization temperature. It also improves the heat dissipation where silicon rubber is used as electrical insulation around heat producing conductors or in applications where heat is generated by vibration flexing or friction.

The thermal conductivity of most silicone rubber compounds ranges from 1.5 to 4.1 Btu's/hr/ft²/in./°F (.07 to .2 cal/sec/cm²/ cm/°C). The thermal conductivity increases with increased filler as illustrated in Fig. 1-9. Where higher values of k are desired, zinc oxide or silver may be added as fillers.

The *flame resistance* or self-extinguishing characteristic of certain silicone rubber compounds is rated as SE-1 when submitted to the M-94 flame test of Underwriters' Laboratories. Minute amounts of platinum, such as occur in the new high strength, addition reaction compounds, improve flame resistance—the mechanics of this are not fully understood. Ground mica or glass frit added as a filler in concentrations as high as 25 parts per hundred (pph) also have been used to help reduce the flammability of silicone rubber.

When silicone rubber does burn, as it would in an intense fire, the polymer decomposes to form silica which, along with the fillers,

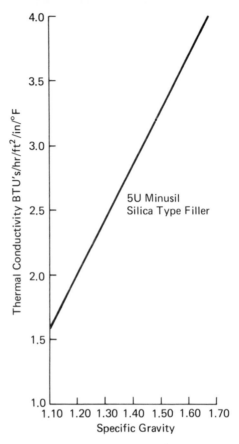

Fig. 1-9. Thermal conductivity of cured and conditioned silicone rubber (temperature range 75 to 350°F).

forms a non-conducting ash, whereas organics leave a conductive residue. While burning, it will yield a comparatively low level of smoke. Carbon monoxide will be a component of the smoke. However, unlike other materials containing halogens, sulphur, or nitrogen it cannot evolve hydrogen chloride, fluorides, sulphur dioxide, nitric oxide, or other noxious chemicals which can irritate the eyes, nose, or throat. Silicone rubber can be readily identified by its burning characteristics: yellow flame, thin, white smoke, white remaining ash.

Silicone rubber is a superior *ablative material*. Mechanical parts of rockets or re-entry vehicles which are subjected to propellant blast or thousands of degrees of heat may be protected through the use either of heat sinks or ablative shields. Heat sinks protect through the increase in temperature of the shielding material which has a high specific heat. The ablative surface insulates mainly through the energy absorbed by changing phase.

Silicone rubber is capable of withstanding temperatures of up to 9000°F (5000°C) for several minutes while still exhibiting good insulating properties. A spongy surface char forms on the surface which reduces thermal conductivity. Gas, formed by the change of phase, is injected into the boundary layer, further reducing the heat transfer rate. The inner layer will remain resilient and, if bonded to a metal surface, the bond will remain viable during the short operational life of the cable or device.

PERMEABILITY

Silicone rubber is highly permeable to gases. Permeability values have been expressed by Kammermyer[4] as P in the unit:

$$P \times 10^{-9} \ \frac{\text{gas vol. cc's} \times \text{cm thickness}}{\text{sec} \times \text{cm} \times \text{pressure drop cm Hg}}$$

Kammermyer reported values of 270 for carbon dioxide with silicone rubber as compared with 1.4 for polyethylene and 13.1 for natural rubber. He later reported that, through the expansion of thin walled silicone rubber capillaries, the gas transfer could be increased by an additional 10 to 20 times.[5] Since thin films of silicone rubber are selectively permeable to different gases, they may be used for separating gases to obtain relative enrichment of one gaseous component over another.[6]

The combination of low levels of hemolysis with the high rate of gas permeability, makes silicone rubber membrane an ideal gas transfer material in oxygenators. More information on gas permeability may be found in Chapter 9 on Medical Applications.

References

1. *G. E. Silicones Technical Data Book S-1E.*
2. Machele, A. L. and McIntyre, J. T., "Properties of Silicone and Organic

TABLE 1-8. SPECIFICATIONS AND SOME TYPICAL PROPERTIES OF A RANGE OF SILICONE RUBBER COMPOUNDS

Outstanding Property	Type ASTM D1418	Typical Application	AMS	ASTM D-2000-70		
				FC-	FE-	GE-
High strength	VMQ	For applications requiring outstanding tear, resiliency, toughness and fabrication rheology.	3348	307	310	309
			3347	512	512	512
			–		610	–	–
			3349	710	–	–
			–	–	–	–
Low temperature high strength	PVMQ	For applications requiring toughness and low temperature flexibility such as: extruded and molded gaskets and seals for a wide variety of mechanical and airframe applications.	3332A	307	–	–
			3345B	512	–	–
			3346B	612	–	–
Low compression set	VMQ	O-rings, gaskets, connector seals, rubber rolls, seal covers, valve gaskets.	3302D	–	–	509
			3303F	–	–	609
			3304D	–	–	709
			3305E	–	–	809
			–	–	–	709
High temperature	VMQ	Oven gaskets, hot air tubing, high temperature hoses or other rubber parts requiring high temperature service.	3302D	–	–	509
Oil and fluid resistance	VMQ and FVMQ	O-rings, valve gasket, hydraulic seals, rubber rolls and gasket sheet stock. For rotary shaft seals, automatic transmission seals, o-rings, and gaskets in contact with high temperature petroleum oils.	3305E	–	–	809
			3305E	–	–	809
			3326B			
Low durometer	PVMQ	For applications requiring low durometer, low temperature flexibility such as: low pressure seals and gaskets, rubber rolls and cushion type sheet stock.	3332A	–	–	–
Food grade	VMQ and PVMQ	For applications requiring translucency, inertness, and durability. Vending machine tubing, food conveyor belting, rubber parts and gaskets used in food processing equipment are typical applications for these compounds.	–	512	512	512
			–	–	–	–
				610	610	610
General purpose	VMQ	For general purpose applications such as rubber rolls, automotive spark plug boots and diaphragms, extruded gaskets, molded o-rings and gaskets, and calendered sheets.	3301D	–	–	409
			3302D	–	–	509
			3303F	–	–	609
			3304D	–	–	709
			3305E	–	–	809
Low temperature general purpose	PVMQ	For applications requiring low compression set and extreme low temperature flexibility.	3334A	–	–	–
			3335A	–	–	–
			3336A	–	–	–
			3337A	–	–	–
			3338C	–	–	–
Sponge	PVMQ	For applications requiring closed cell sponge with excellent low temperature flexibility.	3196B	–	–	–
			3195B	–	–	–

TABLE 1-8. (Continued)

SPECIFICATIONS			TYPICAL PRODUCT PROPERTIES				
ZZ-R-765 b	MIL-STD-417	Durometer Shore "A" ± 5	Tensile (psi)	Elongation (%)	Tear (#/in)	Compression Set (%) 70 hr/300°F	Brittle Point (°F)
Class 3B	TA 510	35	1100	700	170	30	−115
Class 3B	TA 512	50	1300	600	200	30	−130
Class 3B		60	1200	550	200	30	−120
Class 3B	TA 710	70	1200	500	200	30	−120
Class 3B		80	1000	250	100	30	−100
Class 3A		25	1000	800	100	25	−175
Class 3A	TA 510–512	50	1300	550	190	40	−175
Class 3A	TA 610–612	60	1300	600	180	40	−175
Class 2A&B	TA 505–507	50	1000	420	60	10	−100
Class 2A&B	TA 605	60	1000	140	50	15	−100
Class 2A&B	TA 705–707	70	1000	130	60	17	−100
Class 2A&B	TA 805	80	950	140	70	20	−100
		70	1200	350	90	12	−100
Class 2A&B	TA 505–507 TA 807	50	1150	370	70	17	−100
Class 2A&B		80	1000	120	85	25	−100
Class 2A&B		80	1100	130	95	25	−100
	TA 608						
Class 2A&B	−	20	950	900	75	25	−175
−		50-Translucent	1300	600	180	30	−130
−	−	50-Clear	1300	600	210	37	−175
		60-Translucent	1300	550	180	30	−120
Class 2	TA 505	40	1000	500	60	20	−100
Class 2	TA 507	50	1000	400	65	20	−100
Class 2	TA 807	60	1000	300	70	22	−100
Class 2		70	1000	230	75	23	−100
Class 2		80	1000	140	85	25	−100
Class 1A&B		40	1000	400	−	15	−175
Class 1A&B	TA 506	50	900	350	−	20	−175
Class 1A&B	TA 806	60	850	250	−	30	−170
Class 1A&B		70	800	200	−	30	−165
Class 1A&B		80	750	150	−	35	−160
−		FIRM	Compression-deflection (psi) to compress 25% 15 psi				−150
−		MEDIUM	Compression-deflection (psi) to compress 25% 8 psi				−150

Elastomers as Measured at High Temperatures," *Automotive Engineering Congress*, Detroit, Mich., Jan. 10–14, 1972.

3. Payne, A. R. and Scott, J. R., *Engineering Design with Rubber*, Interscience Publishers, New York, 1960.

4. Kammermeyer, K., *Ind. Eng. Chem.* **49**, 1685 (1957).

5. Blaisdell, C. T. and Kammermeyer, K., "Gas Separation through Expandable Tubing," AIChE Meeting, Feb., 1972.

6. U.S. Patent 3,274,750.

2

THE COMPOUNDING OF HEAT VULCANIZING SILICONE RUBBERS

High molecular weight silicone polymers are the gums which, when compounded with fillers, processing aids, and curing agents, produce silicone rubber stocks of the type that can be processed on standard rubber equipment.

Many fully compounded silicone rubber stocks are available from the silicone suppliers, ready for use by the fabricator. They may be supplied as "hats"* of precompounded material for extruding, in rope form for cutting into preforms, or pelletized for hopper feeding.** However, a variety of reinforced gums or bases are also available. By inventorying a relatively few reinforced gums which can be compounded with a variety of fillers and catalysts, the fabricator can more economically meet almost any specification.

Silicone rubber compounds for volume jobs, especially when highly loaded with filler, are often mixed in Banbury mixers. These are closed mixers with very fast cycles. They are usually used in conjunction with two-roll mills. The mixing is performed by the Banbury. The completely mixed stock is then dumped on the roll mill where it is cooled and sheeted off for preforming.

Dough mixers are also a closed piece of machinery. These are only found in the plants of the raw material suppliers. They are equipped to pump fillers, devolatilize compounds, or mix in an inert gas atmosphere. They can provide larger, uniform batch sizes while handling

---

*For an illustration of "hat" feeding of an extruder see p. 106.
**See section on preforming.

a wide variety of silicone products from dispersions through pastes to high strength stocks. But the workhorse in the average fabricating shop is the two roll mixing mill. Practically unchanged in over 100 years, this type of mill has two heavy rotating rolls (Fig. 2-1) usually made of cast iron, although in special applications such as the handling of clean-room stocks, they should be surfaced with hardened stainless steel. The space between the rolls may be varied and one roll rotates faster than the other. A ratio of 1.2/1 to 1.4/1 is preferred for silicone rubber. The higher ratio leads to faster mixing, the lower ratio to smoother sheeting. The rolls must be water cooled to keep the rubber temperature while mixing below 110°F (44°C). Higher temperatures may cause the rubber to become too nervy as scorching occurs or there may be some loss of catalyst due to volatilization.

For silicones, the cheek plates of the mill should be equipped with nylon or other tough plastic plows which will keep the silicone rubber from squeezing under the cheek plates where it will pick up dirt.

The mill is first loaded with the reinforced gum (R gum) and the

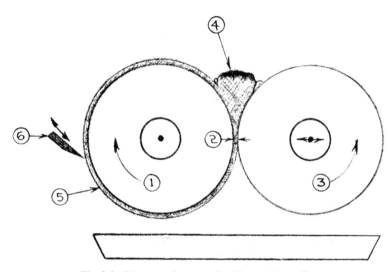

Fig. 2-1. Diagram of a two-roll rubber mixing mill.
1. Fast roll.
2. Nip (space between rolls) which is adjustable.
3. Slow roll.
4. Bank of material, where mixing takes place.
5. Band of material covering fast roll.
6. Scraper blade.

"nip" (the space between the rolls) adjusted to about $\frac{1}{8}$ in. When the R-gum is sufficiently plasticized, the band of material will transfer from the slow roll to the fast roll. When this occurs, the R-gum is ready for the addition of fillers (Fig. 2-2).

Various fine particle silicas are added to silicone rubber to reinforce it and to extend it, to increase the hardness and reduce the stickiness. Carbon black is added when electrical conductivity is required, red iron oxide improves heat resistance, zinc oxide is used for heat conductivity, aluminum hydrate for extra electrical track resistance, and various pigments are used for coloring. They often impart other desirable properties. For example, titanium dioxide, which is a strong white pigment, also improves the dielectric constant of the vulcanized rubber. Care should be taken to add fillers slowly enough to prevent balls of high filler and low gum content from forming and floating on top of the compound bank which leads to poor dispersion. If much filler is being added, it is a good idea to add it in two or three separate additions, cross blending between them to assure

Fig. 2-2. Filler has been added to the gum which has banded on the first roll producing the light colored streaks in the band. By sheeting the band off the mill and reintroducing it into the nip, at right angles to the direction of the streaking and repeating several times, more thorough mixing is accomplished. (*Courtesy Connecticut Hard Rubber Co., an Armco Co.*)

good dispersion. If the rubber looks grainy, tightening the nip should improve the mixing. Crumbs of compound which fall into the mill pan should be collected with a squeegee and returned immediately to the mill rolls. If they are allowed to collect in the pan for any length of time, they may not mill in smoothly, leaving lumps which will give poor appearance to the finished product. When extending fillers are added, they should be added after the reinforcing fillers. A wider nip may be used. Color, when used, may be added at this point. In order to assure good color dispersion and good color matching, master batches are often used.*

Finally, the catalyst is added. Care should be taken to be sure the compound temperature is cool enough, particularly in the case of the low temperature catalysts such as benzoyl peroxide and 2,4-dichloro-benzoyl peroxide (see Table 2-4). In some cases the compound should be removed from the mill and cooled down before returning it to the mill for catalyzing.

Some firm, dry stocks can be removed from the mill roll with the aid of a mill knife but many stocks are soft and sticky after milling. Therefore, silicone rubber mills have to be equipped with a scraper blade (see Fig. 2-3) on the fast roll, since this is the roll the plasticized stock bands on. The scraper blade runs the full length of the roll and, like the roll plows, is constructed of nylon or other tough plastic.

The sheeted stock should be laid out flat on release paper or waffled surface polyethylene until cool. It may then be rolled up with an inter leaf. The outside of the wrapper should be clearly identified with the compound number, the weight of the batch, and the date of compounding. The compound is now ready for molding or extrusion unless additional filler wetting time is needed. Some compounds process better after a period of shelf aging, which may amount to several days. Some must be used directly after compounding.

Flash trimmings and scrap, where the volume warrants, may be reclaimed and the reclaim mixed with virgin compound of the same type—preferably the same compound. The addition of reclaim will have a tendency to reduce the hardness, tensile strength, and elongation but it also reduces the compression set. Thus, certain gasketing applications will be improved with the addition of reclaim. The scrap

---

*Master batches may be obtained from: (1) Kenrich Petrochemicals, Inc., Foot of East 22nd St., Bayonne, N.J. 07002. (2) Ferro Corporation, 4150 East 56th St., Cleveland, Ohio 44105. (3) Ware Chemical Corporation, Box 3375, Bridgeport, Conn. 06605.

Fig. 2-3. Mill operator sheets the rubber off the mill by forcing the scraper blade against the roll. (*Courtesy Connecticut Hard Rubber Co., an Armco. Co.*)

material may be reclaimed by breaking it down on a two roll mixing mill. This involves a considerable amount of milling time. It is better, if sizable quantities are available, to send them to a rubber reclaim specialist. Extrusions containing reclaim rarely have as smooth a surface finish as virgin material.

There is a fine art to the milling of silicone rubber. It involves being able to turn out batches of rubber exhibiting consistently good dispersion of ingredients, coupled with just the right plasticity for the particular job. Lucky is the fabricator who has such a mill operator.

The various fillers used in the compounding of silicone rubber are described in Table 2-1. In addition, the effect of adding increased amounts of fumed silica reinforcing filler to a 50 Duro R gum base is described in Table 2-1A. The addition of extending filler only to the same gum is covered in Table 2-1B. Note particularly the difference between the two fillers in the specific gravity change to achieve the same durometer.

The most important reinforcing fillers are the fumed silicas, silicas which are reconstituted from silicon and present a very large surface

TABLE 2-1. FILLERS SUITABLE FOR USE WITH SILICONE POLYMERS.

	Type	Manufacturer	Specific Gravity	(Millimicron) Particle Size Mean Diameter	Surface Area (sq m/gm)	Typical Load Curve Part 100 = 1 Duro
Highly Reinforcing						
Cab-O-Sil MS-7	Fumed	Cabot	2.20	15	250	1-1.5
HS-5	Silica			10	325	0.5-1.0
Reinforcing						
Santocel C, CS, 62	Silica Aerogel	Monsanto	2.00	18-30	110-200	1-1.5
Hi-Sil	Ppt. hydrated silica	Pittsburgh Plate Glass		22	160	
Ouso H-40	Ppt. silica	Philadelphia Quartz Company	2.10	18	200	
Semi-reinforcing						
Celite-350	Calcined diatomaceous silica	Johns-Manville	2.15	3000	5	1.5
Celite Super Floss	Flux calcined diatomaceous silica	Johns-Manville	2.30	3000	5	2.0
Non-reinforcing (Extending)						
Minusil	Ground silica	Penn. Glass Sand	2.65	5,000-30,000		3-4.0
Neo-Novacite	Ground silica	Malvern Mineral Co.	2.65	5,000-30,000		
Imsil A-10	Ground silica	Illinois Minerals	2.65	10,000-30,000		
Witcarb "R"	Ppt. calcium carbonate	Witco Chemicals	2.65	30-50	32	
XX-78	Zinc oxide	New Jersey Zinc	5.65	300	3	
Pigments						
Red Iron Oxide R-, Ry-	Iron oxide	C. K. Williams	4.95	1000		
Titanox RA	Titanium oxide	Titanium Pigment	3.9	300	9	
Mapico Red #297	Iron oxide	Columbia Carbon	5.18	3000		
P-33 Carbon Black	Thermal black	R. T. Vanderbilt	1.8			
Drakenfeld Black	Cobalt-iron-chrome	B. F. Drakenfeld & Co	5.2			
10335	Oxides					

(Courtesy Silicane Products Dept., *General Electric*.)

TABLE 2-1A. COMPOUNDING FOR HIGH STRENGTH, VMQ
WITH CAB-O-SIL MS-7.
(Typical Properties)

	50 Duro		60 Duro		70 Duro	
Recipe						
SWS-727 Base	100	100	100	100	100	100
Cab-O-Sil MS-7	–	–	5	5	10	10
50% 2,4-dichlorobenzoyl peroxide	1.1		1.1		1.1	
50% 2,5-bis(*t*-butylperoxy) 2,5-dimethylhexane		0.8		0.8		0.8
No Postcure						
Hardness, Shore A	47	48	59	57	70	68
Tensile strength, psi	1150	1190	1255	1200	1150	1200
Elongation, %	520	600	500	520	425	520
100% modulus	110	95	190	175	210	195
Tear resistance (die B), ppi	90	95	100	100	105	115
Specific gravity	1.15	1.15	1.21	1.21	1.23	1.23
Oven Cured (4 hr/400°F)						
Hardness, Shore A	49	50	61	60	71	70
Tensile strength, psi	1150	1150	1140	1130	1150	1170
Elongation, %	475	550	410	460	330	400
100% modulus	130	90	185	190	290	240
Tear resistance (die B), ppi	100	100	115	120	100	115
Compression set (Method B, 22 hr/350°F), %	31	23	33	27	40	39
Oven Cured (16 hr/450°F)						
Hardness, Shore A	50	50	63	62	73	71
Tensile strength, psi	1000	1100	1170	1150	1010	1030
Elongation, %	400	500	375	430	300	360
Tear resistance (die B), ppi	95	100	110	120	100	115
Compression set (Method B, 22 hr/350°F), %	19	14	20	16	25	18
#1 Oil 70 hr/300°F (after 16 hr/450°F postcure)						
Δ Hardness, Shore A	−8	−10	−10	−12	−6	−14
Δ Tensile strength, psi	−14	−20	+2	−4	−11	−10
Δ Elongation, %	+10	−13.5	+4.5	+0	−11	−5
Δ Volume	+5.6	+5.23	+5.5	+7	+5.5	+5.5

(Courtesy SWS Silicones Div., *Stauffer Chemical Co.*)

TABLE 2-1B. COMPOUNDING FOR COST, VMQ WITH
MIN-U-SIL 5 MICRON.
(Typical Properties)

	50 Duro		60 Duro		70 Duro		80 Duro	
Recipe								
SWS-727 Base	100	100	100	100	100	100	100	100
5 Micron Min-U-Sil	—	—	50	50	100	100	150	150
50% 2, 4-dichlorobenzoyl								
peroxide	1.1		1.1		1.1		1.1	
50% 2,5-bis(*t*-butylperoxyl)-								
2,5-dimethylhexane		0.8		0.8		0.8		0.8
No Postcured								
Hardness, Shore A	47	48	60	57	73	70	83	80
Tensile strength, psi	1150	1190	1050	1000	910	865	900	890
Elongation, %	550	600	350	400	240	225	145	150
100% modulus	110	95	300	250	500	450	710	650
Tear resistance (die B), ppi	85	90	95	100	75	85	85	85
Specific gravity	1.15	1.15	1.43	1.43	1.62	1.62	1.75	1.75
Oven Cured (4 hr/400°F)								
Hardness, Shore A	49	50	65	64	73	72	85	84
Tensile strength, psi	1100	1150	1160	1100	990	1000	900	810
Elongation, %	475	550	290	350	150	180	130	120
100% modulus	130	90	350	205	495	490	625	800
Tear resistance (die B), ppi	100	140	90	85	60	50	75	85
Compression set (Method B,								
22 hr/350°F), %	31	23	41	32	41	31	58	36
Oven Cured (16 hr/450°F)								
Hardness, Shore A	50	50	65	65	75	75	85	85
Tensile strength, psi	1100	1100	1000	1130	990	900	795	895
Elongation, %	400	500	240	260	145	145	120	110
Tear resistance (die B), ppi	90	100	60	69	58	63	66	67
Compression set (Method B,								
22 hr/350°F), %	19	14	24	16	25	18	43	28
#1 Oil 70 hr/300°F (after 16 hr/450°F)postcure)								
△ Hardness, Shore A	−8	−10	−11	−11	−7	−9	−5	−3
△ Tensile strength, psi i	−14	−20	−8.7	−9	−32	±0	−12	+25
△ Elongation, %	+10	−13.5	+23	−3	±0	−2	−12	+19
△ Volume	+5.6	+5.2	+5	+4.5	+3.5	+3.7	+3.5	+3.3

(Courtesy SWS Silicones Div., *Stauffer Chemical Co.*)

area (see Table 2-1). Isolated hydroxyl groups on the surface of the silica filler lead to hydrogen bonds between the filler surface and the silicone polymer which contribute to the production of strong, snappy rubbers with high elongation. The filler-polymer bonds form slowly at room temperature. As they increase in number, the compound becomes stiffer. This phenomenon is referred to as "crepe hardening." It is accompanied by absorption of silicone polymer by the silica filler which is referred to as "wetting" of the filler. Crepe hardening can proceed rapidly, particularly with high loadings of fumed silicas in combination with certain gums. The stock will then have to be freshened on the mill before using. The remilling breaks up filler polymer linkage and softens the green stock to the point where it will flow nicely during the molding or extruding.

After freshening, the crepe hardening will begin again and some compounds may have to be refreshened several times before the batch has been completely used. Boonstra, Cochrane, and Dannenberg[1] have shown that the fumed silicas can effectively constitute cross links between silicone polymer molecules and at elevated temperatures a high elongation vulcanized rubber may actually be achieved. This type of cross linking through hydrogen bonds is not a thermally stable one, however, as evidenced by high temperature compression set values approaching 100%. There is no doubt that the filler polymer linkage plays a part in the decrease of modulus, which occurs in the tough, high strength rubbers on repeated flexing (see Table 1-1, page 3).

As a silicone rubber stock compounded with reinforcing fillers wets out, a process which may take several days to fully stabilize, the vulcanized product will have lower durometer hardness, elongation, and compression set values. These changes in physical values can be minimized by the use of masterbatch bases heavily loaded with reinforced silica from the raw material supplier. Humidity control is an important factor in achieving optimum physical properties in the finished silicone rubber product. Fabricators are all too familiar with the "summer effect" when high temperatures combined with high humidity lead to poor results in the fabricating plant. Boonstra et al.[1] have shown that the highest physical properties of the vulcanized product are obtained with the lowest moisture content fillers. For instance, as the silica moisture content increased from .29 to 8.67%, the tensile strength, elongation, and modulus at 50% decreased by

25%; tear resistance decreased by 33% and the durometer reduced by 10 points. The time taken on the mill to band the compound with high moisture containing filler was one quarter of the time taken when the lowest moisture content was used (Table 2-2). This is interesting because it indicates that the addition of moisture is one way to reduce the freshening problem of very boardy or crepe hardened compounds, provided some modification of the physical properties in the vulcanizate is acceptable.

Exposing the silica filler to hexamethyldisilazane vapor inactivates the isolated hydroxyl groups on the surface by converting them to trimethylsilyl groups, thus reducing the tendency to crepe harden and also decreasing the absorption and consequently the effect of moisture. The degree of conversion of free hydroxyl groups to trimethyl groups will have a varying effect on the physical properties of the finished product: formulating a compound with 40 phr of fumed silica having a surface area of 345 sq m/g in VMQ Boonstra et al.[1] report: maximum tensile strength at about 50% conversion to trimethyl groups, maximum elongation and minimum compression set at 100%, maximum tear resistance at about 30% and highest hardness and modulus at 0% (Table 2-3).

TABLE 2-2. EFFECT OF MOISTURE LEVEL.[a]

Sample	A	B	C	D	E
Silica properties					
Moisture, wt. %	0.29	1.18	2.93	6.58	8.67
Water monolayers	0.57	2.3	5.8	13	17
Compound properties					
Incorp. time, min	7.5	5.5	7.5	7.25	6
Knit time, min[b]	4.75	1.75	1.75	1.25	1.25
ODR at 96°C					
L_{max}	61	34.0	31.3	31.5	29.5
L_{min}	35	10.5	7.3	8.0	7.5
ΔL	26	23.5	24.0	23.5	22.0
Vulcanizate properties					
Tensile strength, kg/cm^2	93	76	73	77	70
Elongation, %	260	190	180	200	200
Modulus 50%, kg/cm^2	16.2	14.1	14.8	14.8	12.0
100%, kg/cm^2	30.3	33.1	32.4	31.0	26.1
Hardness, Shore A	68	61	60	60	57
Tear resistance, kg/cm	14.1	10.0	9.1	8.8	9.5

[a] Fumed silica, 200 m^2/g, 40 phr in VMQ.
[b] Banding time.

TABLE 2-3. EFFECT OF CONVERSION OF SILANOL GROUPS TO TRIMETHYLSILYL GROUPS.[a]

Sample	1	2	3	4	5	6	No Filler
Silica properties							
Conversion, % of max.	0	27	47	61	83	100	–
OH, groups per nm^2	3.87	3.05	2.63	2.42	1.96	2.05	–
Trimethylsilyl, groups per nm^2	0.0	0.50	0.89	0.89	1.57	1.88	–
Compound properties							
Incorp., time, min	26	10	8	9	8.5	9	–
Knit time, min[b]	15	2.5	0.75	0.5	0.5	0.25	–
Bound rubber, %	66.2	43.2	29.6	17.1	8.2	4.6	–
ODR at 96°C							
L_{max}	69.5	63.0	49.7	34.5	22.8	19.5	10.5
L_{min}	50.3	35.5	24.0	12.5	5.3	4.0	2.4
ΔL	19.2	27.5	25.7	22.0	17.5	15.5	8.1
α_v	7.2	12.5	11.4	8.9	6.1	4.7	–
T_{90}, min	14.30	8.0	7.0	7.0	6.0	6.0	6.0
Vulcanizate properties							
Tensile strength, kg/cm^2	78	97	106	100	80	80	3.3
Elongation, %	280	320	370	410	430	490	100
Modulus 50%, kg/cm^2	25	18	13	9.2	6.3	5.6	2.3
100%, kg/cm^2	38	28	20	15	11	9.5	3.3
200%, kg/cm^2	62	58	45	37	25	20	–
Hardness, Shore A	76	71	63	57	50	45	22
Tear resistance, kg/cm	6.9	12.2	10.6	9.3	8.8	5.5	2.3
Compr. set, %	79	62	62	56	49	46	3.6
Compr. set (postcured), %	30	29	28	29	21	18	2.5

[a] Fumed silica, 345 m^2/g, 40 phr in VMQ.
[b] Banding time.

Uncatalyzed compound will crepe harden or structure more slowly and band faster on the mill than catalyzed compound. It may be more practical in some cases to add catalyst to sub batches as they are freshened. Different catalysts also affect the rate of creping. For example, some compounds with 2,4-dichlorobenzoyl peroxide will crepe harden in half the time compared with when benzoyl peroxide is used. Wet process silicas have less tendency to crepe harden than fumed silicas; however, they contribute to lower properties.

Extending fillers are used primarily to cheapen the silicone rubber compound, although diatomaceous earths because of their surface area do contribute some reinforcement of the stocks to which they

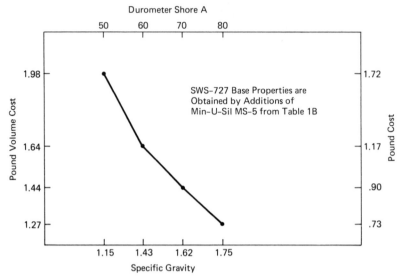

Fig. 2-4. (*Courtesy SWS Silicones, Div. of Stauffer Chemical Co.*)

are added. Ground quartz on the other hand, has little if any reinforcing qualities and can be added in large quantities without pro-
moting crepe hardening. It also has a negligible detrimental effect on
the heat resistance of the vulcanized product. Ground quartz loaded
stocks are cheaper but are highly abrasive and can lead to rapid wear
of processing equipment, molds, and extrusion dies. In estimating
the savings through the use of extending fillers, the cost based on
weight should be converted to a pound volume cost (see Fig. 2–4) by
multiplying by the specific gravity. Only the pound volume cost will
give the true savings in the filled compound. Other additives include:

Red iron oxides	1–3	pph to improve heat aging
Barium zirconate (white)	4	pph to improve heat aging while retaining color ability
Acetylene black	25–50	pph to obtain electrical conductivity
Blowing agents	1–5	pph for sponging
Boric acid		for self-adhering stocks

CROSS-LINKING SYSTEMS

The most commonly used vulcanizing agents for the heat curing silicone rubbers are organic peroxides. Used in very low concentration,

the action of the peroxides appears to be that free radicals, produced as the peroxides reach their decomposition temperature, capture hydrogen atoms from methyl groups of adjacent linear molecules, thus causing cross linking.   The silicone gum becomes a true resilient rubber.

$$ROOR \xrightarrow{\Delta} 2\ RO-$$

$$
\begin{array}{c}
CH_3 \\
| \\
-O-Si-O-Si-O \\
| \\
CH_3
\end{array}
\quad + 2\ RO- \longrightarrow \quad
\begin{array}{c}
CH_3 \\
| \\
-O-Si-O- \\
| \\
CH_2
\end{array}
$$

$$
\begin{array}{c}
CH_3 \\
| \\
-O-Si-O-Si-O- \\
| \\
CH_3
\end{array}
\qquad\qquad
\begin{array}{c}
CH_2 \\
| \\
-O-Si-O- \\
| \\
CH_3
\end{array}
\quad + 2\ ROH
$$

Vulcanized silicone rubber may have 20 to 50 cross links per polymer chain, spaced some 200 to 500 siloxy units apart.

Where vinyl groups are incorporated into the dimethyl siloxane chains, the high reactivity of the vinyl groups allows the use of weakly cross linking peroxides (such as di-*t*-butyl peroxide). The degree of cross linking may then be more closely controlled, since it will be dependent on the concentration of vinyl groups.

Different organic peroxides decompose (become reactive) at different temperatures and at different rates. The choice of which to use is made with consideration of the processing method, the application, and the product dimensions—particularly the wall thickness in mind. The most popular of the organic peroxide curing agents is 2,4-dichlorobenzoyl peroxide. It has the lowest vulcanization temperature combined with the highest rate of vulcanization. Because its decomposition products have a very low vapor pressure, external pressure is not required to prevent porosity. Therefore, it is the agent of choice for extrusions which will be hot air vulcanized. It is used widely in compression molding. Because of its high rate of vulcanization, scorching may be experienced in thin sections or the longer flow experienced in injection or transfer molding. However, much injection or transfer molding is done using 2,4-dichlorobenzoyl peroxide.

Benzoyl peroxide is another low temperature catalyst which may be used to vulcanize all types of silicone and fluorosilicone compounds. It has less tendency to scorch than 2,4-dichlorobenzoyl peroxide. Consequently, it is better in molding very thin sections. However, because of its tendency to gas, it is not as good for hot air vulcanization. It is used in continuous steam vulcanization, the standard method for vulcanizing wire and cable coating.

The low temperature curing agents have several drawbacks. When heavy section parts are to be molded, acid by-products of decomposition tend to cause reversion of the cross-linking bonds during the slow vulcanizing period of thick section parts. They also cause reversion of parts which are confined (as in a metal housing, closed to the atmosphere) and subjected to high service temperatures, or operate under continuous exposure to hot water or steam. The fast rate of vulcanization may lead to scorching of thin molded parts or back rinding along the parting line of thick parts.

Higher temperature organic peroxide curing agents such as dicumyl peroxide and 2,5-bis(t-butyl peroxy) 2,5-dimethyl hexane are suitable only for use with vinyl containing silicone compounds. They are ideal for thick section parts, give good physicals, especially compression set values, and can be used to vulcanize compounds containing carbon black. Table 2-4 lists a number of peroxide curing agents along with their properties, applications, and commercial names.

Sometimes a combination of peroxide curing agents is used. This is particularly useful when extrusions or moldings require post forming.[2] An initial cure, enough to allow handling of the product without deformation, is effected at low temperature with a very small amount of 2,4-Cl$_2$ benzoyl peroxide. The product is then post formed on a fixture and oven cured, while still on the fixture, at a higher temperature, which causes the reaction of the second catalyst and the setting of the rubber in its final shape.

New millable types of addition reaction* silicone rubber compounds were recently introduced.** The catalyst used is a platinum salt at a concentration of less than 1 part per million of Pt ion. The vulcanizates combine maximum toughness, reversion resistance, clarity, and a smooth glossy surface.

High energy radiation may also be used to vulcanize silicone rubber. This is not a common method because of limitations in its use as well as the high initial cost of the equipment. Radiation vulcanization, however, can produce a tough, reversion resistant rubber.

---

*For an explanation of addition reaction see p. 146.
**General Electric Co.: SE 4772.

TABLE 2-4. ORGANIC PEROXIDE CURING AGENTS FOR SILICONE RUBBER COMPOUNDS.

Peroxide	Commercial Grade	Form	Active Conc.	% Active Oxygen	Recommended Use	General Cure Temp. (°F)
2,4-Cl₂ Benzoyl peroxide	Cadox TS (50)³	Paste	50%	2.1	Hot Air	220–250
	Luperco CST²	Paste	50%		Vulcanization	
Benzoyl peroxide	Cadox BSG³	Paste	50%		Molding, steam, CV	240–280
	Luperco AST²	Paste	50%	3.15	Molding, steam, CV	
	Cadox 99³ (200 Mesh)	Powder**	99%	6.3	Molding, steam, CV Solution coating	
Dicumyl peroxide*	DiCup 40C¹	Powder	40%	2.4	Thick section and carbon	320–340
	DiCup R¹	Crystalline	99%	5.9	Black stocks, CV	
2,5-bis(t-butyl peroxy)*	Varox*	Powder	50%		Bonding	330–350
2,5-Dimethyl hexane	Luperco 101 XL²	Powder	50%	5.5	Thick section and carbon black	
	Lupersol 101²	Liquid	95%			
	Varox (Liquid)⁵	Liquid	95%	11.0		
t-Butyl perbenzoate	Same²	Liquid	100%	7.8	General for high activation— sponge temperatures	290–310
Ditertiary butyl* peroxide	Same²,⁷	Liquid	100%	10.6	Thick section and carbon black	340–360
	CW-2015⁶	Powder	15%	1.6		
Cumyl, t-Butyl peroxide* α,α'-bis(t-Butyl peroxy) diisopropyl benzene	Trigonox T	Liquid	95%	7.2	Molding, steam, CV	300–340
	Vul-Cup 40KE¹	Powder	40%	3.8	Molding, steam, CV	340
	Perkadox 14/40	Powder	40%			
1,1 di-t-Butyl peroxy* 3,3,5-trimethyl cyclohexane	Trigonox 29/40	Powder	40%	4.2	Molding, steam, CV	275–325
t-Butyl peroxy* Isopropyl carbonate	B.P.I.C.⁴	Liquid	100%	9.1	Molding and CV	280–300

*Normally limited to use with vinyl-containing base polymers.
**Use powder, not paste, for self-bonding stocks.

Manufacturers:
¹Hercules Inc.   ²Lucidol Div., Pennwalt Corp.   ³Noury Chemical Corp.   ⁴PPG Industries.   ⁵R. T. Vanderbilt.   ⁶Harwick Standard Chemicals.   ⁷Shell Chemical Corp.

Courtesy, Silicone Products Dept., General Electric.

The rheology and curing characteristics of silicone rubber compounds are critical factors affecting the processing properties when fabricating. There are a number of instruments on the market for determination of the curing characteristics of silicone and other rubber compounds. These instruments, such as the Mooney Shearing Disc Viscometer, the Williams Parallel Plate Plastometer, the Garvey Die Extrusion, the Firestone Extrusion Plastometer, the C. W. Brabender Plasti-Corder[R], and the Monsanto Oscillating Disc Rheometer are very useful tools for the batch to batch comparison of the processing characteristics of a compound. However, it is difficult to relate the reading of these instruments to the suitability of a compound in a particular injection mold or extrusion process. Once a compound has proven effective in a specific process, a good rheometer should provide adequate guidance to the compounder in duplicating the desired characteristics.

The most popular rheometer appears to be the Monsanto Oscillating Disc Rheometer (ASTM D-2084-71T) although there is some indication that a capillary rheometer manufactured by the Instrom Corporation produces readings which can be directly applied to the injection molding process.[3] A description of the Monsanto Oscillating Disc Rheometer follows: The oscillation of a biconical disc, embedded in a rubber specimen, confined in a heated square cavity, exerts shear strain sinusoidally on the specimen. The force (torque) needed to oscillate the disc is directly proportional to the stiffness

TROUBLE SHOOTING COMPOUND PREPARATION ON A TWO ROLL RUBBER MILL.

Symptom	Probable Cause	Action
1. Lumpy compound	Freshing technique	Avoid addition of non-freshened compound to plasticized compound.
2. Low viscosity tacky	Overfreshening	Shorten mill time.
3. Poor color dispersion	Cross blending Improper pigment	Use a color Masterbatch. Increase cross blending.
4. Nervy compound	Over heated compound Cross linking	Use cooling water on rolls. Decrease milling time.
5. Contamination	From handling and/or milling	Keep compound in closed containers or covered. Clean all traces of rubber, fillers, etc., from mill.

(shear modulus) of the specimen. As the modulus increases during vulcanization, torque is recorded against time, to give a cure curve of modulus against time.

The Rheograph modulus time chart provides a direct method of determining the entire curing cycle.

It is evident from the accuracy of the rheometer that it is an ideal instrument for quality control and may be used for the identification of material lots, catalysts, and catalyst levels. However, the application of rheometer cure data to the molding process would be difficult because of size and shape differences between a commercial part and a rheometer test sample. Heat transfer rates will vary greatly in molding, depending on the method used, and in transfer and injection molding there may be considerable frictional heat generated. Outside of measuring material quality, there is practically no rheometer information applicable to the extrusion process.

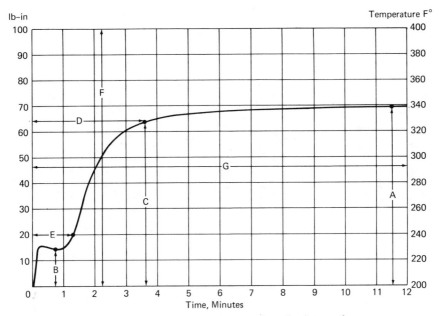

Fig. 2-5. Features of the Rheograph and the interpretation of points on the curve.
(A) T max; Maximum Torque = 100% Cure. (A theoretical value)
(B) T min; Minimum Torque = 0% Cure.
(C) T 90%; 90% Torque (at 90% cure) = 90% × (T max − T min)
(D) t 90 = Time to 90% cure.
(E) t 10 = Time to 10% cure (Scorch?)
(F) Torque; lb$_f$. in___Adjustable from Full Scale (25 lb$_f$. in) to Full scale (200 lb$_f$. in).
(G) Cure Time; min. ___Adjustable from Full Scale (3 min.) to Full Scale (600 min. = 10 hrs.).

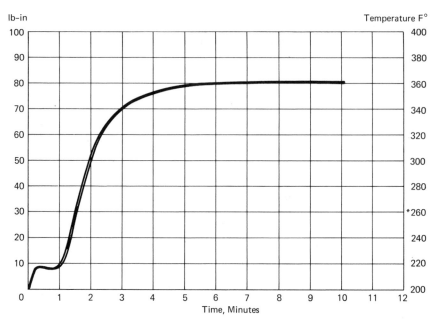

Fig. 2-6. Reproducibility of the Rheometer. Four runs indicate the reproducibility of the Rheometer machine, proving same material with same lot number.

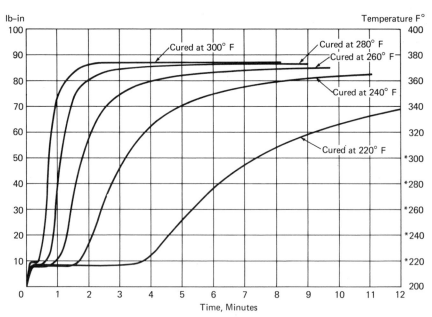

Fig. 2-7. Influence of temperature on curing characteristics.

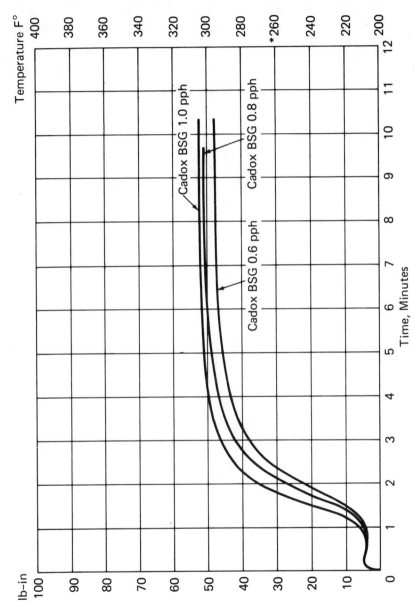

Fig. 2-8. Effect of different concentrations of catalyst .6, .8, and 1.0 pt. Cadox in a 50 duro general-purpose compound. Figures 2-5-2-8 courtesy of Moxness Products Inc., subsidiary of Versa Technologies, Inc.

References

1. Boonstra, B. B., Cochrane, H., and Dannenberg, E. M., "Reinforcement of Silicone Rubber by Particulate Silica," *Rubber Chemistry and Technology*, A.C.S., Vol. **48,** No. 4 (Sept., Oct., 1975).
2. British Patent 868377.
3. Hertel, D. L. and Oliver, C. K., "Versatile Capillary Rheometer," *Rubber Age* (May 1975).

3 | THE MOLDING OF HEAT VULCANIZING SILICONE RUBBERS

The standard methods of compression, transfer, and injection molding are used to produce a great variety of silicone rubber parts (Figs. 3-1 and 3-2). Included are "O" ring seals, cup packings, bonded to metal rotary shaft seals, mechanical gaskets, electrical connectors, boots for environmental protection of electrical and mechanical controls, timing diaphragms and diaphragms—supported and unsupported—for gas pressure regulation, carburetor check valves, suction cups for picking up hot plastics sheet or moldings as they come out of the press or even delicate hot bakery products emerging from the conveyor oven, face masks for flying, diving, and gas protection, human body prostheses, both implantable and worn externally, surgical retractors, vibration cushions, light filters, bottle stoppers, baby bottle nipples, rolls, and many, many others.

COMPRESSION MOLDING

Compression molding is still a very widely used technique for molding silicone rubber parts, in spite of the great strides made with transfer and injection molding. Part of the reason for this lies in the fact that well maintained compression presses will run "forever." There are many jobs being run on compression presses, "written off" long ago, which could not support the huge investment of a modern injection molding press. But another reason is that some silicone rubber parts, large diameter "O" rings for example, cannot be run as economically any other way. There is a minimum of material loss when an extruded preform rod is placed in the cavity. Due to its

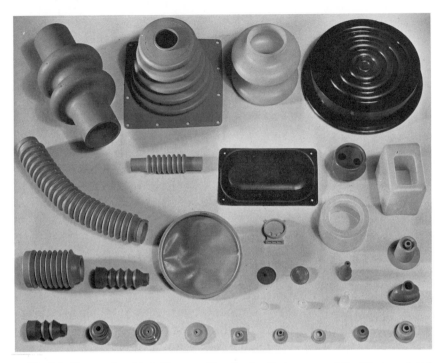

Fig. 3-1. Group of molded silicone rubber boots, diaphragms and flexible convoluted tubes. (*Courtesy Moxness Products, Inc., Subsidiary of Versa Technologies, Inc.*)

high thermal conductivity and the low temperature catalyst systems used, compression molding cures for silicone rubber parts are short (1 to 2 min.), except in very heavy cross sections.

Many compression molds are operated as hand molds. That is, they are removed from the press each cycle. Small molds are slid out onto the molding bench by hand, larger molds may have an air cylinder assist. On the bench they are opened with prybars or with a breaker stand. For opening large molds or molds with a long draw, the breaker stand may be equipped with a mechanical assist (often rack and pinion). The molded parts are then removed, usually by hand with the assistance of a compressed air jet, the mold is cleaned of flash particles, lubricated,* reloaded with preforms, closed, and

---

*Acceptable lubricants are: 2 to 3% aqueous solution of sodium phosphate containing detergent or Duponol WAQ (WAQ is best with fluorosilicones). Mold lubricants should be used as dilute as possible while still obtaining adequate release. Use sparingly to avoid build-up in the mold cavities.

Fig. 3-2. Molded fluorosilicone rubber check valves used in automotive carburetors, operate immersed in gasoline. They can seal against minor surface imperfections or grit, which is not possible for a metal ball check. (*Courtesy Vernay Laboratories, Inc.*)

slid back into the press. The press is then closed and the cure cycle begun.

Ideally, the press should be self-contained to the extent that both pressure and speed of close are adjustable. The press platen temperatures should be adjustable and controllable to ±5°F (3°C). Naturally, there will be a lag between the mold temperature and the platen temperature. Since this will vary with the size of the mold and the percent of time the mold is on the bench versus in the press curing, the platen temperatures may have to be adjusted for each job. The pressure, speed of close, and temperature are the three press variables which must be fine tuned for optimum results. Ideally, the temperature will be the highest practical in order to keep the cure time to a minimum but at the same time not scorch the preform before the press is closed. Benzoyl peroxide or 2,4-dichlorobenzoyl peroxide are the preferred catalysts for hand molds because of their low reaction temperatures. The higher temperature catalysts require so hot a mold that it becomes uncomfortable to handle even though the operator wears insulating gloves. Platen temperatures with hand molds will usually run 270 to 300°F (130 to 150°C) in order to achieve an average mold temperature of 240 to 250°F (115 to 120° C).

Once the mold is in place, the press should be closed as quickly as possible until the top surface of the mold is just about to contact the top platen. At this point the press should be slowed to allow the material to flow gradually enough to fill the cavity evenly, forcing the air out of the cavity in front of it and creating enough back

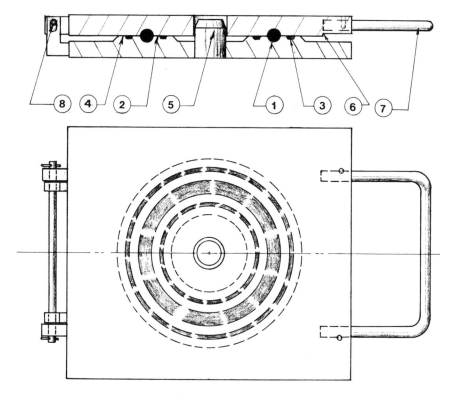

Fig. 3-3. A typical hand-operated compression mold. (1) A single "O" ring cavity is illustrated. In this case, the molding compound would be loaded as a preformed rope with a cross sectional area about 10% greater than the c.s. area of the cavity. (2) Flash land, the width of this land will be determined by the method of finishing to be used: i.e., a tear trim which is often performed by the molder between shots by sharply snapping the stripper ring away from the molding, would dictate the narrowest possible land without risking too easy nicking. Land widths of .010 in. (.25 mm.) are popular for this method. On the other hand, if freeze tumbling* is to be used, a wider land is desirable, .030 or .040 in. (.75 to 1 mm). (3) Stripper ring or flash overflow groove. This should be heavy enough to allow the operator easy grasping for stripping but at the same time not waste material. Average width would lie between .040 to .060 in. (1 to 1.5 mm). (4) Stripper land: creates back pressure on material in stripper ring and in turn on materials in the cavity, thus improving the density. It also reduces the unit pressure on the flash land. It is usually wise to supplement the land area with additional pressure pads to protect the mold in case pressure is applied while empty or excessive pressure is accidentally exerted. (5) Guide pins: Often a single hardened pin and bushing located in the center of the mold in the case of an "O" ring. With other types of moldings, four pins and bushings are used. The guide pins should be on the core side of the mold and should be slightly longer than the core or cores in order to protect them if the core half of the mold is placed on the bench core side down. The guide pins should have a long lead, they should fit loosely until the mold is almost closed. Otherwise binding during opening and closing of the mold is likely. Both guide pins and bushings should be positively anchored in their respective mold plates. (6) Pry bar slots, to initiate mold opening. Many molds will be opened with mechanical assistance such as arbor press operated breaker stands, however, pry bar slots still should be incorporated as a mainte-

pressure as it flashes across the lands to produce good dense mold-ings. The speed of closing, and consequently the rate of flow of the rubber, should not be slowed to the point that scorching occurs and thick flash results. A final closing speed of 5 in./min. (12.7 cm/min.) might be used as a starting point. A preform of proper size and shape coupled with a well controlled speed of closing should normally pro-duce gas-free parts. However, it is sometimes necessary to "bump" the mold in order to eliminate all of the gas or trapped air. This in-volves opening the press a fraction and closing it quickly one or more times before the rubber has begun to vulcanize. If the press does not have a variable closing speed control, it may be equipped with an adjustable height bench. The lower press platen should then be blocked up until the daylight opening is just enough to allow the loaded mold to slide easily between the upper and lower platens. The bench height is then adjusted to suit. In this way the press closing time has been cut to a minimum. The press closing pressure should be as low as possible to reduce wear and tear on the mold, yet high enough to give an acceptable flash thickness (.003 in., .076 mm max.). While pressure requirements will vary greatly, depending on the plasticity of the stock being used and some of the design features of the mold, it should rarely be above 3,000 psi (210 kg/sq cm). If the press is run off a central hydraulic system and the pressure is fixed, the mold should include some substantial pressure pads which would be in contact while the cavity lands are .00015 to .002 in. (.05 mm) apart.

When starting a new molding job, the three press variables, pres-sure, speed, and temperature, must be adjusted until optimum re-sults are obtained. It is well to keep in mind that as the press operator gains proficiency at loading and unloading the mold, the ratio of bench time to cure time will change. The change is usually gradual, but can be substantial over a period of several days with the result that the average mold temperature will increase and a platen

---

nance shop convenience if nothing else. (7) Handle for pulling the mold from the press to the bench and for convenience in opening. If the molds are very large, eyebolts are installed to allow the use of chain hoists. (8) Hinge: hinges should be incorporated wherever possible on hand molds. They not only make the mold more manageable for the operator but they prevent accidental misalignment or reverse positioning of the plates. The hinge must have enough vertical play to allow the plates to lie parallel to each other when the mold is closed by hand on the preforms.

*See section on deflashing, p. 85.

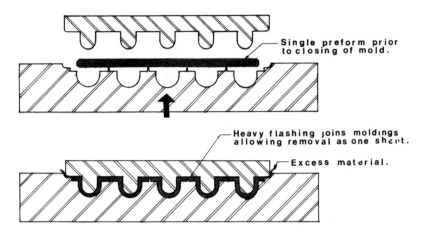

Fig. 3-4. Sub-cavity type compression mold. For certain shapes such as baby nipples or simple boots a multi-cavity compression mold can be designed as a sub-cavity mold in which case the preform may be a single large sheet. After vulcanization the moldings are removed still in sheet form. The "sheet" of moldings is then die trimmed. While material waste tends to be higher on this type of mold, the lower preform cost and loading and finishing times more than offset this.

temperature reduction will have to be made to prevent scorching of the material.

Adjustable guide brackets on the lower press platens speed up proper location of hand molds and reduce wear on the press bearings. Large compression molds are often mounted in the press. This is usually referred to as semi-automatic. An example of a semiautomatic mold may be seen in Fig. 3-5. Prehardened mold steels such as P-20 are preferred for runs of 5000 to 15000 per cavity. For prototypes and short runs, aluminum alloys may be used. Very long running jobs, parts with metal inserts which require sharp cut-off, or where sliding cores could lead to galling, would dictate hardened steel molds. Often, hardened steel is used in combination with prehardened.

Chromium plating is of advantage only where the contours are simple and the silicone rubber compound is a non-sticky stock. Otherwise, cleaning of the cavities with vapo-blast quickly removes the chromium. Mold lubricants have a tendency not to form an even film on chromium plate. Prehardened stainless steel* is pre-

---

*CSM 414: Crucible Steel Co.

ferred to chromium plating.   This material produces tough, long-lasting cavities which take a good finish.   It avoids the problem of rust when the mold is in storage and during periods of high humidity. The additional 15 to 20% extra cost for prehardened stainless steel tools is well worth it when performance and tool maintenance are considered.

Fig. 3-5. Large twenty-cavity compression mold for the production of brush holder boots for use on traction equipment D.C. motors (application illustrated in Fig. 9-16, p. 214). This is a good example of a large mold incorporating unitized construction. Preforms are loaded with a loading board.   The press is a 150-ton McNeil clamshell design, mechanically operated press.   The tilt out feature of the head makes unloading of parts and cleaning of the top section of the mold easier.   The parts are tear trimmed.   (*Photo by Paul Flagg. Courtesy Moxness Products, Inc., Subsidiary of Versa Technologies, Inc.*)

Cast mold cavities, which originally were used for prototyping and short runs where dimensions and finish were of secondary importance to detailed decoration, are now being produced to close dimensional tolerances. Mirror finish and a life as long as machined cavities are possible. They can be produced in a variety of materials, including 304 or 420 stainless steel, P-20, beryllium copper, and beryllium nickel.* When intricate detail and complex shapes are required for multi-cavity molds, casting can save both money and time.

The mold shrinkage of silicone rubbers varies from about 2 to 4%. Since the linear thermal expansion of silicone rubber averages about seventeen times that of steel, the main variable is mold temperature— the lower the molding temperature the lower the shrinkage. Release of volatiles during vulcanization and post cure may also be an important factor and a substantial difference exists between some compounds. The addition of fillers also lowers the linear expansion of the compound. Because silicone rubber is a compressible material, the method of molding, the shape of the piece, and the pressure applied will certainly influence the dimensions of the finished product. The important factor in producing uniform parts is the control of the many variables affecting shrinkage. Their very close control can lead to tolerances of ±.002 inches per in. (±.02 mm/cm) on parts .25 in. (6 mm) in size or smaller, although ±.010 in./in. (±.1 mm/cm) is more practical. Closer tolerance, except on very small parts, is accomplished by grinding. Closure dimensions, the dimensions which vary with the flash thickness, are harder to hold than those dependent on the fixed dimensions of the mold. An additional tolerance allowance of 3 to 4% may be required for closure dimensions. The RMA Rubber Handbook[3] lists four classes of dimensional tolerances for molded rubber products, which can easily be applied to silicone rubber parts:

Class 1, for precision parts requiring exact dimensions such as "O" rings and other precision seals.

Class 2, for high quality parts requiring close dimensional control such as diaphrams, cylinder cups, and valve seats.

Class 3, for ordinary commercial parts.

Class 4, for noncritical parts.

---

*Sarcol Inc., Chicago, Ill.

Standard tolerances are given as follows:

RMA Class 1		
Size (In.)	Fixed	Closure (Plus or Minus)
0– .499	.005	.005
.500– .999	.005	.008
1.000–1.999	.008	.010
2.000–2.999	.010	.013
3.000–3.999	.013	–
4.000–4.999	.015	–
5.000–7.999	.020	–

8.000 and over–multiply by .0025

RMA Class 2		
Size (In.)	Fixed	Closure (Plus or Minus)
0– .499	.005	.008
.500– .999	.008	.010
1.000–1.999	.010	.015
2.000–2.999	.015	.020
3.000–3.999	.018	–
4.000–4.999	.021	–
5.000–7.999	.025	–

8.000 and over–multiply by .0037

RMA Class 3		
Size (In.)	Fixed	Closure (Plus or Minus)
0– .499	.010	.015
.500– .999	.010	.018
1.000–1.999	.015	.020
2.000–2.999	.020	.025
3.000–3.999	.025	.030
4.000–4.999	.030	.035
5.000–7.999	.035	.050

8.000 and over–multiply by .0050

RMA Class 4		
Size (In.)	Fixed	Closure (Plus or Minus)
0– .499	.015	.03
.500– .999	.015	.03
1.000–1.999	.020	.03
2.000–2.999	.025	.05
3.000–3.999	.030	.05
4.000–4.999	.035	.05
5.000–7.999	.045	.07

8.000 and over–multiply by .0060

These tolerances should be used as guidelines only. Where unusual shapes are involved or great differences in wall thickness on the same part occur, close tolerances may be achieved only through the "cut and try" approach of a prototype mold accompanied by variations in materials compounding.

A process for the continuous automatic compression molding of small (up to 2 in., 5 cm) rubber parts has been developed.* This process is limited to the use of stocks with sufficient green strength to allow a continuous ribbon of rubber to be fed from the mill to a series of single cavity molds mounted on a four foot (1.2 m) diameter vertical wheel. There are approximately 100 cavities mounted on the wheel, each one going through a full cycle with one complete turn.

*Orco-Matic (formerly Gora Lee) process, Ohio Rubber Co.

The single cavities are self-registering and capable of producing very precise parts. One machine can turn out as many as 400,000 parts per day. High performance silicone rubber "D" ring seals are produced by this method for use in the diesel engines of the traction equipment described on p. 209.

The compression molding method is used to produce "O" ring seals, especially the larger sizes, bonded shaft seals, diaphrams, supported and unsupported and with or without metal inserts, stoppers for medical applications, various boots for switches, flat sheets, and a variety of simple mechanical parts, some of which are discussed in detail in other chapters.

PREFORMING

The successful compression molding of a product is largely dependent on preforming of the unvulcanized stock into slugs of a certain shape and volume prior to molding. The shape of the preform and its location in the compression cavity are quite important to the efficiency of the mold. Ideally, as the mold closes, the material should flow in such a manner as to expel the air in front of it and reach the flash land all around the cavity at the same time. For example, a preform shaped as shown in Fig. 3-6, placed in a shallow square cavity, will assure even filling, whereas a round preform would cause excess flash at the sides and often shorts or air pockets in the corners. Preforms of this type are often made by sheeting the stock off the mill to a specified thickness. The sheets are then die cut, usually with a hand operated "cookie" cutter. Preforms for O-ring molds and cavities requiring simple round slugs are generally extruded and cut off to length. Where heat-sensitive stocks are used, the preform extruder may be a hydraulic ram rather than a screw type. Less working of the stock takes place when a ram is used, reducing the risk of "scorching" or partial cure of the compound before the molding step. An example of a ram type extrusion preformer with a built-in cutoff is the preformer shown in Fig. 3-7. Figure 3-8 shows a close-up view of the cutter head. Preform cutters are available* for use in conjunction

---

*G. F. Goodman & Son advertises two models which slice preforms at the face of the extrusion die. One model can handle solid slugs 4 in. (10 cm) diameter X 4 in. long; its delivery rate is 22 to 2000 preforms per minute. The other can handle solid slugs of up to 6 in. (15 cm) diameter X 6 in. long.

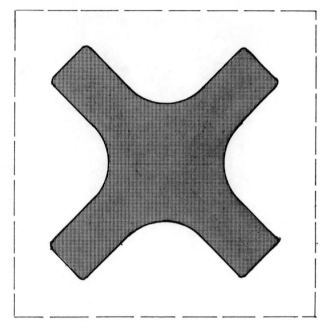

Fig. 3-6. Cross shaped preform is required in order to fill a square cavity evenly.

with any of the standard makes of screw extruders. Preforms extruded or cut from medium or high durometer compounds may be kept from sticking to one another by a light dusting of silica or talc powder. Preforms of soft, sticky stocks usually have to be separated with waffle-surfaced polyethylene film.

Where a large number of cavities are involved, preform loading fixtures should be used to speed up the loading time and prevent scorching of the material before the mold is closed. Molds using one or just a few small preforms per shot are handily serviced by a small air cylinder operated preformer mounted on the molding bench and operated by the molder. Units of this type are usually built in the fabricator's own maintenance shop.

A number of silicone rubber stocks can be pelletized. These are typically the stocks used in wire coating by extrusion (p. 112), and the molding of automotive spark plug boots by injection or transfer molding (p. 76). The pellets are produced by extruding the stock through a multiple hole extrusion die to obtain cords $\frac{1}{8}$ to $\frac{1}{4}$ in. (5 mm) in diameter. The cords are dusted as they leave the die. On

Fig. 3-7. Automatic precision preformer processes up to 1500 lb (680 kg/hr) of preform blanks in a variety of shapes with a volumetric accuracy of ±1.5%. The die and cutter lie behind the expanded metal safety gate. They are illustrated in detail in Fig. 3-8. (*Courtesy Barwell, Inc.*)

entering a rotary pellet cutter they are chopped into pellets at rates of over $\frac{1}{2}$ ton per hour. The free flowing pellets can be hopper fed, leading to fully automatic feeding of extruders or injection machines. They can be accurately weighed, which allows better control of flashing and dimensional tolerances. They can be handy for loading transfer pots, or even compression cavities, as well as hopper fed machines. For instance, some intricate compression cavities require preforms which are time consuming to prepare. A load of pellets, however, may be distributed around the cavity to give the same result. Pelletized compounds have a comparatively long shelf life and are available from the raw material suppliers.* Consequently, the fabricators of products which are suited for production from pelletized silicone

---

*Gensil P. S. E. 790, Silicone Products Dept., General Electric.

Fig. 3-8. Close-up of die and cutter arrangement. A simple cylindrical shaped preform is shown being formed. A variety of shapes can be produced at rates up to 15,000/hr. The thickness of the preforms may be varied from one edge to the other by varying the die land depth. (*Courtesy Barwell, Inc.*)

stocks, are able to eliminate the compounding step and the need for costly compounding equipment.

The technology exists for the preparation of silicone rubber compounds as free flowing powders.[1] The powders are generated comparatively easily through the high shear mixing of silicone gums with treated silica fillers and special process aids. If desired, catalysts may also be included. Bulk density is low, running about 20 to 30 lb/cu ft (320 to 480 kg/cu m) with particles averaging about 20 μm in size. Swanson et al.[2] have reported that the powder form appears to have unlimited shelf life without crepe hardening. They also observed greatly improved compression set properties and predict the possibility of some unique physical property profiles when powdered, as opposed to standard bale-form, silicone rubber stocks are used. A free flowing powder form of unvulcanized silicone rubber compound is especially attractive, from the point of view of ease of preparation, handling, and its long storage life, when compared with the standard, tacky bale-form. However, its very low bulk density and poor heat transfer leads to difficulties during plasticization which takes special extrusion and molding equipment to overcome. There will be low fabricator acceptance until this difficulty is solved.

It is probable that as the technology of fabricating with powdered silicone rubber is perfected, it will lend itself to completely automated processes for the fabrication of some types of silicone rubber products.

TRANSFER MOLDING

Transfer molding is the most widely used technique for the molding of silicone rubber parts. Faster cycles than compression molding, a single preform per shot, and the ability to mold more complicated parts, especially around delicate inserts and pins, all contribute to its popularity. When compared with injection molding, the difference in equipment costs usually gives transfer a decided advantage. There are two basic types of transfer mold: one is the pot and piston mold which can be set up in an ordinary single ram compression press; the other is the plunger type, which requires a double ram press, one to clamp the mold the other to transfer the material as a separate function. Transfer molds may be operated as hand, semiautomatic or automatic molds.

A semiautomatic pot and piston mold is diagramatically illustrated in Fig. 3-9. Such a mold must have a pot area about 25 to 30% greater than the projected area of all the cavities in order to prevent the mold flashing when full pressure is applied. This type of mold is ideal for the large volume production of small parts such as bushings, insulating caps, etc. Unlike a design using a runner system, the pressure in this mold will be applied evenly to all cavities, making it unnecessary to balance gates. Upon curing, the cull can be ripped out of the pot with sprues attached, leaving the parts clean at the gate. The loose cavity plate is then removed from the mold and the pieces knocked out by airblast or with a knockout board.

In Fig. 3-10 a pot and piston mold is shown mounted in the press on rails which allow the pot and cavity plates to slide out for easier operator servicing. The 100 cavity mold produces small electrical terminal boots. In Fig. 3-11 the mold is inverted with the pot and

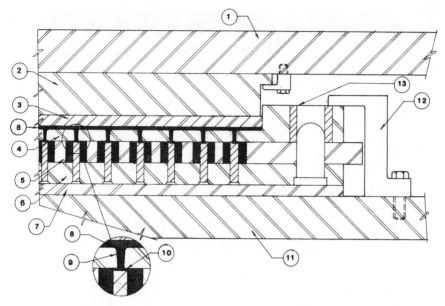

Fig. 3-9. Pot and piston type transfer mold. (1) Heated upper press platen. (2) Piston. (3) Piston wear plate. (4) Pot. (5) Loose cavity plate. (6) Mold base plate. (7) Back-up plate. (8) Material cull. (9) Sprue. (10) Gate. (11) Heated Bottom press platen. (12) Guide rail and mold stripper. (13) Guide bushing.

piston on the bottom for easier servicing of the extra long cavities and cores.

A plunger type mold is illustrated diagramatically in Fig. 3-12. A preform is loaded into the pot (2) which is a permanent part of the upper platen (8). It is either introduced into the top of the pot with the plunger fully retracted or it is placed on top of the cavity plate before the press is closed. In some plunger presses the main ram is on top and the transfer ram is on the bottom. In such a case the material is conveniently dropped into the open end of the pot when the plunger is retracted and the mold is slid into the press, runner side down. In many cases, it is more practical to gate the cavities at the parting line. Then a central main sprue carries the material to a runner system at the parting line. When both mold halves are permanently mounted on the platens, the plunger must enter the mold all the way to the parting line to allow removal of the cull and runners. In still another variation, the transfer cylinder is mounted at right angles to the clamping cylinder and the plunger enters the

Fig. 3-10. A typical semiautomatic pot and piston type mold, ideal for the molding of a large number of small pieces. The pot slides out of rails for easier removal of cull and reloading. The bottom core plate also slides out on the molding bench for easier air removal of moldings. (*Photo by Paul Flagg. Courtesy Moxness Products, Inc.*)

mold horizontally along the parting line. Figure 3-13 shows the cavity detail of the 8 cavity, plunger type, hand mold used for the production of pacemaker connector boots and illustrated in Fig 3-14. The rubber is a 50 durometer VMQ medical grade stock* catalyzed with 1.4 parts of TS50. The shot weight is 14.5 g, 6 g or 40% of which is runners and cull. The cure cycle is 2.5 min at 240°F (115°C). The transfer pressure is 1900 psi (134 kg/sq cm). The average num-

---

*MEC 501, Medical Engineering Corp.

ber of heats per hour is twelve. The nose of the core pin enters the sprue hole with a close fit. This keeps the core pin centered, which is important because of the very thin wall section at the top of the boot. Three flats, .010 in. (.25 mm) deep, are then ground at the tip of the core pin where it enters the sprue hole—these act as gates. Gate dimensions and location in transfer or injection cavities are often a matter of compromise between obtaining optimum physical properties (appearance and trimming costs) in the finished molding. Very small gates which produce the cleanest parts may cause scorch-

Fig. 3-11. A pot and piston transfer mold may be inverted for easier removal of parts. The long insulating boot produced in this mold is used on traction equipment connections. (*Photo by Paul Flagg. Courtesy Moxness Products, Inc., Subsidiary of Versa Technologies, Inc.*)

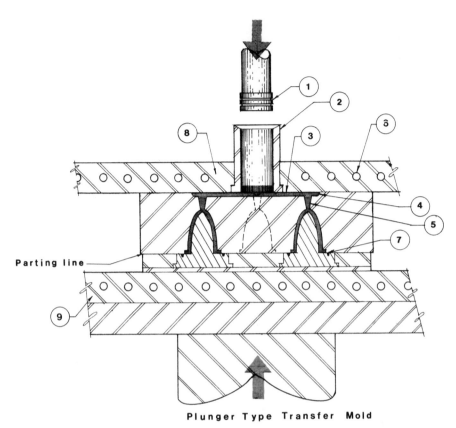

Plunger Type Transfer Mold

Fig. 3-12. Plunger-type transfer molds. (1) Plunger. (2) Pot. (3) Cavity plate. (4) Runner. (5) Sprue. (6) Heaters. (7) Stripper. (8) Top platen. (9) Bottom platen.

ing of the stock and incomplete filling. Usually, the fabricator will start with the smallest gate he feels is practical, based on his experience, then open it gradually until he gets the best results. The cavity (Fig 3-13) is vented at the parting line and at the base of the core pin. A good rule of thumb for venting is that the vents should have about 20% of the cross sectional area of the gates. Without adequate venting, the molding will develop soft burned spots. The cavity usually stains and may quickly corrode where brown spots have occurred.

Moldings which take up a large area of the mold but have a low projected area and weight in relation to their overall dimensions, are more economically run in stacked or multi-layer molds. Illustrated in Fig. 3-15 is a hand transfer mold for the production of silicone

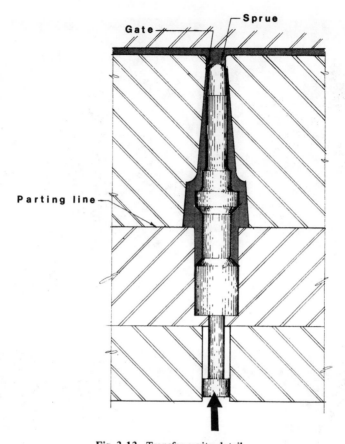

Fig. 3-13. Transfer cavity detail.

rubber flat electric frying pan handle gaskets. There are five plates, each with four cavities, fed by a centrally located sprue hole, a total of twenty cavities. Twenty cavities of this size all on one plate would be difficult to manage and require a much larger, more expensive press as well as having a high material loss due to a longer runner system.

Automatic Transfer Molding: An automatic pot and piston type molding system* has appeared on the market recently. It should become popular for a variety of silicone rubber molding projects be-

*Trans/Matic, The Kent Machine Co., Div. of the Lamson & Sessions Co. U.S. Patents 3,748,075 and 3,836,307.

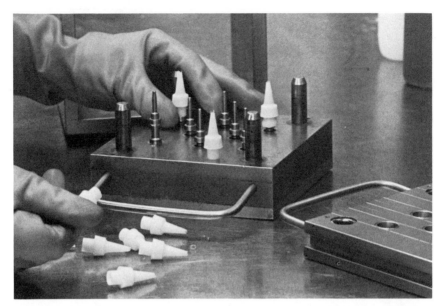

Fig. 3-14. Eight cavity plunger-type hand transfer mold. (*Courtesy Medical Engineering Corp.*)

Fig. 3-15. Multi-layer hand transfer mold. Note that the plates are hinged, this greatly facilitates handling of the mold by the operator and reduces the possibility of damage to the plates. Moldings are deflashed by scraping the surface of the cavity plate with a sharp nylon scraper before removing them from the cavities. (*Photo by Paul Flagg. Courtesy Moxness Products, Inc., Subsidiary of Versa Technologies, Inc.*)

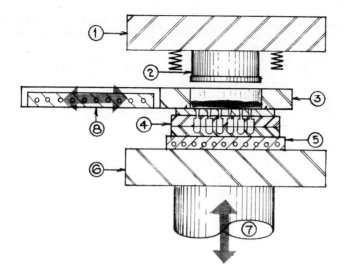

Fig. 3-16(a). Automatic transfer molding. Start of cycle; press is closing with mold and loaded pot in position. (1) Stationary press head. (2) Transfer piston. (3) Transfer pot with detachable sprue plate. (4) Mold. (5) Lower heating plate. (6) Lower moving press platen. (7) Clamping ram. (8) Upper heating plate. Attached to pot frame, it can be moved horizontally by the action of a cylinder. The cylinder may be seen in Fig. 3-17—part 9.)

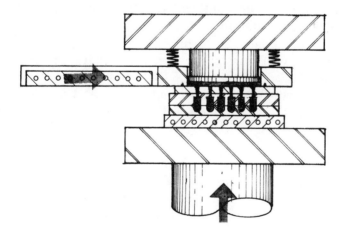

Fig. 3-16(b). Material transfer piston has entered pot and material has been transferred to cavities. Upon completion of transfer the press reopens, the pot is moved horizontally from the mold, being replaced by the upper heating platen which is insulated from both pot and piston. Press recloses.

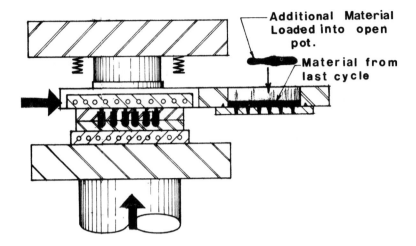

Fig. 3-16(c). Cure cycle begins. During the cure cycle fresh molding material is loaded into the pot. If necessary, a cold plate is moved into contact with the sprue plate to prevent scorching of the material in the pot by absorbing the heat which the sprue plate gained from the mold during the transfer cycle.

cause of its lower capital investment compared to injection molding equipment and the elimination of excessive wear and stock set-up problems, especially encountered with the screw fed machines. A diagramatic representation of the system is presented in Fig. 3-16, a photo of the molding equipment in Fig. 3-17.

The versatility of transfer molding indicates its application in the production of a great variety of silicone rubber parts, many of them bonded to metal; boots for mechanical and electrical applications, gaskets, closures, shock mounts, bellows, small "O" rings, carburetor check valves, diaphrams, rotating shaft seals, oxygen masks, and electrical connector insulators to name but a few. All are used where outstanding dependability is required under severe operating conditions. Dimensions of transfer molded silicone rubber parts may be held to the same tolerances as compression molded parts except that an extra allowance for closure dimensions usually need not be made.

INJECTION MOLDING

Silicone rubber is an ideal material for the injection molding process due to its good flow characteristic and very fast cure at high tempera-

Fig. 3-17. Trans/matic molding machine. Illustrated is a 392-ton model equipped with 24 × 24 in. (60 × 60 cm) platens. The simple, rugged, single ram hydraulic press construction is apparent. The equipment may be "dry cycled" in 26 sec. The upper heating platen (8) is shown in the cure cycle position. On the right is a materials preparation unit (10) for slug cutting and, when required, preheating. The equipment cost of approximately $70,000.00 is considerably lower than injection units of the same capacity. The mold costs are also lower than standard injection molds and much lower than cold runner molds. This model of automatic transfer molding machinery is being used successfully in the production of silicone rubber spark plug boots. Performance compares very favorably with the injection molding equipment used on the same projects. (*Courtesy The Kent Machine Co., Division of The Lamson & Sessions Co.*)

tures. As early as the middle 50's, two California men—Clem Shaw, the designer of a ram injection machine and Hugh Stewart, a rubber chemist—had developed a practical system for the injection molding of silicone rubber. It is probable that the Electronic Components Division of the Deutsch Co. was the first to commercialize the injection process by making silicone electrical connector seals. The initial method developed is well described in a U.S. patent* granted to Hugh Stewart. Figure 3-18, taken from the patent, illustrates diagramatically a ram-type injection molding set-up. The injection

---

*Patent #3,107,234

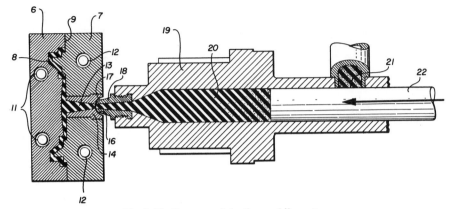

Fig. 3-18. Ram type injection molding set up.

cylinder (19) is loaded through opening (21) with strips of unvulcanized silicone rubber compound. The cylinder temperature must be kept below the vulcanization temperature of the rubber. The ram (22) then forces the unvulcanized rubber at very high speed at pressures of 5,000 to 20,000 psi (350 to 1400 kg/cm^2) into the mold cavity (8). The mold is heated to a constant temperature of about 425°F (220°C) where vulcanization takes place in a matter of seconds. Stewart showed that vinyl containing silicone rubbers, which were just then becoming available, when cross linked with as little as 0.2% of a high temperature vulcanizing agent such as dicumyl peroxide, would cure in 5 to 20 sec at temperatures of 400 to 450°F (205 to 230°C). Very little volatile by-product was formed and this would dissipate rapidly during cure. In contrast, benzoyl perozide, which decomposes rapidly above 250°F (120°C), when used at these higher temperatures would produce gas rapidly causing blistering and sponging of the silicone rubber molding. Stewart also found that preheating of the uncatalyzed compound at 450°F (230°C) for 4 to 5 hr boiled off certain unpolymerized constituents and reduced the amount of mold shrinkage markedly. These volatiles represented as much as 6% by weight of the original compound.* Linear mold shrinkage values of about 2%[†]

---

*Silicone rubber stocks today normally are supplied with volatile fractions stripped from them and need not to be pre-cure heat aged.

[†]This factor can vary greatly with mold temperature (the coefficient of thermal expansion of silicone rubber is approximately 20 times that of steel[4]) and with injection pressure.

were obtained. He also found that his process exhibited superior physical properties, particularly compression set, even before oven post cure.

The combination of the energy absorbing characteristic of the silicone rubber combined with its compressibility, makes it essential that a constant volume of material be in the injection cylinder each cycle. Otherwise, the variation of pressure and fill of the cavity would vary enough to affect the quality of the moldings being produced.

A number of examples are given in the patent. They compare the injection molded results with the suppliers advertised typical data for the same material. The following selected examples should help to indicate the advantages of Stewart's process:

METHYL VINYL POLYSILOXANE—SUPPLIER'S RATING FOR HARDNESS OF CURED RUBBER FROM STOCK SUPPLIED, 80 SHORE A

[Vulcanizing agent: bis(α, α-dimethylbenzyl) peroxide]

Amount uncured stock	g	231.8
Amount v.a., 0.10%	g	0.23
Injection mold in temperature	°F	430
Time held in mold	sec	25

Properties of product removed from mold:

	Stewart	Supplier's rating (15 min./250°F)
Shore A Hardness	79	56
Tensile strength (psi)	1,020	950
Elongation, percent	530	500

Properties after oven postcure for 24 hr at 480°F.:

	Stewart	Supplier's rating
Shore A Hardness	82	80
Tensile strength	920	800
Elongation. percent	230	225
Compression Set (22 hr/350°F), percent	27	30

In the following example the raw gum stock was preheated and then cooled to room temperature before mixing in the vulcanizing agent

METHYL VINYL POLYSILOXANE—SUPPLIER'S RATING FOR HARDNESS OF CURED RUBBER FROM STOCK SUPPLIED, 40 SHORE A

[Vulcanizing agent: α, α dimethylbenzyl (α, α-dimethyl-p-methylbenzyl) peroxide]

Weight before preheating	g	250.0
Weight after 4 hrs./450°F	g	227.9
Loss during preheating {	g	22.1
	percent	8.84
Amount of v.a., 0.10%	g	0.23
Injection mold temperature	°F	430
Time held in mold	sec	25

Properties of product removed from mold:

	Stewart	Supplier's rating (15 min./250°F)
Shore A Hardness	39	37
Tensile strength (psi)	1,090	950
Elongation, %	540	500
Linear shrinkage	1.8	—

Properties after oven postcure for 24 hr at 480°F:

	Stewart	Supplier's rating (15 min./250°F)
Shore A Hardness	42	40
Tensile strength	920	825
Elongation, %	300	375
Compression set (22 hr/350°F), %	17	20
Linear shrinkage	1.8	—

Messrs. DeSieno and Fuhrmann have reported similar improvement in physical properties.[5]   They also show that superior physical values are obtained after injection molding even without post cure. This is due to the fact that there is greater utilization of catalyst, therefore less is required. Since less curing agent is used, there are less catalyst decay by-products, which are the cause of rubber reversion in compression molded products and which must be driven out by oven postcure cycles of sometimes as long as 24 hr at 400 to 480°F (205 to 250°C).

Initially, a few progressive silicone rubber fabricators built their own injection equipment and kept them quite proprietary. Most of this activity was centered on the U.S. West Coast. In 1956 the Lewis Welding and Engineering Company, Cleveland, Ohio (now the Lewis Division of McDowell Wellman Engineering Co, Cleveland, Ohio) entered into an agreement with Clem Shaw and started building the Lewis automated ram-type injection machine. In 1957 the first machine was delivered to the W. J. Voit Company (now AMF Voit) on the West Coast. Figure 3-19 illustrates one of the early 200-ton Lewis horizontal rubber injection molding machines producing pre-

Fig. 3-19. Multi-layer injection mold. Mold has just been opened. Runners may be seen between center plates with the main sprue to the left. Cores can be clearly seen on either side of the runner plates. (*Photo courtesy James E. Rogers*)

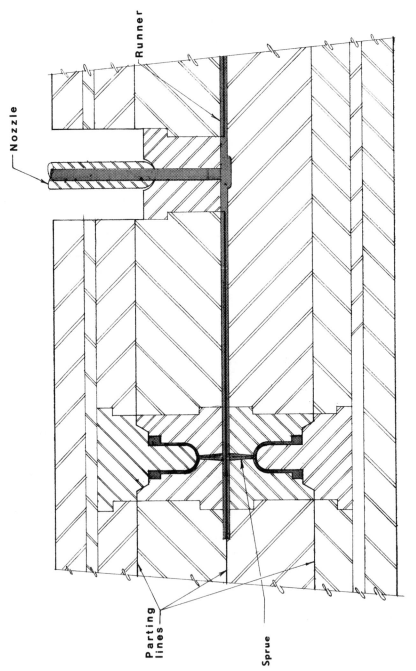

Fig. 3-20. Construction of multi-layer mold shown operating in Fig. 3-19. (*Courtesy James E. Rogers*)

cision mechanical timing diaphrams. The material used is Union Carbide K-1235 silicone rubber vulcanized with Varox. The mold is a 200 cavity multi-plate mold, the construction of which is shown in Fig. 3-20. The molding conditions used were as follows:

Injection cylinder temperature	150°F(65°C)
Injection pressure	7500 psi (527 kg/cm^2)
Mold temperature	485°F (250°C)
Injection time	3 sec
Clamp time	30 sec
Clamp pressure	200 tons (182 metric tons)
Total cycle*	45 sec

The timing diaphram was a very high production military ordnance job running into many millions of parts per year. Unfortunately, there were few such high volume silicone jobs around. Consequently, the use of injection molding equipment developed very slowly.

Another factor affecting the growth of injection molding is the fact that in many cases rubber parts do not lend themselves to automatic removal from the mold. The very characteristics of rubber, such as stretching over heavy undercuts, which allow for simpler mold construction than with more rigid material, requires operator assistance, e.g., applying an air jet in a particular area while pulling in another. The examination of the mold at the end of each cycle to be sure there has been no buildup of material sticking in the cavities or on the flash line is often necessary. Generally, molds may be run automatically when the moldings are short in depth, do not have much undercut, and have enough body so that knockouts can be used. To keep the mold free from part hang-up or flash residue, one manufacturer has developed a fixture (Fig. 3-21) which is adaptable to any press. Upon opening, rotating brushes move across the face of the mold, cleaning it, and the proper amount of mold release is applied for the next shot.

The fast filling of cavities associated with injection molding dictates the necessity of adequate venting to prevent gassy parts. Some parts, however, defy the elimination of gassy spots no matter what venting pattern is used. In such cases, a vacuum drawn on the mold

---

*The identical part run in a sub-cavity compression mold had a total cycle of 2 min. 15 sec.

Fig. 3-21. Automatic injection molding. Photo on top shows the hydraulic ejector system ejecting the pieces from the cavities and on the *bottom the rotating brush* sweeping down to make sure all pieces are free from the mold and the mold face is clean. [*Photos courtesy RUTIL Switzerland.* (*in U.S.A. RUTILUSA Chicago*)]

just prior to injection should solve the problem. Vacuum package units which can be hooked into the automatic cycle controls of the molding machine are available.

Ram-type injection molding presses, first used in the United States, were followed by reciprocating screw types. Because the abrasive nature of silicone rubber fillers leads to screw maintenance problems, we now see many variations of feed: screw feed into a ram type injection chamber*, plunger feed past a shear cone into a ram type injection chamber,[†] the shear cone reputedly wearing at only one third the rate of a screw, and others. A growing proportion of the machines for injection molding are being manufactured with a vertically operating clamp. These machines are preferred for parts with molded-in-place inserts or which require molds with removable inserts or removable cavity plates.

Cold Manifold Molds for Injection Molding   Injection molding cycles for silicone rubber do not have the large cure time advantage over transfer molding that is experienced with organic rubbers. As a matter of fact, some thin-walled silicone parts may be compression molded in a sub-cavity type mold (p. 48) almost as quickly as by the injection process. Great materials savings may be realized, however, with silicones in the injection process through the use of cold manifold (or cold runner) molds. These are molds in which the runner system is completely enclosed and the material in the runners does not set up because the runner plate is cooled and insulated from the cavity section of the mold. Silicone rubber is an ideal material for this type of mold. It does not have to be heated in order to become plasticized to flow through the runner system and into the cavities. It can be vulcanized through the use of a high temperature catalyst. The temperature differential between the runners and the cavities, therefore, can be so great that there is very little chance of the runner system setting up. Figure 3-23 shows the construction used for a large cold manifold mold made to be run in a vertical Lewis machine.

The temperature of the runner system should not be allowed to go above 130°F (54°C), otherwise scorching will occur. This could lead

---

*REP Corporation "V" head Bartlett, Ill. (Fig 3-22)
[†]Sund-Borg Machines Corp. Fremont, Ohio.

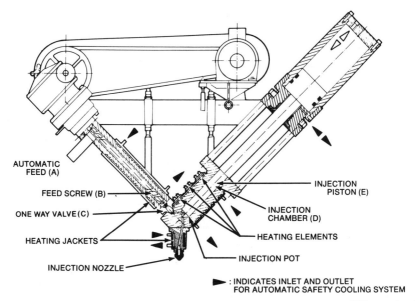

Fig. 3-22. The popular REP injection molding machine incorporates a "V" type head. It is supplied in three models with injection volumes of 30.5 in.[3] (500 cc) 73 in.[3] (1200 cc) and 122 in.[3] (2000 cc) and ranging in price from about $40,000.00 to $100,000.00.

eventually to the setting up of the material in the runners. Usually, city water with thermostatically controlled volume is sufficient. To reduce down time in case of runner set up, it is a good idea to be able to separate the two runner plates without having to remove the mold from the press. Where cavity layout allows it, this may be accomplished by locating the assembly screw heads at the parting line for easy removal. Latches are positioned on each side of the mold, allowing quick attachment of the lower runner plate (2) to the lower cavity plate (6). The lower runner plate should be designed to run on the guide pins. Upon opening the press the runners are exposed. The runners and sprues are quickly cleared and in a matter of minutes the mold is back into service. This is also an advantage in color changes and week-end shutdowns, although there are instances reported of extended shutdown periods of ten days or more followed by successful start-up without opening and clearing the runner system.

Silicone rubber, particularly under injection pressures, easily flows into joints with less than .0005 in. clearance. Consequently, at runner level, a dam system (13), which is a vertical step along the

parting line of the two runner plates, is incorporated to prevent flashing of the runners.   The sheet formation caused by flashing would
force the runner plates apart causing leakage of the stock and mal-
function of the cold runner system.   This dam differs from standard

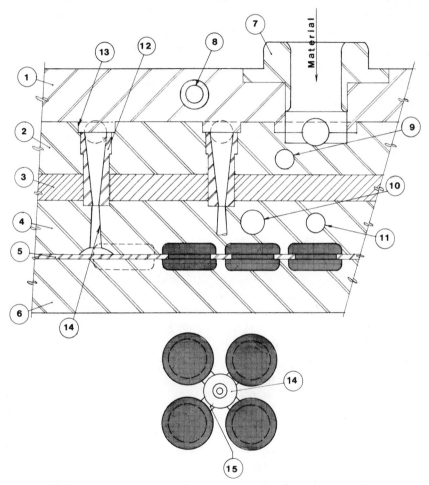

Fig. 3-23. Cold manifold injection mold. (Design by Delaware Valley Mfg., Co., Inc.
Cherry Hill, N.J.) 1. Mold plate, upper half of runner system. 2. Mold plate, lower half of
runner system. 3. Insulation layer. (transite) 4. Upper cavity plate. 5. Groove plate (typical
of grommet molds). 6. Lower cavity plate. 7. Sprue bushing. 8. Cold water circulation
system. 9. Probe for thermostats, two or more locations. 10. Cartridge heaters, number and
size determined by need for supplemental and/or sustaining heat. 11. Probe for thermostats, two or more as required. 12. Downsprue stack from runners to upper cavity plate.
13. Runner Dam. 14. Downsprues manifold with lateral gating to four cavities. 15. Gates
.003 in. to .010 in. × .250 in.

practice with cold runner systems when they are designed for other thermosetting materials. Where there is a large or complicated runner system, the dam system can add appreciably to the mold cost. A 75% premium over the cost of a basic injection mold may be experienced. There are few materials, however, outside of silicone rubber, which in high volume can so quickly pay back the difference in cost. This is particularly true of medical and other high quality applications where reclaim is not used and the base materials are expensive premium types. Some cold manifold molds producing small parts in many cavities will have 50% or more of the total shot weight in the runners. Many molds will show at least a 25% saving in material. Inasmuch as the material in the runners does not become part of the shot capacity of the molding machine, the number of cavities can be increased over a basic type of injection mold. This increase can equal the total volume of material inventoried in the runner system as long as the maximum projected area of the machine clamp is not exceeded.

The Future for Injection Molding The advent of large volume usage of silicones in the automotive industry is leading to some marked changes in production methods. A much needed boost has been given to the engineering of automatic high speed molding of silicone rubber. Silicone rubber spark plug boots for instance, because of their superior heat and dielectric characteristics, represent approximately 40% of the total boots produced now and this proportion is increasing each year. At the Packard Electric Division of General Motors Corporation, silicone rubber spark plug boots are being turned out on a battery of huge multiple station injection molding machines. Both Desma and Stokes machines are used at Packard Electric (Fig. 3-24). Each of the four clamp stations is equipped with a 96 cavity mold. Pelletized silicone rubber (p. 53) is fed by conveyor at the rate of approximately 5 lb/min. (2.3 kg/min.) to the hopper of the machine. The specification on p. 82 is typical for a high performance spark plug boot material. The Desma machine has a $3\frac{1}{2}$ in. (8.9 cm) screw which can plasticize the material turning at about 160 rpm and fill the cavity in about 15 sec. Every 30 sec. a mold opens in front of the operator. The core plate slides out and the parts and runner system are removed. The mold is then ready to be rotated to the fill position and the next cycle begun.

Fig. 3-24. Top Desma Model 905 rotary molding machine with 4 clamp stations. (*Courtesy Compo Industries, Inc., Waltham, Mass.*). Bottom Stokes Model 757R4 rotary injection molding machine with 4 clamp stations. (*Courtesy Stokes Div., Pennwalt Corp., Philadelphia, Pa.*)

The runners are reclaimed, mixed with virgin material (30 phr), and pelletized. The Stokes machine is operated on the same basis. Following is a complete description of the Stokes model 757R4:

Four, 500-ton clamp sections are mounted on a rotating frame. Each clamp section has its own, independent, heat control and set-up controls. The use of double solenoid valves permits infinite control of the opening and closing strokes.

Clamp tonnage is applied by a combined hydraulic, mechanical system (see Fig. 3-25). Initial high speed closing is performed by a hydraulic cylinder at low pressure to protect the mold. With the mold closed, a second hydraulic cylinder, located under the top platen, rotates the clamp lock plate closing off the three access ports in the top platen. A short stroke, 26 in. diameter cylinder in the bottom platen, strokes upwards approximately $\frac{1}{8}$ in. raising the mold, moving platen and lock bars until contact is made with the clamp lock plate, developing the full 500-ton clamping force. Spacers may be added to the lock bars to reduce the clamp stroke from its 18 in. maximum, in 2 in. increments, to 12 in.

Single or multiple breath sequences may be programmed into the clamp cure cycle.

The clamp closing sequence, which takes a maximum of 6.7 sec, occurs while the clamp carrousel is indexing from station to station, as does the clamp opening sequence.

A Ferguson drive controls the indexing movement and provides positive positioning at each station. There are four stations on the machine: one operator's station, one injection station, and two cure stations. The clamps open during indexing between the second cure station and the operator's station. The clamps close during indexing between the operator's station and the injection station.

The injection unit has a 3 in. diameter screw which rotates in a bimetallic lined barrel. Based on a 1.25 specific gravity, the unit has a maximum shot capacity of 61.5 ounces. A hydraulically actuated nozzle shut-off valve is standard. Four shot size limit switches permit the screw to be programmed to prepare a different sized shot for each clamp section, so that a different mold may be used in each clamp.

The injection unit is a separate sub-assembly, which is connected to the clamp with a solid tie to maintain alignment and permit good nozzle to sprue bushing contact when the injection unit is advanced.

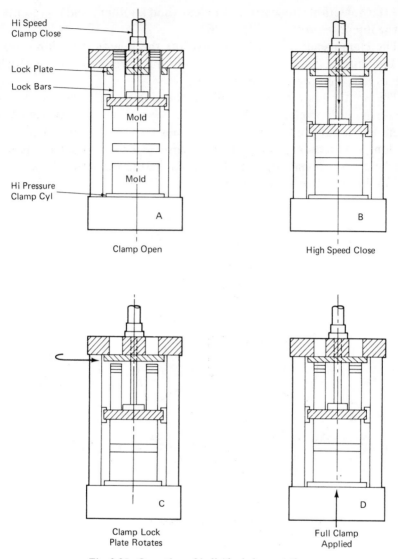

Fig. 3-25. Operation of individual clamp station.

To allow the clamp stations to index without interference, sprue break takes place prior to rotation of the carrousel. The shut-off nozzle prevents material drool while the injection unit is in its retracted position.

After injection, the carrousel indexes and another mold is presented to the injection unit (see Fig. 3-26).

The clamp section which has just left the injection station is now in the cure segment of its cycle. During cure, single or multiple breath may be programmed to occur.

The next index movement still has the clamp section we are following, in its cure cycle. As the clamp leaves station three it begins to open and is fully opened when it reaches station four, the operator's station. A standard part of the clamp section is a set of hanger brackets to lift and separate the mold halves for ease of handling and mold servicing by the operator.

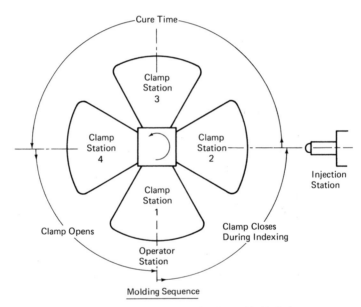

Station 1.   Operator services mold and pushes and holds dual push buttons to signal the press to continue cycling. Clamp begins to close.

Station 2.   Clamp arrives at injection fully closed, injection takes place. A different size shot may be injected into each mold.

Stations
3 and 4.   Mold held closed under full clamp for cure.

As clamp leaves Station 4 it begins opening and is fully opened for parts ejection when it reaches Station 1.

Fig. 3-26. Molding sequence.

The operator initiates the next index motion, once he has removed the molded parts, cleaned the mold, and loaded any necessary inserts, by holding depressed a pair of push buttons. The clamp is fully closed by the time it reaches the injection station and the injection unit advances.

In the center of the indexing carrousel is a rotary manifold to distribute the hydraulic oil, cooling water, air, and vacuum to each of the clamp sections. Mounted on this manifold is an electrical slip ring assembly carrying control and heater wiring to the clamps. The clamp and indexing mechanism are powered by a free standing hydraulic power unit. There are no accumulators in the system and the circuitry permits the clamp to be jogged on set-up and stopped in any required position. For added mold protection there are limit switches to ensure that the mold stripper plates are correctly positioned prior to machine index and clamp close. Heating and cooling platens are standard on each clamp section. One Sterlco water temperature controller is provided for the internally cooled screw and two more maintain the temperature along the barrel. A 25 gpm water cooler and a heat exchanger control the temperature of water going to the clamp cooling platens.

Specifications for the Stokes machine include:

Injection Unit

Screw diameter	3 in. (76.2 mm)
Screw L/D ratio	13/1
Shot size	85 in.^{3} (1393 cm^3)
Rate of injection	14–75 in.^{3}/sec (242 cm^3/sec)
Injection pressure	20,000 psi (1406 kg/cm^2)

Clamp

Capacity	500 tons (453.6 metric)
Stroke	18 in. (45.7 cm)
Daylight opening	26 in. (66 cm)
Mold size	17 in. × 21 in. (43.2 cm × 53.3 cm)

General

Motors	2,40 hp
Floor space	25 ft × 12 ft (7.6 in. × 3.7 m)
Height	12 ft (3.7 m)
Weight	45 tons (40.8 metric)

These tremendous machines cost in the neighborhood of $350,000.00. At the present time less than 200 have been sold in the United States[7] and a very small proportion of these are being used in the fabrication of silicones.

Another interesting automotive application of a rotary type injection molding machine is described on p. 136. Outside of the automotive field, growth in the use of injection equipment in the silicones industry will probably be in the smaller single station injection machines of about 200 tons clamp and costing in the range of $60,000.00. A machine of this caliber is described on p. 142.

It is obvious that the injection molding process, where volume warrants large capital investment, does have advantages over the compression and transfer molding of silicones. Shorter molding cycles are possible, particularly for thick section parts. Less operator involvement in the cycle should result in better cycle control and consequently more consistent quality. However, the main advantage of the injection process is not fully realized without the use of cold manifold molds. The popularity of the injection process will no doubt be increased as fabricators learn of the tremendous materials savings which can be made in conjunction with cold manifold molds.

TABLE 3-1. SPECIFICATIONS FOR A SPARK PLUG BOOT.

1. Scope: The material defined by this specification is a high temperature and high tear silicone rubber.
2. Application: This material was originally used as a molded spark plug insulator for vehicles requiring a high temperature material.
3. Requirements:
    3.1 Slab stock (6 × 6 × .075 ± .005): Molding conditions to be the same as those used to mold parts and must be submitted at time of qualification testing.
        3.1.1 Tensile strength: 950 PSI min.
            (ASTM D 412 Die "C")
        3.1.2 Elongation: 270% min.
            (ASTM D 412 Die "C")
        3.1.3 Durometer–Shore "A": 60 ± 5 points
            (ASTM D 2240)
        3.1.4 Oven aged 70 HR at 450° F:
            (ASTM D 573)
            Tensile strength change: −20% max.
            Elongation change: −30% max.
            Durometer change: −3 to + 7 points max.
        3.1.5 Aged 70 hr # 1 oil at 300° F:
            (ASTM D 471)
            Tensile strength change: −15% max.
            Elongation change: −20% max.
            Durometer change: 0.10–10 max.
            Volume change: +10% max.

3.1.6 Aged 70 HR #3 oil at 300° F:
(ASTM D 471)
Tensile strength change: −60% max.
Elongation change: −35% max.
Durometer change: 0.10–25 max.
Volume change: +50% max.

3.1.7 Compression set (70 hr at 350° F): 35% max.
(ASTM D 395, Method B)

3.1.8 Cold test: No cracking
Test method: After 70 hr at −40° F material is bent 180° over $\frac{1}{2}$ in. mandrel.

3.1.9 Tear strength: 80 lbs/in. min.
(ASTM D 624, Die "B")

3.1.10 Dielectric strength: 500 vpm min.
(ASTM D 149 short term)

3.1.11 Ozone resistance:
(ASTM D 1171)
No checking or cracking after 72 hours at 100 ± 2° F at an ozone concentration of 50 ± 5 parts per 100 million parts of air.

3.2 Molded parts: Specific requirements, when required, shall be specified on the engineering drawings or engineering specifications for parts of this material.

3.2.1 Corona test (spark plug insulators only): The insulator with an 18 in. length of cable is applied to proper spark plug. The assembly is laid in the bottom of a 400 ml beaker. The wire is then coiled one turn and led out the spout of the beaker. A watch glass is taped over the top of the beaker. This assembly is set into a 1000 ml beaker containing 250 ml of mercury and weighed until the 400 ml beaker sinks to a depth of at least 1 in. A potential of 15,00 volts rms, 60 cycle is applied between the conductor and the mercury and maintained for 5 hours. The molded rubber part must not show signs of cracking at the end of 5 hours.

3.2.2 Elongation after heat (spark plug insulators only): After 5 days in a mechanical convention oven at 400 ± 5° F, the molded part shall make a tight seal, but should not adhere on a spark plug as indicated by a 10 minute immersion in tap water.

3.2.3 Hardness—micro: 57 ± 5
(ASTM D 1425)

*Taken from Ford Motor Company engineering specifications ESE-M2D8-B dated 6/16/75.

BLOW MOLDING

Some relatively simple shapes have been successfully blow molded from silicone rubber. These include the convoluted tubes for use on anesthesia equipment and the balloons for medical cannulas seen in Fig. 3-27. The multiple balloons on the left in Fig. 3-27 are soft and very thin-walled (.008 in., .2mm). A tubular preform or parison 20% smaller than the smallest diameter of the finished part is extruded directly onto the blowing mandrel. The blowing mandrel is connected

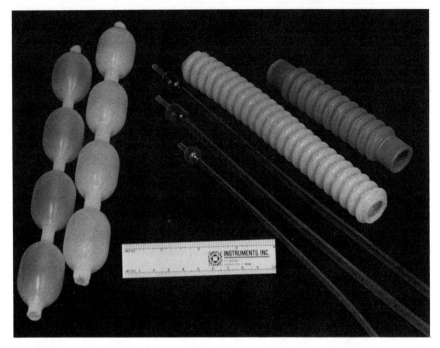

Fig. 3-27. Blow molded silicone rubber parts. (*Photo by Paul Flagg. Courtesy Medical Engineering Corp.*)

to a low pressure (5 psi, 350 g/cm^2) air supply. It is the full length of the molding and is positioned vertically between the two halves of the blow mold. The mold is run very hot (400°F, 205°C). A very soft, low modulus stock is used.* Cycles approaching 45 sec are possible. The balance between the plasticity of the rubber stock, the mold temperature, the blowing pressure, and the dwell before applying the blowing pressure, plus the speed at which it is applied, are very critical. The degree to which the unvulcanized material can be expanded on blowing is dependent on the green strength of the material. Allowing vulcanization to proceed partially before blowing fully can increase the expansion capability of the material.

The balloon type cannulas in the center are run with a high durometer, addition reaction, silicone rubber compound.† Note the difference between the diameters of the tube on each end of the

---

*MEC 119, Medical Engineering Corp.
†MEC 500, Medical Engineering Corp.

balloon.   The diameter over the full length of the long tube was attained during the blowing cycle.

Heavy walled parts such as the convoluted tubing on the right of Fig. 3-27 are often produced using a cold-hot cycle on the mold. Extruded preforms of a 55 durometer (Shore A) dry, high green strength, VMQ stock are placed over blowing mandrels which are positioned horizontally between the two halves of a cool, open blow mold. The mold is closed, the preform is then blown against the cavity wall and the temperature of the mold quickly raised to about 330°F (165°C). Cycles may be as long as 7 or 8 min.

Blow molding offers a cost reduction in both tooling and fabricating of simple parts.   Removing the parts from heavily undercut cores is eliminated, as is the removal of parting line flash. However, considerable wall thickness variation occurs between minimum and maximum diameters and dimensional tolerance allowances must be greater than RMA Class 2 molding tolerances by a factor of 50%.

DEFLASHING OF MOLDED PARTS

Before the design of a part and the tooling to produce it are finalized, the method of deflashing or finishing must be considered since this will influence the location and design of the parting line. Very often the cost of finishing small, intricate, precision parts may exceed the cost of molding and material so it is important to focus particular attention on this phase of the fabrication process. Deflashing methods used include:

1. Freeze tumbling is a popular method of finishing. The parts are loaded into an insulated tumbler, often with tumbling aids such as nylon moldings. The temperature in the tumbler is lowered quickly with liquid nitrogen to below the brittle point of the silicone rubber. The thin flash becomes brittle first and breaks off before the molding itself reaches the brittle point. This method is satisfactory for simple shaped moldings with flash around an outside edge.

    Wheelabrating is a more sophisticated method of accomplishing freeze tumbling, the principle of which is illustrated in Fig. 3-28. The parts, which are tumbled on an endless steel belt inside an insulated cabinet are pelted with fine steel shot .014 to .022 in. (.4 to .6 mm) diameter, which quickly knocks

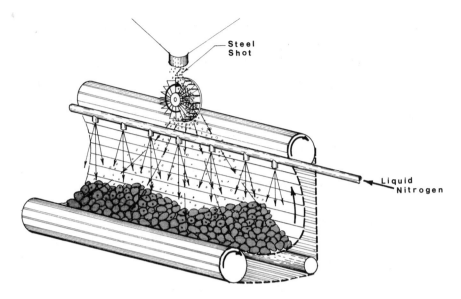

Fig. 3-28. Principle of wheelabrating.

the flash out of holes and grooves as well as off the outside edges. For best results, wide flash lands should be used to allow the shot easy access to the thin flash. The flash should not be more than .003 in. thick. The average time for a wheelabrator load is about five minutes. The main drawback to wheelabrating is the discoloration of parts by the fine rust particles from the steel balls and the steel belt. The rust is so fine it penetrates the surface of the silicone and on white parts is very difficult to remove. On most industrial parts (red, brown, black) it is not noticeable, however, and a light wash is sufficient.

A freeze-tumbler which is becoming increasingly popular is one equipped with rotating nylon brushes as shown in Fig. 3-29. Molded parts joined by heavy flash are shown lying over wrist of operator. Finished parts are seen in the operators hand and lying among the brushes of the tumbler. The haze is created by moisture condensation caused by liquid nitrogen cooling of the tumbler. This is more compact and represents a smaller investment than the wheelabrator, but it does a very effective job and can handle relatively heavy flash.

Fig. 3-29. Rutilusa brush tumbler. (*Photo by Paul Flagg. Courtesy Lavelle Industries*)

Thin walled parts such as diaphrams, which would freeze quickly, cannot be deflashed via the freeze tumble method. Nor is it practical to tumble very small or very large parts.

Die trimming is generally used on compression molded parts with heavy flash. It is an ideal method for the trimming of sub-cavity moldings which are ejected from the mold in one sheet (Fig. 3-4). For best results, multiple trim die units must be accurately made and mounted in a heavy die set or they will not trim evenly. Die trimmed flash lines are always visible but when the dies are well maintained, they are very clean, devoid of whiskers of flash. This is an economical method to use when the part design allows it.

3. Buffing is used where all vestiges of parting line flash must be removed. This is particularly the case with "O" ring seals. Small "O" rings may be buffed on a mandrel which they fit loosely. The mandrel should have a very fine, smooth file fin-

ish. As the "O" rings have the O.D. flash removed by the buffing wheels, they rotate on the mandrel. The finish on the mandrel meanwhile removes the I.D. flash.

4. Tear trimming is dependent on narrow flash lands .007 to .012 in. (.2 to .3 mm) and very thin flash—preferably .003 in. or less (.07 mm). When the cavity is shaped as in Fig. 3-30 and cavity and core sections are accurately lined up, the stripper ring can be located on the core side, allowing reduction of flash land "A" to a minimum (.001 in. to .002 in., .03 mm), which will lead to very clean pieces. Tear trimming is best with high durometer, high modulus stocks. It may not work at all with low durometer, low modulus stocks, especially PMQ types. It is a preferred method for large moldings or moldings with complicated contours at the parting line.

   Sometimes tear trimming can be used to advantage on bonded to insert moldings: where the cavity land cannot bite into the insert as in Fig. 3-31a, a stripper ring should be incorporated as on the shaft in Fig. 3-31b. The stripper ring can be pulled cleanly from the shaft by masking the stripper ring area of the shaft during priming or since both primer and detergent solutions have a tendency to wick along the surface, an acrylic

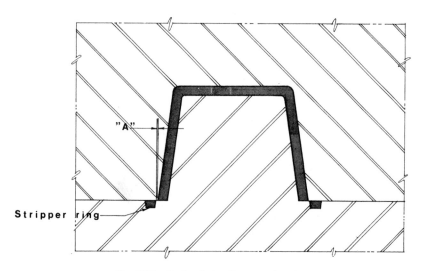

Fig. 3-30. Cavity design for tear trimming.

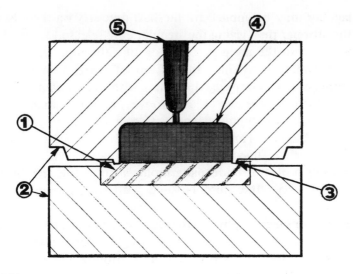

Fig. 3-31a. (1) Flat metal insert. (2) Cavity inserts. (3) Cavity land coined into metal insert to prevent flash on surface. (4) Bonded rubber. (5) Sprue.

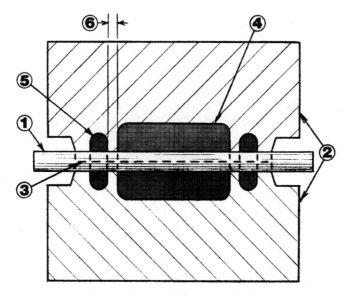

Fig. 3-31b. (1) Metal shaft. (2) Cavity inserts. (3) Parting line. (4) Bonded rubber. (5) Stripper ring. (6) Flash land (.007 in. to .012 in. wide).

Fig. 3-31. Flash trimming of inserts.

lacquer may be applied to the shaft precisely on the area under the stripper ring, giving the stripper easy release.

5. Scraping in the mold is a method of deflashing which has not been widely used since the advent of freeze tumbling. A requirement is a sharp edged molding with one whole surface flush with the mold surface. Flash grooves are not desired. Vigorous scraping of the mold surface, with a sharp edged nylon scraper, before the pieces are ejected will usually produce an acceptably clean part. This method is most effective with loose plate transfer molds or multi-plate molds such as the one illustrated in Fig. 3-15. It cannot be used with soft, low modulus materials.

6. Scissor or electric clipper trimming may have to be used on low volume or extra large parts with irregular parting lines. Scissor trimming is often used in the fabrication of medical parts because of the low volumes and necessity of eliminating every small whisker of flash from a part to be inserted in the human body or to handle parenteral fluids or blood.

FLASHLESS MOLDING

Many attempts have been made to develop flashless methods of molding silicone rubber parts and thus eliminate the need for finishing—a difficult project because of the tendency for silicone rubber to flow into the minutest openings during molding. There has been a degree of success. However, the successes appear to be confined to specific applications, part designs, and material formulations. In all cases the tooling must be top quality and carefully maintained.

The multi-holed precision grommets used for insulating the contacts of AN electrical connectors are an example of silicone rubber parts whose finishing costs would be extraordinarily high if they were molded by standard methods. Fig. 3-32 illustrates such a grommet molded in a conventional injection mold. Note the flash in the holes and on the outer diameter. Flash free silicone rubber grommets are molded at the Amphenol Connector through the use of a special compression molding process* which is illustrated diagramatically in Fig. 3-33. Each cavity is made up of three precision inserts, numbers

---

*U.S. Patent 3,145,422.

Fig. 3-32. Part molded by conventional method showing flash in holes and outer diameter. (*Courtesy Amphenol Connector Division, Bunker Ramo Corp.*)

(1), (2), and (3), located in precision bored multi-cavity plates. The top and bottom cavity inserts (1) and (2) contain the pins for molding the holes in the grommets. The top pins telescope into the bottom pins, which are hollow. As the mold closes, excess stock (5) is forced through the hollow pins and cut off cleanly as the pins telescope. The top and bottom inserts, which are hardened, have very narrow flash lands (6). By controlling the weight of the preforms (4) to $\frac{1}{4}$ g and keeping the cavity inserts in top flight condition, flash free parts such as the one shown on the left in Fig. 3-34 are produced routinely. A set of cavity inserts are illustrated in Fig. 3-35.

Some fairly flash-free "O" rings and cup seals have been produced on injection molding equipment through a delayed clamping mechanism. At the start of the cycle the mold is stopped within a few thousandths of closing. The injection cycle is started and just as the cavity fills, the mold is closed under full clamping pressure; a sort of combined injection-compression molding. This method, in addition to producing cleanly cut-off parts, helps eliminate gas and eliminate gates in the case of "O" rings with the localized modulus variation

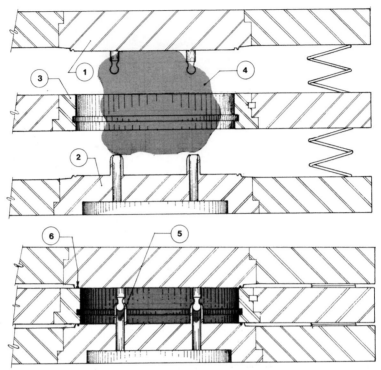

Fig. 3-33. Cavity design for flashless molding of electrical connector grommets. (1), (2) and (3) precision cavity inserts similar to those shown in Fig. 3-35, (4) material preform, (5) excess material escaping through hollow molding pins, (6) narrow flashlands.

that often accompany them. Although special parts may benefit from "flashless" molding, it is generally cheaper to consider freeze-tumbling in the original mold design rather than maintain a mold in flashless condition.

OVEN CURING

Postcuring of silicone rubber parts after vulcanization drives off volatile materials such as the chemical by-products of vulcanization which might cause reversion if the part is confined or subjected to hot water or steam service. It also stabilizes the properties such as compression set, for high temperature service.

Postcuring is performed in a hot air circulating oven Fig. 3-36. Electric resistance elements are usually the heat source. The circulation of the air must maintain the temperature everywhere in the

Fig. 3-34. Flashless molded part compared to conventionally molded parts. (*Courtesy Amphenol Connector Division, Bunker Ramo Corp.*)

oven within a few degrees. Fresh air must be continuously introduced into the oven and air saturated with volatiles exhausted to the
outside. Although two or three air exchanges per minute are normally sufficient, the oven should have almost double that capacity to
handle extra heavy loads. Trays for holding parts should be fabri-

Fig. 3-35. Typical Precision Cavity Inserts. (*Courtesy Amphenol Connector Division, Bunker Ramo Corp.*)

Fig. 3-36. Post curing ovens. Two large "walk-in" hot air circulating ovens are illustrated. A truck with racks for curing trays may be seen on the left. Stainless steel construction and smooth welded corners ensures easier maintenance.

cated from expanded stainless steel and when parts to be postcured are placed on them, they should be stacked in such a way that the air can circulate freely around them.

When oven curing long lengths of heavy walled tubing, a slight flow of fresh air should be circulated through the tubing. This can be run in copper tubing from a compressed air line through a control valve into the oven and be hooked up to one end of the silicone rubber tubing. If several feet of copper tubing are run inside the oven, the fresh air will be adequately heated before entering the silicone rubber tubing.

The oven should be kept clean. Stacks can clog with silica, collect low molecular silicone oils, and catch fire.

Electrical contact points should be kept clean. Sparking due to silica dust can cause contacts to freeze shut and the temperature to rise until the oven load catches fire—this can happen to the safety as well as the main relay. It is not a bad idea to hook a klaxon alarm up with a separate oven thermoswitch.

Postcuring usually includes one or more hours at 300°F (150°C), depending on the thickness of the parts. This will be followed by up to 24 hr at 480°F (250°C) for parts to be subjected to extreme heat and compression stress service. Heavy parts require stepping the temperature up to maximum in two to three steps. The actual time and temperature used will depend on the service to which the part will be used.

TROUBLE SHOOTING

Problem	Possible Cause
1. Molded parts feel sticky and spongelike	Die too cold—cure cycle too short.
2. Parts appear brittle or tend to split or tear too easily	Die temperature is too high—cure cycle is too long.
3. Chaulky appearance on outside of molded part	Excess mold release.
4. Soft spots	Air entrapment, check pattern of material flow in mold, improve venting or preform shape and location.
5. Back rind	Thick part, rapid cure rate. Lower mold temperature or use higher temperature vulcanizing agent, reduce mold pressure.
6. Molded parts appear distorted or warped	Scorching due to too high mold temperature or too slow close. Also could be too much of a temperature differential between top and bottom cavity sections.
7. Excess flash	Too much material. Decrease size.
8. Underfill	Not enough material, not enough pressure or mold temperature too high.
9. Molded in flash	Not removing excess flash on cavity sections between shots—material seating down between core pins when shearing excess flash over core pins.
10. Die temperature difficult to stabilize	Open press cycle fluctuating too much—heating element burned out—temperature controller not functioning properly.
11. Plugged hole	Broken core pin—core pin shifted back.
12. Parts not sticking to desired side of mold.	Lubricate other side, use plain water or very dilute sugar water solution on side sticking desired.

References

1. U.S. patent 3,824,208.
2. Swanson, J. W., Leicht, J. T. and Wegener, R. L., Silicone Rubber In Powder Form, Rubber Div., American Chemical Society, Philadelphia, Pa., Oct. 1974.
3. *Rubber Handbook,* Rubber Manufacturers Association, Inc.
4. Penn, W. S., *Injection Moulding of Elastomers* (Chapter 14, "Injection Moulding of Silicone Rubbers"), Gordon & Breach 1969.
5. De Sieno, R. P. and Fuhrmann, R. C., "Molding Silicone Rubber by Injection Methods," *Rubber Age* **91**, 84 (Apr. 1962).
6. Rogers, J. E. and Kleiner, G., "Injection Molding of Silicone Rubber," presented to meeting of the Swedish Institute of Rubber Technology, May 1963.
7. *Rubber World* (Dec. 1974).

4

THE EXTRUSION OF HEAT VULCANIZING SILICONE RUBBERS

A wide variety of shapes and sizes may be extruded in continuous lengths from silicone rubber (see Figs. 4-1 and 4-2). The process equipment and tooling are basically similar to that used in the extrusion of organic rubbers; however, the relative heat sensitivity of the peroxide catalyzed, unvulcanized rubber, and its low "green" strength necessitate special methods of handling.

THE EXTRUDER

A variety of extruders and screw designs have been used successfully in silicone rubber extrusion. Probably the most popular "workhorse" in the custom extrusion shop is a machine with a $3\frac{1}{4}$ in. (83 mm) diameter single flight screw, having a length to diameter ratio of 10 or 12 to 1, a compression ratio of 2.5 to 1 and flights about $\frac{1}{2}$ in. (13 mm) deep. This seems to work best with materials which slip well in the screw. Where stickier stocks are used or where reduced porosity and close dimensional control are required, compression ratios of 3 or 4 to 1 are preferred. The compression should be attained through a variable pitch, holding the root dimension constant. Variable root screws can cause excessive heating, particularly with sticky stocks. Double flight screws of comparable length and compression ratios will not have as high an output as single screws and are more vulnerable to misfeeding. Some designers have compromised and made the last few flights, at the delivery end of the screw, double (see Fig. 4-3). This would reduce the pulsating effect of the screw feed while eliminating some of the drawbacks of the double flight

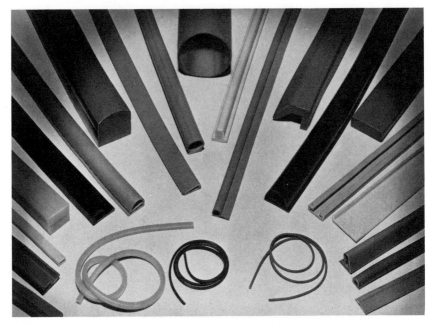

Fig. 4-1. A variety of shapes and sizes may be extruded in continuous lengths. (*Courtesy Moxness Products, Inc. Subsidiary of Versa Technologies, Inc.*)

design. However, the limiting factor, as far as rate of output is concerned, usually hinges on the capacity of the vulcanizing unit rather than the extruder.

The overall clearance between screw and barrel should be about .003 in. (.08 mm). Higher length to diameter ratios than 12 to 1 allow the use of lower compression ratios and show less sensitivity to clearance variations between screw and barrel. Because of the abrasive nature of the silica-type fillers used in silicone rubber, both barrel and screw must be fabricated from the most wear-resistant alloys: Xaloy barrels* and screws of nitrided 4140 steel are recommended. Both screw and barrel must be watercooled since heating of the material in the barrel above 130° F (55° C) would cause scorching and probable loss of vulcanizing agent. The discharge end of the screw should be within .030 in. (.76 mm) of the breaker plate to reduce shear working of the material to a minimum and should be somewhat rounded at the tip. The extruder should be equipped with

---

*Xaloy Inc., New Brunswick, N.J.

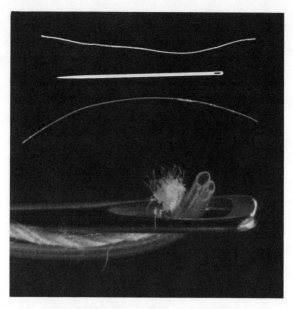

Fig. 4-2. A microscopic sized trilumen silicone rubber tube is shown threaded through the eye of a needle along with a fine thread. The actual size of the tubing, needle and thread are shown on the top. The thread is the farthest left. The tubing was developed for use in gas analyses, taking advantage of the high rate of gas permeability of the silicones. An even wall thickness around the lumen gives the tube a clover leaf shape. The extruder die holder for extrusions of this type is equipped with a micrometer adjustment. The die must be set up under a magnifier. (*Photo by Paul Flagg. Courtesy Medical Engineering Corp.*)

a roller feed (illustrated in Fig. 4-4) for automatic feeding of stocks which can be fed from a hat. Clearance between the roller and the screw usually runs a little over $\frac{1}{8}$ in. (3 to 4 mm) and the surface speed of the roller should be 50% greater than the screw. Where clean extrusions are desired, the roller should rotate between tightly fitting nylon plates and be equipped with an adjustable nylon scraper to reduce contamination of the stock caused by metal-to-metal wear. In the case of stocks which are too soft and sticky to be fed from a hat, the throat of the extruder should be equipped with a stuffing

Fig. 4-3. Extruder screw showing double flights "A" at delivery end of screw. (*Courtesy Medical Engineering Corp.*)

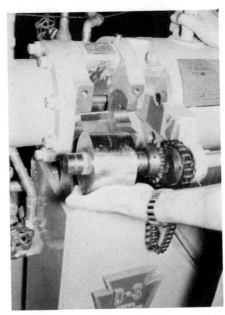

Fig. 4-4. A view of the roller feed mechanism of a silicone rubber extruder disassembled to show its construction.

box and a plunger operated by a compressed air or oil hydraulic cylinder. The box should be large enough to carry material for one-half hour or more of extrusion time. To maintain cleanliness of the stock, the nose of the plunger should be made of nylon. Relatively low pressure (100 psi–7 kg/cm^2 or less) is required to keep the stock in contact with the feed section of the screw. A slight undercut of the barrel in the feed section, on the entrance side of the screw, is desirable. Soft stocks exhibit slippage in the screw, more die swell, and deformation of shape than do harder materials. Precautions must be taken at all times to prevent small tools, bolts, etc. from accidentally entering the throat section of the extruder.

At the discharge end of the screw lies the breaker plate, shown in Fig. 4-5, which is a metal disc perforated with holes or slots and recessed to hold various combinations of stainless steel screens. The screens filter out dirt, large gel particles, and undispersed filler aggregates. They also create back pressure which reduces porosity and provides closer dimensional control of the extrusion. The finer the mesh used in screen packs, the cleaner and smoother the extrusion.

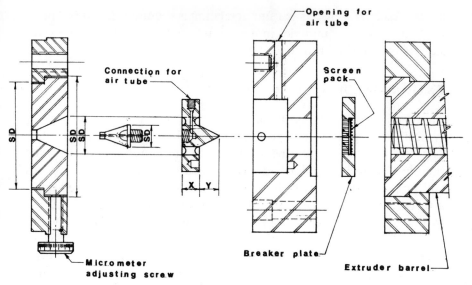

Fig. 4-5. Front flange assembly with bolted on die holder of the type commonly used on small extruders. In this case a $\frac{3}{4}$ in. laboratory extruder. From right to left: The delivery end of the screw. The breaker plate which contains the screen pack and also serves to center the two adjoining sections. The spider (or torpedo) holding ring which is bolted to the barrel when in use. The spider which is streamlined to allow the material to flow around the pin holder and through the openings between the spokes. Various sized pins which form the lumen of the tubing can be screwed into the spider. The base diameter, the height and the threaded section of the pins are all standard (SD). The die is retained by the front flange, Fig. 6, all dimensions are SD other than the front opening diameter which is varied along with the front pin diameter to produce the desired tubing dimensions. Centering of the die is accomplished by three or four micrometer adjusting screws located in the front flange. On larger extruders the die holder is often mounted on a hinged member (as in Fig. 4-6). A quick acting split collar, also shown, clamps over the tapered flanges on the extruder barrel and the die holder. Sometimes on larger machines the hinged die holder* is secured by swing bolts.

*Also referred to as a die adapter.

However, fine mesh packs will reduce extruder output and will block up more quickly, necessitating more down time for screen pack changes. Dirty screen packs may be cleaned by soaking in toluol for several hours and wire brushing. A common screen pack combination is an 80 mesh backed by 60 mesh. Usually the weaves are placed diagonally to one another. A combination used for maximum production is a 60 mesh backed by a 40 mesh, but some very clean applications—medical grade for instance—will use screens of 200 mesh or finer. The course screen is placed next to the breaker plate to prevent the fine screen from being extruded through the slots or holes. Usually, where such fine screening is required, it is more practical to screen the material in a separate step from the actual extrusion of the finished profile.

EXTRUSION DIES

The simplest type of extrusion profile is standard round tubing. A typical die design for the production of tubing is shown in Fig. 4-5. The dies and pins should be machined to the standard dimensions of the die holder and spider. An economical method of producing dies and pins is to have a large number of blanks (100 or so) turned upon a turret lathe. The die opening and pin diameters are then finished to the size as required in a matter of minutes in the fabricator's tool shop. The author has found that prehardened stainless steel* is an excellent material for pins and dies from the point of view of super finish and long wear, coupled with reasonable economy. Die lands can be comparatively short, varying from $\frac{1}{16}$ in. on very small diameters to $\frac{1}{4}$ in. for diameters of 2 to 3 in. The die should be designed in such a way so as to produce even flow. There should be no dead spaces. Die pins should be drilled for application of air through one of the spokes of the spider (also shown in Fig. 4-5). Otherwise the tubing would collapse as it leaves the die. The rubber will swell as it comes out of the die. The amount of swell will depend on the flow characteristics of the material, wall thickness, and the pressure applied to the material as it enters the die. However, dimensions can be modified somewhat by speeding or slowing the take-off which will vary the degree of stretch of the green extrusion, or air pressure may be applied to tubular extrusions to increase their diameter. Because of these variables, it is difficult to specify the relationship between the die size and the diameter of the extrusion. However, a rule of thumb is that the tubing will swell approximately 3% over the die dimensions, more on very soft stocks, less on the higher durometer stocks.

For prototyping and short runs, the die holder may be equipped with an adapter ring which is designed to accommodate simple, flat dies cut from duraluminum plate. Such dies, while short-lived, take only minutes to make and besides accommodating short runs, are

*Crucible Steel Co.—CMS 414.

Fig. 4-6. Hinged die holder. Front flange of extruder may be seen on left. Split collar is open. The die holder or adapter has been swung away from the front flange to allow screen or die changing.

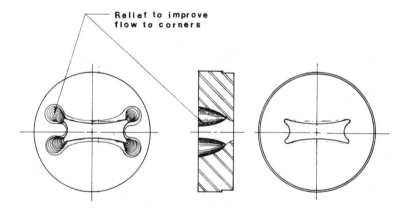

Fig. 4-7. Extrusion die designed to produce a rectangular shaped extrusion. Because the material will flow more easily through the center of the opening there will be more swell here. Consequently the die opening is constricted in the center. The corners on the other hand have been heavily relieved and the lands made quite short to increase the flow. Since the flow characteristics vary from one formulation to another a certain amount of "cut and try" in the fine development of the die opening contour will be necessary.

very useful for zeroing in on the final die dimensions and on the production rates of complicated shapes before a more expensive die is produced.

When extruding shapes other than round, the orifice of the die is rarely identical to the cross section of the extrusion. This is due to the fact that differential frictional forces at different points of the flowing material come into play. For instance, the die to produce a solid rectangular shape would look like the illustration in Fig. 4-7. Where irregular shaped dies and pins are involved, the face of the die should be provided with holes to accommodate a spanner wrench for aligning the die radially with the pin. Where the shape is such that

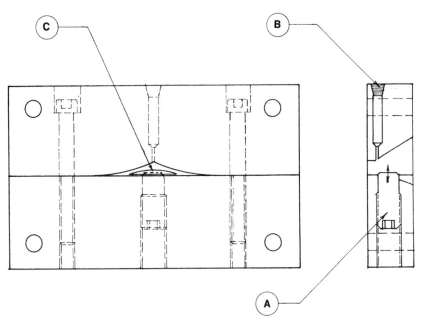

Fig. 4-8. An extrusion die used to produce electrical insulation tape having a triangular cross section. When the tape is half lapped an even thickness of insulation is applied to a conductor. This is important if the conductor must then be fit into an exact size of opening or slot such as a form wound motor coil. Therefore dimensions of the tape must be held closely. The sides of the triangular opening are concave in order to compensate for the swell which would normally occur there due to the heavier cross section. The screw "A" becomes a baffle at the base of the triangle which may be effective enough alone or may be used in conjunction with a shaped pad "C". This allows adjustment of the flow and consequently control of the height dimension of the triangular tape while the extruder is running. A colored identifying stripe is applied by forcing a low viscosity colored silicone compound, from a simple ram type of extrusion cylinder attached to connection "B", to flow under pressure onto the apex of the tape.

cross sectional thickness varies greatly, and a non-uniform flow rate occurs, the flow difference can be modified by shortening the land about the thin sections and/or placing screw adjusted baffles (sometimes the screw body itself is enough) in the path of the flow to the thicker sections. Fig. 4-8 illustrates the use of such a baffle in the die to produce a solid triangular insulation tape described on page 000. Special effects may be obtained, such as the center stripe on the triangular tape mentioned above, through the use of auxiliary extrusion equipment.

An ingenious method of incorporating stretchy, reinforcing, fabric substrates in extruded silicone rubber tapes is described in U.S.

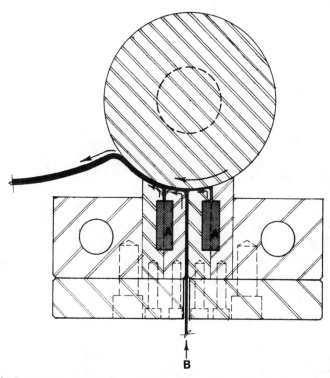

Fig. 4-9. Diagramatic section through the center of the reinforced tape extrusion die, facing the delivery end of the extruder. Silicone rubber enters two separate chambers in the die A_1 and A_2 from the extruder. The die has an opening between the two chambers through which the reinforcing fabric B is drawn. A ribbon of silicone rubber is laid on the surface of the rotating roller from A_2, the thickness being determined by the clearance between the surface of the die and the roller, in the direction of flow. The fabric is pressed against the rubber as the roller rotates. It is then coated on the other side with the ribbon of rubber extruding from A_1. The composite tape is then ready for vulcanization.

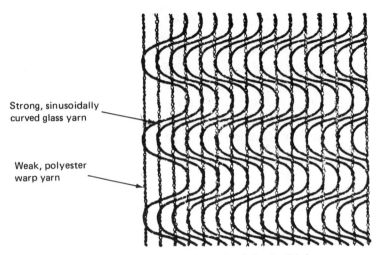

Strong, sinusoidally
curved glass yarn

Weak, polyester
warp yarn

Fig. 4-10. Construction of stretch reinforcing fabric.

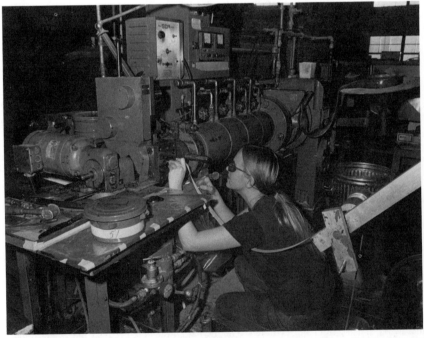

Fig. 4-11. Operator is shown threading reinforcing fabric into the tape die illustrated in Fig. 4-9. Note the strip of raw stock being fed from a "hat" on the right rear of the photo into the roller feed throat of the extruder. The electric motor drive for the die roller can be seen in the left foreground. (*Courtesy Moxness Products Inc., Subsidiary of Versa Technologies, Inc.*)

Patent 3,253,073. The principle, illustrated in Fig. 4-9, involves the extrusion of two separate ribbons of silicone rubber, one on each side of a special fabric reinforcement, and simultaneously squeezing the three layers together on a revolving roller or drum which fits up against the delivery section of the die. Equipment using this process is pictured in Figs. 4-11 and 4-12.

In order that the reinforced tape can be stretched and thus conform smoothly to the product to be taped, a special type of fabric* illustrated in Fig. 4-10 is used. The polyester warp yarn (about 40 denier) is just strong enough to hold the sinusoidally curved glass yarn in position, preventing it from stretching, while it goes through the extrusion die and becomes embedded in the silicone rubber tape. Upon being exposed to the high temperature of vulcanization, the polyester warp yarn is destroyed or weakened to the point that it will break easily. The tape is then free to be stretched until the glass yarn is taut.

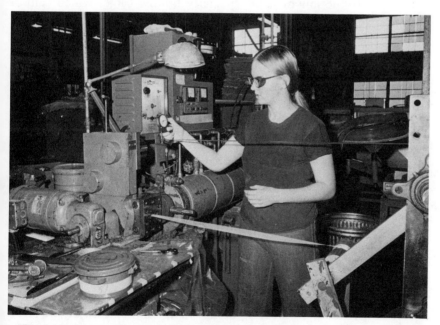

Fig. 4-12. Operator has the extruder in production and is checking the tape thickness as it leaves the die. The tape will be vulcanized with very close control over time and temperature to assure optimum tack and physical properties. (*Courtesy Moxness Products, Inc., Subsidiary of Versa Technologies, Inc.*)

---

*U.S. Patent 3,256,130.

By varying the height of the sinusoidal curve, the degree of stretch may be controlled between 15 and 25%.

Extrusion over wire requires the use of a crosshead attachment (Fig. 4-16A) on the extruder. The die is mounted on the crosshead at right angles to the barrel of the extruder. The wire can then be fed into the flow of material through a hollow die guide or mandrel.

Reinforced hose may be produced continuously with the use of a crosshead. A heavy-walled tube is first extruded in the standard fashion from high green strength rubber. After a preliminary vulcanization, reinforcing wire or Nomex* cord can then be braided over it. It is then run through a crosshead to have a cover coat of low green strength rubber extruded over it. Collapse of the tube is prevented by applying air pressure to the I.D. and the use of the less nervy rubber reduces the pressure necessary to apply the outer coating. The reinforced hose is then fully cured.

In the production of some specialty hollow cables which cannot have a cover coating applied by the above method, the first or inner layer of rubber is applied over dead soft copper wire. When the cable is complete, the wire is mechanically stretched, reducing its diameter, allowing it to be slipped out of the cable. This method is particularly useful for the production of stretchy cable.

VULCANIZATION OF THE EXTRUSION

The extruded profile leaves the die in the green state. It is quite delicate and easily deformed, thus it must normally be vulcanized immediately.

The most popular form of vulcanization, other than in the wire and cable industry, is continuous hot air vulcanization (HAV) illustrated diagramatically in Fig. 4-13. The extrusion is carried through an HAV heated tunnel on a conveyor belt, usually made of pressed flat stainless steel mesh. HAV's, which usually are 25 to 30 ft long ($7\frac{1}{2}$ to 9 m.), are heated either by convection or radiant electric heat sources and have two or more heating zones. The temperature of the HAV may be adjusted from 400°F (200°C) to 1000°F (550°C). It is important to introduce fresh air into the HAV just as it is in the post-cure circulating ovens. The air supply line, preferably stainless steel,

---

*Trademark of E. I. Dupont.

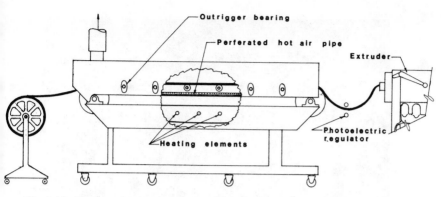

Fig. 4-13. Horizontal hot air vulcanizing unit (HAV). The extruded tubing or profile forms a loop between the extruder die and the conveyor belt of the oven. To control dimensions the depth of the loop must be kept constant. In order to accomplish this the speed of the conveyor must be synchronized with the speed of the extruder. This may be accomplished visually by the extruder operator or a photo electric regulator can be installed to control the speed of the conveyor. The conveyor belt is supported by a number of rollers as it passes through the oven. Because of the high temperatures in the oven the roller bearings should be outside the oven walls. Because of the volume of smoky volatiles produced during vulcanization an exhaust stack must be provided.

is run along side the heaters of the HAV to heat up the air within. The air is then released through small holes drilled in the wall of the air supply tube as it doubles back through the length of the HAV. The turbulence created leads to faster heat transfer and considerably faster cure time for the extrusion. The movement of air also helps drive volatile gases on up the exhaust.

Small variations in cross section may be accomplished by adjusting the loop height, e.g., if the HAV conveyor is speeded up to reduce the amount of loop, a certain amount of stretching of the green extrudate will take place and cross sectional dimensions will be reduced. Depending on the characteristics of the stock being extruded, especially the green strength, some extrusions may be reduced in cross section well over 50% by stretching.

Invariably, the conveyor belt of a horizontal vulcanizing unit leaves an impression on the surface of a silicone rubber extrusion; particularly if the section is thin, a certain amount of sag occurs before vulcanization takes place. If these conditions are objectionable, then a vertical HAV unit (illustrated in Fig. 4-14) may be used. The extrusion is passed over a variable speed, motor-driven drum at the top of the HAV unit. As it moves up through the unit, vulcanization proceeds continuously, giving it the strength to hold the weight of the

Fig. 4-14. Vertical hot air vulcanizing unit.

material below without any serious stretching. Although the illustration shows the extrusion returning to floor level outside of the HAV, some units have been set up so the extrusion is exposed to heat in a second parallel tube on its trip down.

Because of the chimney effect with vertical units, forced air circulation is not required. An adjustable damper should be cut to fit around the extrusion at the top of the HAV to control the rate of exhaust and a Teflon® guide ring installed at the bottom entrance to prevent the fresh extrusion from striking the side of the HAV. Despite the Teflon® guide ring and especially when non-conductive Pyrex® coated radiant heating panels are used in the construction of the HAV, static charges developed on the silicone rubber extrusion will attract it to the heating panel and, upon touching, the extrusion will burst into flame. This is particularly the case with light, small cross section extrusions. When this becomes a problem, air ionization equipment should be mounted on the die holder to allow bleeding off of the static electric charge.

The maximum height of a vertical HAV is limited to about 10 ft (3 m) because of the excessive stretching of the extrudate which

Fig. 4-15. A 10 ft (3 m) vertical HAV shown open for cleaning or servicing. It is electrically heated with two zone control. (*Courtesy E. B. Blue Co.*)

would take place with a higher tube. For increased speed of vulcanization without excessive marking of the extrudate, a vertical HAV could be used in conjunction with a horizontal or angled down unit. HAV vulcanization of silicone rubber requires the use of 2,4-dichlorobenzoyl peroxide. Other curing agents are too volatile; they would lead to low states of cure and a high degree of porosity.

Many factors influence the rate at which an extrusion can be produced:

> The size and power of the extruder, the design of the screw, the clearance between the screw and the barrel, type and quantity of filler, the fineness of the screen pack (and whether or not it is partially clogged with debris), the hardness and nerve or green strength of the stock, the shape and cross sectional area of the extrusion and, perhaps most important of all, the type and length of the vulcanizing unit. A reference table of extrusion rates is given on page 114.

When silicone rubber insulation is extruded over wire or cable, continuous steam vulcanizing (CV) is the preferred method (Fig. 4-16). Because the rubber is supported by the wire there is no need for a conveyor belt. The coated wire passes directly from the die into a long chamber which is filled with live steam at pressures of 100 to 250 psi (7 to 18 kg/cm^2). The wire or cable is usually preheated through electrical resistance as it enters the die guider. Vacuum is applied to stranded wire, in the guider, to prevent blistering of the rubber coating due to entrapped air. Curing of the rubber occurs in 10 to 15 sec. and speeds of up to 1200 ft/min. (366 m/min.) are possible although 600 ft/min. (183 m/min.) is probably a fair average. Because of direct contact with the steam chamber, extrusion dies should have cooling arrangements. CV equipment is considerably more expensive than HAV equipment and is more space consuming. Some CV tubes are over 200 ft (60 m) in length whereas HAV's rarely are longer than 40 ft (12 m). Startup of CV's is more complicated and wasteful of material. However, the extremely high production rates possible make this the most economical for the high volumes of standard products encountered in the wire and cable industry.

Silicone insulation is often applied to lower volume specialty cables. In this case HAV's or FBV's may be used. Speeds of 60 ft/min. (18 m/min.) are attainable.

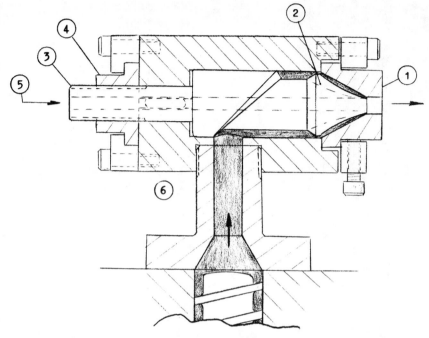

Fig. 4-16a. Simple crosshead for a small extruder. 1. Die. 2. Guider. 3. Quill. 4. Adjusting nut. 5. Wire entry. 6. Keyway.

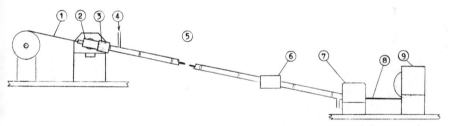

Fig. 4-16b. Continuous steam vulcanizing. 1. Wire entering crosshead. 2. Crosshead. 3. Splice box used to seal pressurized CV tube to die adapter. 4. Steam connection. 5. CV tube. 6. Water level control. 7. Water seal and air wipe. 8. Coated wire. 9. Take-up.

SPECIALIZED VULCANIZATION SYSTEMS

Hot Liquid Vulcanizing (HLV)   Hot liquid baths have been used on occasion for the vulcanization of silicone rubber extrusions. Extrusions which require complete support as they leave the die, because the green strength of the particular stock being used is very low, or

TABLE 4-1. EXTRUSION RATES FOR COMMONLY USED SIZES OF METHYL VINYL SILICONE RUBBER TUBING.

The values in this table are meant as an average guide only, many factors, including quality levels contribute to extrusion rates.

Size of Tubing:	I.D. Wall	$\frac{1}{8}$ in. (3.2 mm) $\frac{1}{16}$ in. (1.6 mm)	$\frac{1}{4}$ in. (6.4 mm) $\frac{1}{16}$ in.	$\frac{5}{16}$ in. (7.9 mm) $\frac{1}{16}$ in.	$\frac{3}{8}$ in. (9.5 mm) $\frac{1}{16}$ in.	$\frac{1}{2}$ in. (12.7 mm) $\frac{1}{8}$ in. (3.2 mm)	$\frac{5}{8}$ in. (15.9 mm) $\frac{1}{8}$ in.	$\frac{3}{4}$ in. (19 mm) $\frac{1}{8}$ in.
1 (50–60 Duro material, 2 in. (50.8 mm) extruder, 60/80 mesh screen pack, short HAV)								
ft/hr		3000	2000	1400	1350	900	730	700
m/hr		915	610	425	410	275	222	213
2 (Change of screen pack to 200/250)								
ft/hr		2050	1320	940	900	600	500	480
m/hr		625	400	285	275	183	152	146
3 (30 Duro material, other conditions same as 1)								
ft/hr		2500	1700	1165	1125	750		
m/hr		760	520	355	345	230		
4 (2½ in. (63.5 mm) extruder longer HAV (20 ft.) other conditions same as 1)								
ft/hr				3000	2900	2000	1560	1500
m/hr				915	885	610	475	460
5 (3½ in. (89 mm) extruder, longer HAV (30 ft.) other conditions same as 1)								
ft/hr						3600	3200	3000
m/hr						1100	975	915

Standard tolerances for tubing are 10% of any given dimension. Soft rubber stocks may require greater tolerances. Precision tubing held to ±.002 in. (.05 mm) can be fabricated under special conditions.

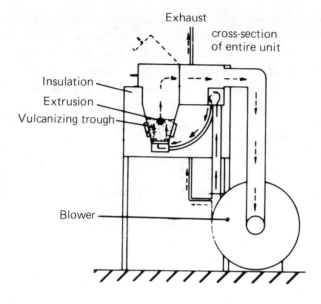

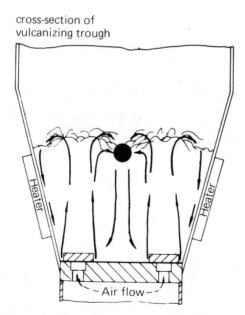

Fig. 4-17. Cross section through vulcanizing trough of fluidized bed continuous vulcanization system.

the cross section sectional shape is easily deformed, must be handled in this manner. Polyethylene glycols containing a small amount of anti-oxidant are most commonly used. These materials are non-toxic, do not react with the silicone rubber and, being water soluble, can easily be washed off with a water spray as the vulcanized extrusion leaves the tank. Operating temperatures should not exceed 400°F (204°C). While considerably lower than HAV operating temperatures, the higher rate of heat transfer, about double, more than compensates.

The extrusion must be kept immersed by running under rollers or the hot liquid must be sprayed over the top surface. The hazards of using super-heated liquid along with rapid oxidation and evaporation have kept this method from common use. However, the advent of the low temperature, fast cure, addition reaction rubbers described on p. 164 could lead to the popularization of this system.

Fluidized Bed Vulcanization (FBV)   When air at low pressure is passed through finely powdered solids, the solid particles become suspended in the air and tend to take on the characteristics of a fluid. This principle has been used for many years to melt coat hot metal

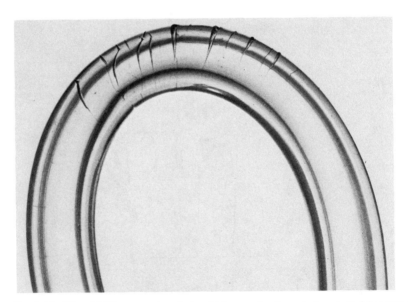

Fig. 4-18. When HAV temperature is too high or extrusion rate has slowed because of dirty screen pack the surface of the extrusion will become brittle and crack on bending or stretching.

TROUBLE SHOOTING

Problem	Possible Cause and Corrective Action
Embrittled surface Fig. 4-18	HAV temperature too high for rate of extrusion. Check to see whether screen pack is partially clogged, slowing down extrusion.
Porosity	Entrapped air in compound. May be due to improper milling or too high a mill speed—compound may need shelf aging. May be due to misfeeding—size of preform strip should be large enough to prevent starving of screw (without blocking of throat).
Blisters	Excessive humidity—store compounds in a cool, dry area, mix under dry conditions. When extruding over wire, especially stranded wire, excess moisture or oil on the wire surface will cause blistering—clean and preheat wire before extrusion.
Rough surface	Poor filler dispersion—crossblend batch thoroughly. Scorching—increase cooling, if present screen pack is clean, go to courser screen pack. Check surface of die land.
Poor cure, sticky surface	HAV temperature too low for rate of extrusion. Low HAV temperature may be due to excessive air flow—increase temperature or reduce air flow. Contamination of compound with oil—most common source is lubricating grease on mill rolls.
Variation in cross section dimensions	Change in rate of extrusion. Lack of synchronization between rate of extrusion and HAV conveyor. Change in rheology of compound due to churning in loose fitting screw—check clearance between screw and barrel at several points because they do not usually wear evenly.
Dark streaks or smears	Screw too tight in barrel or bent, metallic object fed in with material—remove screw and check for any of these problems.

parts using powdered resins and to transport powder materials, e.g., flour, etc. Fluidized bed vulcanization*, illustrated in Fig. 4-17, utilizes fine, spherical soda lime glass particles as the heat transfer medium. The fluidized mass offers very little resistance to bodies moving through it and the "boiling" action immerses the extrusion so that all surfaces are evenly heated. Heat transfer rates approximate those of LCV's. Advantages over LCV's are many—it can be run at much higher temperatures, it is dry, nonvolatile, non-flammable, and extru-

---

*Developed and patented by R.A.P.R.A. of Great Britain and licensed to the Davis-Standard Div. of Crompton & Knowles.

sion holddown devices are not required. In comparison with HAV's, FBV's are four times as fast. There is the problem of removal of the glass particles however. Silicone rubber has an affinity for glass and soft, sticky stocks are almost impossible to clean. Additionally, many profiles will trap the glass particles and thus create a problem. For simple shapes and relatively dry stocks this system would appear ideal. Short run specialty wire and cable applications, for instance, where the setting up of CV's would represent a large portion of the cost, would be a natural.

5 | COATED FABRICS

Silicone rubber applied to woven fabric is used in many applications, both mechanical and electrical. The fabric contributes strength while the silicone rubber provides flexibility, resiliency, and desirable electrical properties over a wide temperature range along with resistance to moisture, ozone, and weathering. Because glass cloth exhibits good dimensional stability, flame and heat resistance, almost zero moisture absorption, and high strength to weight ratio, it is the most commonly used fabric in combination with silicone rubber. However, Nomex*, which has better flex, abrasion, and crush resistance and is good for service above 500°F (260°C) is also a popular substrate for silicone rubber coating. For applications under 350°F (175°C) polyester fabric offers excellent abrasion resistance and high strength, coupled with outstanding flex life. Under 200°F (95°C), nylon is lightweight and offers excellent flexibility and abrasion resistance, coupled with very high strength.

DISPERSION COATING

The dispersion coating method is used to prime high temperature fabrics before they are calender coated or where very thin coatings of silicone rubber (up to .015 in., .38 mm) are desired for certain types of diaphrams, gaskets, ducting, electrical insulating tapes, hose, etc.

All silicone rubbers may be dispersed in solvents such as toluol, xylol, chlorinated hydrocarbons, or mineral spirits. The use of mineral spirits is increasing, despite the slower evaporation rate, because of government or federal restrictions on the use of the more flammable or toxic solvents. The dispersions incorporate up to 15% by weight

---

*Trade Mark E. I. Dupont, Polyimid.

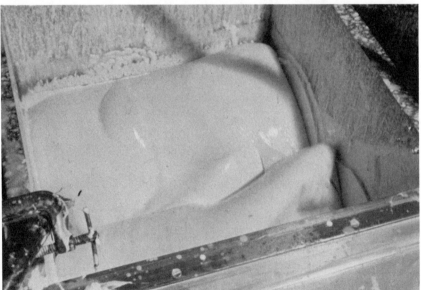

Fig. 5-1. *Dispersion mixing.* The preparation of solvent dispersions of silicone rubber is carried out in "Z" mixers. Dispersions having a viscosity of between 10,000 to 15,000 cps are usually used. Top: mixing room; bottom close up of mixer in action. (*Courtesy The Connecticut Hard Rubber Company, an ARMCO company*)

of silicone rubber. Silicone resin primers in as high a concentration as 10% by weight of the rubber are usually included to improve the bond strength. Solventless RTV's are also used for dip coating although they are more often applied by knife coating. Dispersion coating gives a thorough penetration of the fabric, contributing to both its flex life and to uniform electrical insulating properties. The production coating of fabrics with silicone rubber dispersions is often carried out in a vertical coating tower, illustrated diagramatically in Fig. 5-2. Horizontal type coaters are also used. The roll of material is first fed through accumulator rolls: accumulator rolls facilitate splicing of the substrate material by moving up and down so the material continues to be fed into the coating tower while a new roll of material is being spliced to the end of the old roll. The substrate then is carried through the dispersion dip tank. When a relatively thin coating or primer coating is required, the thickness of the coating may be controlled by a combination of the dispersion viscosity and the speed of the substrate through the tank. Heavier coatings require thick dispersions in combination with the use of wiper blades or rods which are set to strike off the required thickness of coating as the substrate

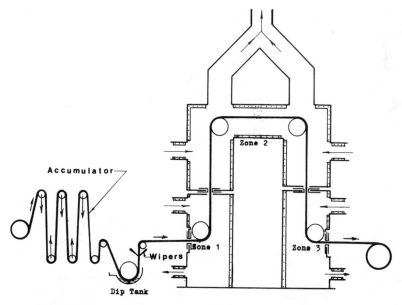

Fig. 5-2. Diagramatic illustration of a three-zone dispersion coating tower.

Fig. 5-3. Accumulator section of dispersion coating tower. (*Courtesy The Connecticut Hard Rubber Company, an ARMCO company*)

leaves the tank. As the freshly coated fabric moves into the first zone of the tower, the solvent must be removed at a temperature below that needed to initiate breakdown of the peroxide vulcanizing agent. Approximately 167°F (75°C) is sufficient. Too early peroxide action would cause blistering and pin holes. The second zone, at 266 to 284°F (130 to 140°C), promotes vulcanization. The final zone, at 450°F (232°C) or higher, eliminates traces of volatiles and maximizes the bond and physicals of the prime coat.

The application of heavy dispersion coatings often leads to marring of the surface due to dripping of the coating material as it leaves the dip tank and enters a vertical tower. In this case, horizontal curing equipment is preferred. The silicone rubber dispersion may be applied using either a transfer roll or a roll and knife combination. Limited to the coating of one side of the substrate at a time and consuming more floor space, the horizontal method does, however, allow somewhat more flexibility in surface preparation. Speeds of coating will vary with the length of the curing equipment, the material combinations used, and the thickness of the coating applied. An average speed would run about 15 linear ft (4.6 m) per min. Various weaves of fab-

Fig. 5-4. Base of 60 ft high dispersion coating tower showing accumulator section in background and finished coated fabric entering roll in foreground. Coating speeds are adjustable. A maximum width of 54 in. (137 cm) may be accommodated. (*Photo courtesy The Connecticut Hard Rubber Company, an ARMCO company*)

ric may be used as the substrate for coating; basket, leno, tricot, rip-stop, and dobby as well as plain woven. The silicone rubber coating may be provided in an uncured state for subsequent forming into diaphrams and other shapes prior to curing, or to be slit into tapes which will bond to themselves after taping and curing in place.

Standard thickness tolerances on dispersion coated fabrics are:

Fabric Thickness (in.)	Tolerance
.005 to .010	±.001
.011 to .020	±.002
.021 to .035	±.003
.036 to .050	±.004

CALENDERING

Calenders are used to manufacture continuous sheets of unsupported silicone rubber as well as to apply silicone rubber to one or both sides

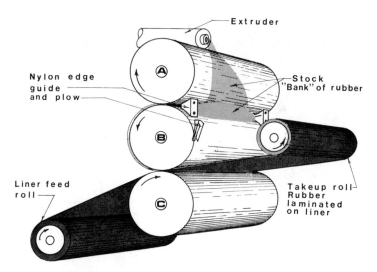

Fig. 5-5. Diagram of a three-roll calender. Roll B runs 1.1 times faster than roll A, so a freshening action is applied to the bank of material. The material bands on roll B and is transferred to the interliner or fabric as they pass between the nip of rolls B and C. The nylon plows should be adjusted so the band is slightly narrower than the fabric to which it is being applied.

of reinforcing fabric. The most widely used calender is the three-roll type illustrated in Fig. 5-5, where it is set up to produce unsupported sheet. Rolls "A" and "C" are adjustable to vary the clearance or "nip" between them and fixed roll "B". Roll "B" should turn faster than "A" by a ratio of $1 \cdot 1 : 1$ to $1 \cdot 4 : 1$. Roll "C" turns at the same speed as roll "B" except when being used in friction coating of fabric. The calender should be equipped with a variable speed drive since various formulations will be run most efficiently at different speeds. A constant bank of rubber between "A" and "B" is maintained by a metering screw or ram "D". The temperature of the rolls must be controlled. When starting, warm the top roll to 120°F (50°C), keep the center roll at room temperature, and cool the bottom roll. Roll temperatures while running should be kept well below the scorching temperature of the rubber. An interleave, usually of polyester film,* is run between the lower rolls. The nip between the rolls is adjusted

---

*A matte finish is recommended since it is difficult to transfer the rubber from the calender roll to a glossy surface. If a glossy finish is desired on one side of the rubber sheet, then the rubber should be calendered to the matte side of a matte finish on one side film. Holland cloth may also be used as an interliner.

until the proper thickness of rubber is applied to the interleave. Speed and roll temperatures are adjusted until the material transfers nicely to the interleave. The full take-up roll, with rubber and interleaving, may then be pressure taped and placed in a curing oven, or preferably, a steam autoclave until vulcanization has taken place. The core of the take-up should be a hollow metal tube and no more than a 5 in. (12 cm) thickness of material should be built up on it, otherwise difficulties will be experienced achieving proper vulcanization.

Fig. 5-6. Three-roll calender set up to produce glass reinforced electrical insulating tapes (R tapes) for traction equipment. Glass cloth is being fed into the calender between the two lower, even speed rolls. The band of silicone rubber may be seen on the center roll. The glass cloth has been previously primed with a 5% dispersion of silicone rubber catalized with 2-4-dichlorobenzoyl peroxide in mineral spirits followed by curing in a three-zone vertical tower at 212°F (100°C), 300°F (150°C) and 500°F (260°C). (*Courtesy of Electro-Motive Division, GMC*)

When the three roll calender is used for the coating of fabric, the fabric is run between rolls "B" and "C" in place of the interleave material.   Photographs of such a calender in operation may be seen in Figs. 5-6 and 5-7. If an interleave is required, it can be run directly into the take-up as is the case in Fig. 5-8. Coating performed with the lower two rolls running at the same speed is referred to as skim coating.   Friction coating where the lower two rolls run at uneven speeds may be used to apply very thin or prime coats to organic fabric. Calendering production speeds range from 5 to 10 ft/min. ($1\frac{1}{2}$ to 3 m/min.).   The speed is mostly dependent on the green strength in combination with good release from the rolls. Improvements in these characteristics continue to allow increased speeds of production. The angle at which the coated fabric leaves the calender also seems to af-

Fig. 5-7. Coated cloth leaving the calender. Notice the bank of rubber between the top roll and the center roll. Rate of production is about 10 ft/min (3 m/min). The calendered materials will not be vulcanized. It will be slit into various widths of tape rolled and stored at 40°F (4°C) until used. This produces a tape which after it is applied to a conductor will flow enough to fill out irregularities and squeeze out air pockets and fuse on heating into a continuous insulating jacket. (*Courtesy Electro-Motive Division, GMC*)

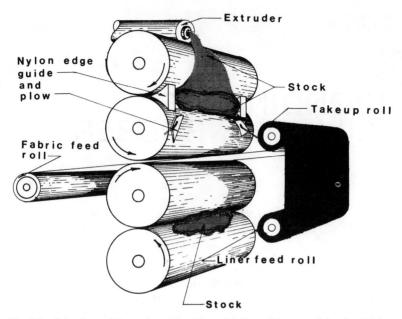

Fig. 5-8. Calender making supported rubber with liner. Diagram of 4-roll calender used to coat both sides of fabric simultaneously. Banks of stock are kept between both the upper two and lower two rolls. The material bands onto the center rolls and is transferred to the fabric which is then rolled up with an interliner.

fect the speed, with improved release being gained when the take-up is positioned lower than the top of the bottom roll. It should be noted that the three roll calender will apply the rubber to only one side of the fabric. If both sides must be coated, then a four roll calender becomes practical on long runs (see Fig. 5-8). While the illustration shows all rolls in line, they often are positioned in an L or V pattern.

Besides insulating tapes, calendered silicone rubber sheet is used in the manufacture of stamped-out diaphrams and gaskets, flexible electrical heating pads, pads for hot stamping or heat sealing equipment, and for very hot or very cold air ducting. The metallizing of a reflective surface on one side further improves the excellent service characteristics of silicone ducting. Unvulcanized reinforced sheet is used to build hoses and reinforced seals or to mold diaphragms.

6 | BONDING OF SILICONE RUBBER

Silicone rubber can be bonded to many materials, including metals, a number of plastics, ceramics, glass, masonry, various fabrics, itself, and some other rubbers. Much of the surface phenomena of silicones is not fully understood; consequently, a great deal of empirical art is mixed with the science of its bonding. The best bond between silicone rubber and a substrate is usually obtained from a vulcanized bond, accomplished simultaneously with the vulcanization of the silicome rubber itself. The bonding of silicone rubber directly to a substrate surface is facilitated by the use of primers. The primer, when applied to the substrate, forms a new chemical species on the surface. The primers which are preferred are highly proprietary and contain more than one ingredient. However, there are siloxanes included and the reaction of the primer on a metal surface might be described* as follows:

$$
\begin{array}{c}
CH_2 \\
\parallel \\
CH \\
\mid \qquad\qquad \mid \\
(\text{primer})\!-\!Si\!-\!O\!-\!Si\!-\!OR \\
\mid \qquad\qquad \mid \\
OR \qquad\quad O
\end{array}
$$

OH   OH   (metal surface)

/M//M//M//M//M//M//M//M/

---

*Description of Dr. Frederick H. Sexsmith, Manager, Research & Development Div., Hughson Chemicals, Lord Corporation.

where

$$R = -CH_3$$
$$-C_2H_5$$
$$-COCH_3$$

Typical metal parts have hydrated metal oxide surfaces.

Chemisorption is effected between the alkoxy groups of the siloxanes and the hydrated metal oxide.

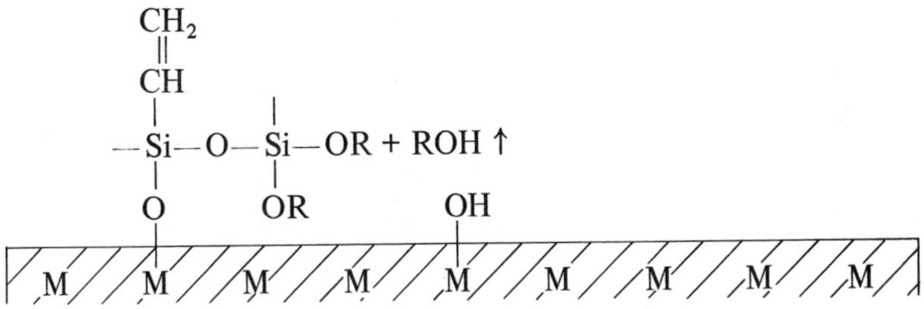

During cure of the silicone elastomer, covalent bonding occurs between the silicone polymer and the chemisorbed siloxane moiety. The silicone elastomers generally cure by a free radical (peroxide) process and silicone radicals are the active agencies by which these bonds are formed.

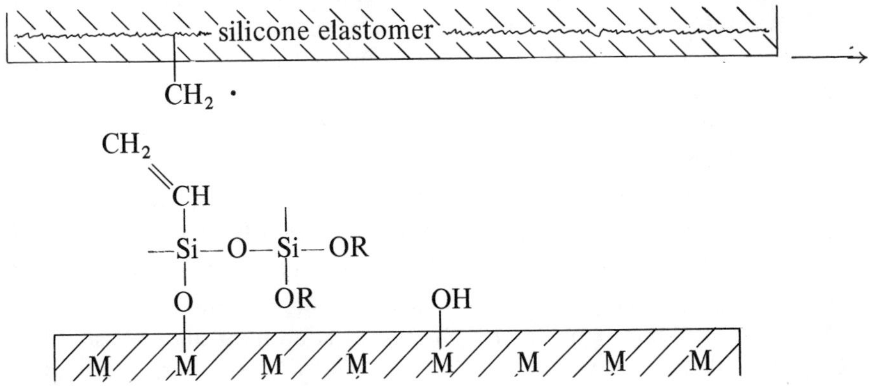

$$CH_2$$
$$\cdot CH_2-CH$$
$$Si-O-Si-OR$$
$$O \qquad OR \qquad OH$$

Since the primers readily hydrolyze, they should be kept tightly covered. They should not be used directly from the container but in small amounts poured into a receptacle for application. Any primer left over should be discarded. While primers may be applied by brushing, dipping, or spraying, they must be applied in a uniform, thin coat. Add methyl or ethyl alcohol if the primer thickens due to evaporation or if a porous substrate, such as fabric, is being coated. The primer should air dry in 10 to 30 min. For best bonding results, priming should be applied in a controlled humidity area (55% relative humidity is preferred) to freshly cleaned substrate.[1] Molding should be performed as soon as possible after the primer dries with rubber which has just been freshened.

During molding/bonding volatile by-products are formed at the rubber-substrate interface; therefore, short, high temperature cures should be avoided. Post curing, when required, should be step curing. The environment-proof sealing of toggle switches for use by the military/aerospace and commercial aircraft industries is an example of the precision molding of silicone rubber to very intricate inserts, as seen in Figs. 6-1 and 6-2.

Certain display lighted pushbutton switches can change color to signal different conditions. One way of accomplishing this is to use a white translucent plastic button, under which is located one to four miniature lamps. The lamps are covered with a thin colored silicone rubber boot which acts as a color filter. The color of whichever lamp is on is then projected to the translucent button which lights up with that specific color (Fig. 6-3). The use of silicone rubber color filters is indicated because of their ability to stand the concentrated heat of the miniature lamps and the lack of reactivity with the coloring chem-

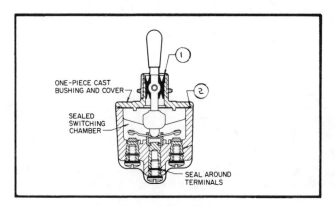

Fig. 6-1. Environment-proof toggle switches are sealed with molded-in-place silicone rubber. 1. Seal at pivot point of toggle, designed to offer maximum freedom of movement, presents challenge to mold designer. 2. Seal between cover and case is also molded in place. (*Courtesy Micro Switch Division of Honeywell Inc.*)

icals incorporated in them. Some of the light filters are required to have a metal washer bonded to their base. If individual rings were to be used, the mold loading and product cleaning times would be quite high. An efficient way of handling a problem like this is to mold/bond the rubber parts to a metal plate the thickness of the required washer and pierced with holes the diameter of the mold cores and spaced to suit them. Figure 6-4 illustrates such a molding. After post curing, the individual light filters are stamped out of the sheet. There is no further finishing required.

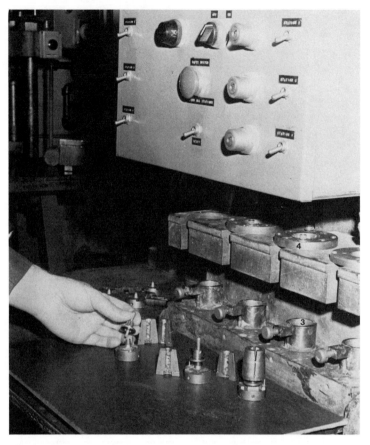

Fig. 6-2. Proprietary multi-station transfer press and tooling. This is ideal for complicated insert molding such as the toggle switch lever seal described in Fig. 6-1. The mold
sections must seal off at four different points on the toggle switch insert. Despite closely
held tolerances there is always a slight variation from one insert assembly to another. Therefore the use of single cavities simplifies the problem of sealing along parting lines. The
operator during the one minute cure cycle has just enough time to service the other three
cavities. If a multi-cavity mold had been used, the individual mold cavities would have to be
spring loaded, the mold bench time would be high, leading to greater mold temperature
fluctuation, and damage to one cavity would put the whole mold out of service during
repair. Additional flexibility with a multi-station press lies in being able to run different
models at each station. The operator is shown placing a primed toggle insert into a section
of the mold which will form the underside of the seal. This section also contains the material sprues and gates. The tapered split sections of the mold are then fitted around the top
undercut toggle lever. The assembly is inverted and dropped into a tapered chase. A spring
loaded location and lock pin can be seen on the front of each chase. The bottom of each
chase is mounted on a hydraulic ram which, when actuated, moves the unit upwards, clamping it against the bottom of the individual transfer pot. The piston actuated by an overhead
cylinder, hidden by the control panel, transfers the silicone rubber into the mold. The
material used is a 20 durometer phenyl methyl stock for maximum service flexibility at low
temperature. Catalyzed with benzoyl peroxide, it is press cured for one minute at 275°F
(135°C). (*Photo by Paul Flagg. Courtesy Moxness Products, Inc.*)

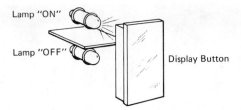

Lamp "ON"

Lamp "OFF"

Display Button

Fig. 6-3. The color of the "On" lamp is projected to the translucent white display button which glows with the lamp color.

Silicone rubber rolls for plastic film laminators, embossing, tape recorder drives, etc., require a strong, dependable bond to the metal shafts to which they are molded. A typical compression molding set-up, including detail of a four cavity mold, is pictured in Fig. 6-5. First, the steel shaft insert is cleaned, using a solvent* wipe and primed with Dow Corning 2260 primer. After air drying for 30 min. at greater than 30% humidity, it is then carefully wrapped with a raw rubber preform of specific thickness, width and weight. A press cure of 6 min. at 340°F (170°C) is followed by an oven post cure of 1 hr at

Fig. 6-4. A cluster of silicone rubber light filters is molded to a thin metal plate in a sub-cavity compression mold.

*Dow Chemical Co.'s Chlorathene NV.

Fig. 6-5. A 300-ton hydraulic compression molding press with self-contained pumping use, a work-horse in the custom rubber business. Inset view of the four cavity mold used to produce rolls for a plastic film laminator. (*Courtesy Moxness Products, Inc.*)

300°F (150°C) and 2 hr at 400°F (205°C). The rolls are then ground to clean up the flash line and achieve a close tolerance of ±.002 in. on the diameter (Fig. 6-6). Crushed tungsten carbide abrasive wheels are best. Using a surface speed of 15,000 ft/min. (4,570 m/min.) rolls

Fig. 6-6. Grinding silicone roll to exact diameter. (*Courtesy Moxness Products, Inc.*)

can be finished at the rate of 20 parts/hr. A good policy when grinding silicone rubber is to reverse the wheel periodically so the cutting
edges will not wear on one side only. Occasional soaking of the wheel
in toluol followed by wire brushing will get rid of rubber loading.

Adhesive primers can be added directly to unvulcanized silicone
rubber stocks to produce self bonding silicone rubber.* They are
handy for short runs or for use as tie coats on certain types of rolls

*An example is General Electric Co.'s SE-458U, a high strength, 55 durometer, which
can be bonded to many metal, plastics, and textile substrates.

but they are not broadly used because they are more expensive and mold release can be a problem. Fluorocarbon coating** of the molds is recommended.

One of the most critical of silicone bonded to metal applications is the shaft seals used in automotive transmissions. Some shaft seals are still molded by compression, many are molded by transfer methods, but the drift has been toward injection molding. Desma-Werke of West Germany has engineered a fully automatic system for insert molding which is currently being applied to shaft seals at the Citroen works in France and at a state automotive plant in Poland. The Desma system involves a multi-station press similar in design to the unit described on p. 77, but with as many as 14 clamp stations (Fig. 6-7). A schematic layout is illustrated in Fig. 6-8 and details of the stripping, cleaning and magazine insert loading mechanisms are shown in Figs. 6-9, 6-10 & 6-11. Vacuum equipment is standard on this machine and can be connected to all stations, eliminating rejects due to gassy parts.

Silicone rubber may be bonded to plastic parts as well: Fig. 6-12

Fig. 6-7. Desma Model 931. Fully automatic rotary insert molding injection machine. (*Courtesy Desma-Werke, Achim, W. Germany*)

---

*Floroglide from Chemplast.

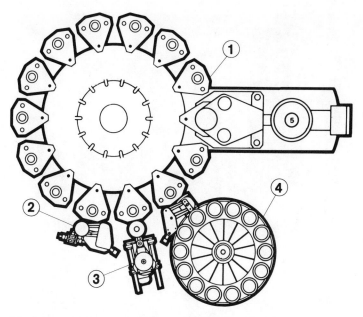

Fig. 6-8. Schematic layout of fully automatic insert molding machine used for the production of silicone rubber bonded to metal shaft seals. 1. Individual hydraulic mold clamp unit mounted on a turntable. 2. Stripping station: molded parts are removed from the cavities and dropped into a chute. 3. Molds are cleaned with rotating brushes and lubricated for the next "shot." 4. Magazine insert loader—14 magazines; each one could contain and load a different size or style of insert. 5. The screw injection unit. It can be programmed to deliver a different shot weight at each station, if desired. It is equipped with a mold scanning device which automatically adjust the approach of the injection unit to the mold—compensating for differences in size of the mold if different styles of product are being run. The injection unit may also be programmed to inject 85 to 90% of the shot quickly at high pressures, then drop back to a lower pressure as the fill is complete to avoid flashing. (*Courtesy Desma-Werke, Achim, W. Germany*)

illustrates two molded plastic mating parts that form a small housing for servo motors used in computer tape drives manufactured by Honeywell, Inc. The seals were originally fabricated separately and cemented in place by hand, which was slow and difficult to hold close tolerances. The direct molding process has reportedly reduced motor housing costs by 900%.[2]

The assembly of the all-silicone rubber Foley catheter described on p. 232 is an interesting example of silicone to silicone bonding, inasmuch as it combines two methods, one molding in place and the other the use of an adhesive. The bilumen catheter shaft is extruded and cut to length after only an HAV cure. One end of the shaft is then

Fig. 6-9. Mold stripping station (2). (*Courtesy Desma-Werke, Achim, W. Germany*)

positioned in a cavity for molding the "Y" section. The tips of the "Y" cores are inserted a short distance into the lumens of the shaft. When the mold is clamped closed, the lands, which fit snugly around the shafts where they enter the cavities, prevent the shafts from being forced out as the cavities fill with silicone rubber. The injection or transfer pressure should be little more than enough to fill the cavities and envelop the shaft ends. As vulcanization proceeds, cross linking occurs between the molded "Y" sections and the extruded shafts*,

---

*Cross linking can be improved, if required, by brushing the end of the shaft with a 1% solution of 2,4,-dichlorobenzoyl peroxide or benzoyl peroxide in toluol and allowing it to dry before molding.

and upon completion of the cure cycle, they have become an integral unit. Subsequent oven curing enhances their bond. A four-cavity injection mold used to mold the "Y" sections to the shafts is shown in Fig. 6-13. Figure 6-14 illustrates a popular injection machine for use in complicated insert molding of this type.

Some suggestions for obtaining good results when molding/bonding silicone rubber are as follows:

1. Cleanliness is of the utmost importance. The substrate surface must be freshly cleaned before application of the primer. This may be accomplished by rubbing with fine emery, grit blasting, or acid etching. Because of better control and lower cost, the chemical method is preferred. Use of degreasing equipment can create problems unless great care is taken to prevent contamination of the degreasing solvent. Freshly cleaned or primed parts must not be handled on the surfaces to which the rubber is to be bonded. Priming should be carried out in a separate, very clean room, with the humidity kept as closely as possible to 55%. The rubber compound should be freshly prepared.

Fig. 6-10. Mold stripping station (2) on left. Mold cleaning station (3) on right. (*Courtesy Desma-Werke, Achim, W. Germany*)

Fig. 6-11. Rotary magazine insert loader (4) on right. (*Courtesy Desma-Werke, Achim, W. Germany*)

Fig. 6-12. Silicone rubber seals (light color) mold/bonded to plastic servo motor housing. (*Photo by Paul Flagg. Courtesy DA/PRO Rubber Inc.*)

Fig. 6-13. Lower section of an injection mold for the molding of the "Y" to the shafts of The Foley Catheter. The cure cycle has been completed. When the mold opens, the lower platen moves, carrying the lower mold section out from under the upper section, allowing the operator easy access for removal of the parts and cleaning of the mold. The core blocks are raised manually with the handles, which are seen on each side of the cavity plate and the parts are removed by applying air pressure to the open end of the shafts. While the unloading cycle proceeds, a duplicate lower mold section, which is mounted on the opposite end of the moving or shuttle platen, may be used to carry another set through the fill and cure cycles. Overall cycles of well under a minute can be achieved in this manner, even with quite complicated cores. (*Courtesy of Travenol Laboratories, Inc.*)

Avoid any oily contamination—preforms should not be handled with bare hands.

2. Avoid the use of ketones or alcohols in cleaning surfaces to be bonded.

3. Apply the primer in as thin a film as possible—do not allow it to collect in grooves, depressions, etc. Do not hesitate to try several different primers on each job. Some primers work better under certain molding conditions and/or compounds than others and it is not unknown to have subtle variables occur which are solved by changing the type of primer. Chemlock 607 and 608 (available from Hughson Chemicals) are good all round primers. Do not prime ahead more than one day's supply of inserts.

Fig. 6-14. Open throat type of injection molding machine, a useful press for all types of insert molding. It may be equipped with a rotary table as shown or a shuttle table. The shuttle set-up is preferable for molding long, dangling inserts such as cables or the catheters picture in Fig. 6-13.   Salient features are: reciprocating screw, 25.7 cu in. (420 cu cm) capacity, 125-ton vertically acting hydraulic clamp, accommodates 16 in. mold platen. (*Courtesy New Britain Plastics Machine Division Litton Industrial Products, Inc.*)

4. Control cycle temperature and time closely. The best adhesion will be obtained with adequate cure at the mean temperature for the catalyst used, e.g., with benzoyl peroxide as the vulcanizing agent, 10 min. at 260°F, with di-tertiary butyl peroxide 15 min. at 340°F. Post cure should be a gradual stepped cure.

5. Gate transfer and injection molds in such a way that the flow of material across primed surfaces is minimized to prevent washing off of the primer.

6. Minimize the time the inserts are at mold temperature before the silicone rubber compound comes in contact with the primed surface.

Following these suggestions will not necessarily eliminate all gremlin attacks but they will go a long way toward obtaining a high level of reliable bonding.

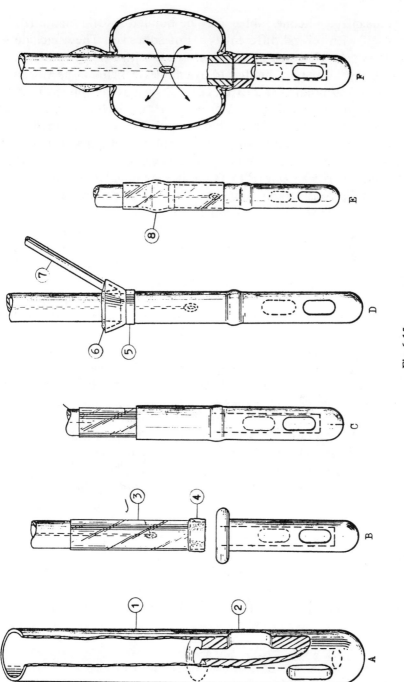

Fig. 6-15.

Vulcanized silicone rubber may be bonded to other materials and to itself with several different types of adhesive. These include solventless pastes* which must be catalyzed with benzoyl peroxide before using. They are limited to assemblies which can be vulcanized by hot press molding at 250°F (121°C), such as the splicing of extrusions or simple flat shapes. A dispersion** applied to the surfaces to be bonded by dipping or brushing, which has to be air dried $\frac{1}{2}$ to 1 hr before being used but which can be vulcanized quickly at high temperature, (2 min. at 302°F (150°C) for example, can be used. Room temperature vulcanizing (RTV) adhesives are popular because although bonds take considerably longer to form—$\frac{1}{2}$ hr or more to tack free, 24 hr or more to near full strength, they are easy to work with and form very strong bonds with a wide variety of materials.* An interesting assembly calling for the use of RTV adhesive is the distal tip of the Foley Catheter, already referred to earlier in this chapter. Figure 6-15 covers a series of steps in its assembly.

Figure 6-15A shows the detail of an integrally molded balloon and catheter tip: (1) represents the thin-walled balloon section, (2) the heavier walled tip. The eyes in the tip allow fluid to enter the drainage lumen of the catheter. In Fig. 6-15B the tip end of the shaft has been covered with a short length of thin walled heat shrinkable plastic tubing (3), leaving a small area at the very end for the application of silicone rubber RTV adhesive. The adhesive is applied at (4). Below the end of the shaft, the tip is shown with the balloon wall rolled back to the shoulder. The end of the shaft is positioned against the shoulder and the balloon section unrolled as shown in Fig. 6-15C. The plastic tubing prevents the adhesive from bonding the balloon-tip to the shaft except in an even, narrow band at (4). When the adhesive has set, the balloon section is rolled down to the adhesive line. The plastic tube is slit and removed and the balloon section unrolled against the shaft. A very narrow band of heat shrink tubing (5), Fig. 6-15D, is then applied over the balloon at its unattached end, leaving just enough free to apply adhesive (6). The adhesive may be applied between the balloon wall and the shaft with a syringe (7). A second, longer section of plastic tubing (8), Fig. 6-15E, is then shrunk over

---

*Dow Corning 61280.
**Dow Corning S-2288.
*Stauffer Chemical SWS Silicones Div. 951 adhesive. Fluorosilicone rubber should be bonded with Dow Corning 142 adhesive.

the adhesived joint, smoothing it and giving it a gently tapered edge. When the adhesive has set, plastics sleeves (5) and (8) are removed and the balloon is ready for inflation (Fig. 6-15F).

References

1. Chemlok Technical Bulletin: "Preparation of substrates for bonding," Hughson Chemicals, Lord Corporation, Erie, Pa.
2. "Molded Rubber Seals Reduce Motor Housing Costs," *Rubber Age* (June, 1973).
3. *Product Engineering* (Dec. 19, 1960).
4. Rienzner, H.J. "Recent Developments in the Use of Multi-Station Injection Molding Machines." *Rubber Chemistry & Technology*, Vol. 48, No. 2, May-June 1975.

7 | ROOM TEMPERATURE VULCANIZING SILICONE RUBBERS (RTV's)

One of the most spectacular and interesting growth areas for silicone rubbers has been the liquid compounds known as RTV's, RTV standing for room temperature vulcanizing. Originally these compounds were cured almost exclusively at room temperature. They are now available in a range of viscosities varying from thin, easily poured liquids, to rather stiff thixotropic pastes. Cure times can be controlled over a wide range and in many applications curing is accomplished at elevated temperatures, sometimes in a matter of seconds. Unlike the viscoelastic gums, the liquid rubber compounds are based on low molecular weight polymers with reactive end groups.[1] They are supplied as one package, ready for use or two package, ready for use on mixing, systems. The most versatile of these is a two package RTV, having an addition reaction curing system. Upon mixing, silicone hydride cross-linkers, in one package, react with vinyl groups (some at the end of the chain and some along the chain) in the other:

$$-O-\underset{\underset{CH_3}{|}}{\overset{\overset{CH_3}{|}}{Si}}-CH=CH_2 \ + \ H-\underset{\underset{CH_3}{|}}{\overset{\overset{CH_3}{|}}{Si}}-O- \ \xrightarrow{\text{Pt.}} \ -O-\underset{\underset{CH_3}{|}}{\overset{\overset{CH_3}{|}}{Si}}-\underset{\underset{H}{|}}{\overset{\overset{H}{|}}{C}}-\underset{\underset{H}{|}}{\overset{\overset{H}{|}}{C}}-\underset{\underset{CH_3}{|}}{\overset{\overset{CH_3}{|}}{Si}}-O$$

End group reaction (lengthens molecule)

$$\begin{array}{ccc} CH_3 & CH_3 \\ | & | \\ -O-Si-O-Si-O- & + \end{array} \begin{array}{ccc} H & CH_3 \\ | & | \\ -O-Si-O-Si-O- \\ | & | \\ CH_3 & CH_3 \end{array} \xrightarrow{Pt.}$$

$$\begin{array}{cc} CH_3 & CH_3 \\ | & | \\ -O-Si-O-Si-O- \\ | & | \\ CH_3 & CH_2 \\ & | \\ & CH_2 \quad CH_3 \\ & | \quad\quad | \\ -O-Si-O-Si-O- \\ & | \quad\quad | \\ & CH_3 \quad CH_3 \end{array}$$

Cross-link reaction

A platinum compound is the catalyst. The concentration of platinum ion may be less than 1 ppm. There are no volatile by-products produced during cure. The cure proceeds evenly in deep sections. The cured rubber has excellent resistance to reversion (even when subjected to high pressure steam), good compression set, and low flammability. Following are typical physical property ranges:

Hardness, Shore A	20–80
Tensile strength, psi	800–1300
kg/sq cm	55–90
Elongation, %	175–1200
Tear strength, pi	75–150
(Die B) kg/cm	14–27

A cheaper but not anywhere nearly as versatile a two package system involves a condensation reaction curing system in which an alkoxy crosslinker reacts with a silanol group in the presence of a stannous soap as the catalyst:

$$\begin{array}{ccc} CH_3 & CH_3 & CH_3 \; CH_3 \\ | & | & | \quad | \\ -O-Si-OH + C_2H_5O-Si- & \longrightarrow & -O-Si-Si- \; + \; C_2H_5OH \\ | & | & | \quad | \\ CH_3 & CH_3 & CH_3 \; CH_3 \end{array}$$

The RTV's have the same outstanding properties as the regular heat curing silicone rubbers—thermal stability, ozone resistance, electrical characteristics, low compression set, etc.

Applications for these versatile materials are numerous. Lightly cross-linked addition reaction systems can be engineered to produce soft, clear vibration absorbing gels, used in the electronics industry to pot delicate assemblies. The assemblies are protected from moisture and contaminants as well as from shock. They can be visually inspected through the clear gel. Electrical test probes can be inserted through the gel to test a component and the gel will reseal upon their removal. They will not harden with time and elevated temperature. The new electronic auto ignition systems are protected by RTV gel. A very soft, bioclean variation of this gel is used in the implantable breast prostheses described on p. 227. Tougher RTV rubbers, often with special fillers to improve thermal conductivity and flame resistance are used to pot T.V. flyback transformers, high voltage power supplies, connections, and many types of electrical equipment which must be sealed against the elements and protected from arc-over, corona, and abrasion. RTV's are also used in place of solvent dispersions of HV silicone rubbers to coat fabrics, thus eliminating solvent removal steps and obtaining excellent adhesion. They are also used for the coating of release papers. By the incorporation of a blowing agent into an addition reaction type of liquid silicone rubber, a fairly even structured, closed cell silicone rubber sponge may be obtained. In contrast with conventionally blown silicone sponge, such a sponge will display close control of density and of compression deflection properties, very low compression set, flame resistance, and close dimensional tolerances.

Molds for many applications are conveniently and economically made with the liquid silicone rubbers because they flow freely, they reproduce the finest details of the pattern, and when they are allowed to cure at room temperature there is practically no shrinkage. The flexibility of the mold allows the casting of rigid materials with some undercuts. Plaster, foundry core sand, concrete, epoxies, polyesters, polyurethanes, polystyrenes, vinyls, waxes, low melting point metals, and even silicone RTV are among the materials which can be cast in silicone rubber molds. Originally used to produce short run prototypes or cast complicated tooling fixtures, silicone rubber molds are being used in a number of applications as production tooling and can produce thousands of parts. In the case of simple products having one flat side or end, such as wall plaques, mirror frames,

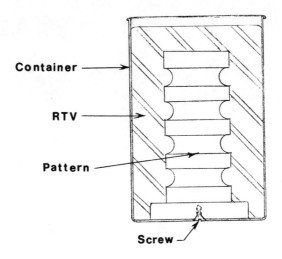

Container

RTV

Pattern

Screw

Split in mold

Tape

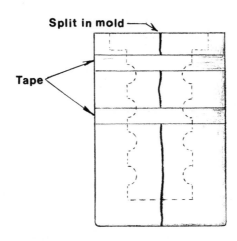

Fig. 7-1. An RTV mold for the casting of a solid part having undercuts and a flat base. A container is selected which will accommodate the pattern and allow an adequate thickness of mold wall around it. If the pattern is wood or other light material, it will have to be attached to the bottom of the container or it will float up when the RTV is poured. If a standard container cannot be obtained readily, one can be made up by rolling a cylinder of flexible plastic sheet and taping it, then taping on a bottom section. To facilitate release of the vulcanized RTV, pattern and container may be lubricated with a 5% solution of petroleum jelly in methylene chloride. After pouring most mold making RTV's will take approximately 24 hr at room temperature to reach the stage of vulcanization, where they can be roughly handled. The mold, along with the cast-in pattern, is then removed from the container, slit down one side with a sharp knife and spread open to release the pattern. By taping or clamping the split shut, the mold is ready for casting a duplicate of the pattern in epoxy, plaster, wax or any number of materials.

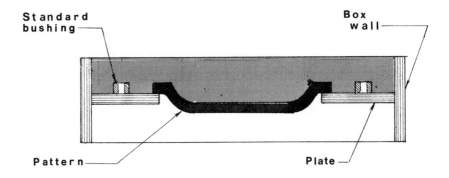

Step I

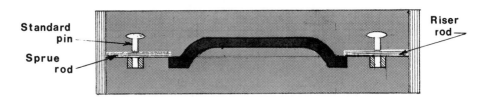

Step 2

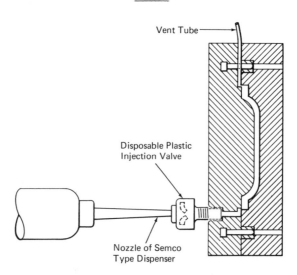

Note: The valve may be located at the parting line instead of where shown to facilitate removal of valve, sprue and cast part.

Step 3

candles, etc., the master pattern or model need only be placed in a box, pan, or other container which would allow about 2 in. (5 cm) clearance all around. If the pattern is of lightweight material, it should be attached to the bottom of the container. The A and B parts of RTV are then mixed in the proper proportion. They are usually supplied in different colors so through mixing can be determined visually by the blending of the two colors. Care should be taken during mixing to minimize inclusion of air. When the color is uniform, the mixture is deaerated with a vacuum of 27 to 29 in. (700 mm) of mercury. The mixing container should have three to four times the capacity of the RTV mixture to allow for foaming during deaeration. The rubber mixture should then be poured in a continuous stream over the pattern from a height of 2 to 3 in. (5 to 8 cm), being careful not to fold air into the material. In the case of intricate patterns, it is best to pour a light coat carefully over the complete surface, breaking any bubbles that form against the pattern surface with a toothpick, then completing the pouring. Most RTV mold compounds cure and are ready for use in 24 hr. If the curing is hastened by heating, mold shrinkage will occur and may run as high as 2%. The fully cured mold is easily removed if the pattern has a straight draw or light undercuts. If the undercuts are substantial, it may be necessary to cut the mold in half or at least along one side in

←

Fig. 7-2. Method of constructing a two piece RTV mold for a more complicated shape.

Step 1. An open-ended box is made up of light plywood to dimensions which will accommodate the pattern and allow sufficient mold wall. A pattern support plate, dimensioned to fit into the box snugly, has an opening which will just accommodate the pattern. It is positioned in the box so there is an equal amount of space on each side of the pattern from the top and bottom edges of the box wall. Standard guide bushings should be located on the plate, their I.D.'s plugged with wax or plastic rod to prevent inflow of RTV. All corner cracks where liquid RTV material could flow are dammed with pattern makers wax. The pattern and box are lubricated with mold release and the mixed, deaerated RTV carefully poured into the top section of the box.

Step 2. When the RTV has cured, the box is inverted and the pattern support plate is removed. Plastic rods or tubes are placed opposite one another on the parting line to mold in riser and sprue holes, all surfaces are treated with mold release, the bushing I.D.'s are cleared, and standard guide pins placed into them. RTV is then poured to fill the back section of the box.

Step 3. Upon curing, the box wall is removed, the mold halves separated, and the pattern and rods removed. The mold is now ready for the casting of parts. Clamping it in a vise, on edge, as shown, will reduce the risk of entrapped bubbles. A plastic filler tube is inserted into the lower opening. A liquid casting resin such as epoxy can then be run through the filler tube to fill the cavity from the bottom while the air escapes via the vent at the top. As an alternative to the filler tube a Hoefer disposable injection check valve may be used as shown in alternate Step 3.

order to release the pattern.   In this case, it will be necessary to clamp the mold or hold it in a frame during the casting process (Fig. 7-1).   Castings made in the silicone rubber molds will be a faithful reproduction of the original and because of the natural release properties of the silicone, can be removed easily from the mold.   When the master or pattern is too large or heavy to handle as described, thixotropic brush-on coatings may be used to build up the required thickness.   These are obtainable from the raw material manufacturers or can be made from a standard RTV moldmaking compound by mixing in 1.5 to 3% by weight of asbestos.[2]   When the pattern requires a two piece mold, the fabrication steps are shown in Fig. 7-2.

The manufacture of durable, good looking furniture by the casting of rigid polyurethane and polyester plastics in silicone rubber molds is a large and growing share of the furniture business.   A single set of molds to produce one furniture grouping can use several hundred pounds of RTV.   The mixing and accurate dispensing of such large volumes of RTV must be done automatically.   Figure 7-3 illustrates a machine which performs this operation directly from the shipping containers.

A very interesting method of molding rigid parts which have extreme undercuts in one piece RTV molds involves applying a vacuum to the outside surface of the mold,[3] pulling it away from the casting. This process is illustrated in Fig. 7-4 and the sequence photos in Fig. 7-5. Widely used in the manufacture of decorative candles, lamp bases, and reproductions of art objects, the Flexmold[R] process, as it is known, is now making a mark for itself in the casting of complicated sand foundry cores.   The standard method of making sand cores having undercuts is to mold separate core sections and cement them together.   The method is not only time consuming and expensive, but the sections are often misaligned and joint marks appear on the metal casting which adds an additional finishing operation. The Flexmold process has been used to eliminate as many as eight separate pieces on a core made by the regular method.   One foundry reported a total time saving of 69% on one core making job and 74% on another.[4]

Soft vinyl plastics have long been replacing leather in shoe uppers, luggage, handbags, etc.   Their scuff resistance and good appearance, combined with low price, have made them attractive to the consumer.   The reason for the realistic appearance of the vinyl surface

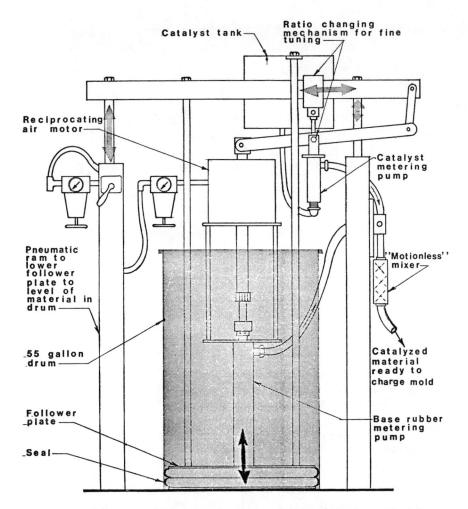

Fig. 7-3. Diagram of an RTV automatic mixing and dispensing machine. The follower plate, which can be supplied to fit the inside diameter of standard 5 gal. (19 liter) pails or 55 gal. (208 liter) open end drums, is forced into the drum of material by the action of the pneumatic rams which are located on both sides of the drum and which support the pumps and metering mechanisms. As the follower plate exerts pressure on the top of the material in the drum, the material is forced into the base rubber metering pump. From there it is pumped into the motionless mixer. Component "B", containing the cross linker and catalyst, has been charged into the catalyst tank. The metering pump for component "B" is actuated by the movement of the reciprocating air motor. By varying the location of the smaller metering pump on the reciprocating beam, the ratio of "B" to "A" metering can be adjusted. The component mixer has no moving parts, consequently, it will not heat the silicone and because the mixing is done in a completely sealed situation, air is not introduced into the silicone. This machine handles up to 5 lb (2.3 kg) per min. It develops enough pressure to inject the mixed RTV into closed molds. (*Courtesy Fluid Automation Co.*)

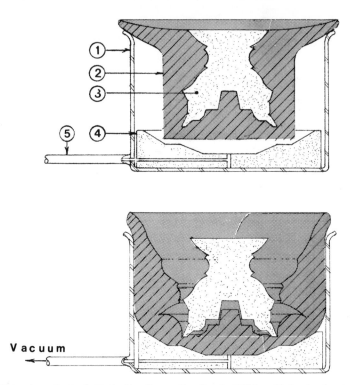

Vacuum

Fig. 7-4. A method of eliminating the parting line in RTV molds having heavy under-cuts. *Top diagram:* 1. Vacuum pot. 2. RTV silicone rubber mold. 3. Cast plaster or plastic lamp base with severe undercuts. 4. Fixture to control areas of expansion of mold when vacuum is applied. 5. Vacuum line. *Bottom diagram:* Vacuum has been applied and has drawn the flexible mold to the walls of the pot. The casting can easily be removed. There are no parting line marks or mismatches to be removed.

lies in the use of silicone molds in a process called flow molding. RTV is first poured over a finished leather part of shoe upper, hand-bag section etc. which has been layed flat in an aluminum or plastic frame. The duplication of the original parts is so exact that even the stitching looks real. The silicone rubber impression is then used to cast an epoxy duplicate of the master which in turn can be used in the production of any number of silicone rubber sheet molds ap-proximately $\frac{3}{16}$ in. (5 mm) thick. Molds are placed embossed side up at each of the stations of the rotary flow molding machine illustrated in Fig. 7-6. A sheet of vinyl plastic is placed over the mold and the combination is sandwiched between a hinged metal plate. As each station arrives at the flow molding position, an RF current is applied across the plates. The vinyl softens and flows to pick up the detailed

surface of the mold. In about 10 sec. the vinyl is ready to be removed from the silicone (Fig. 7-7) and a new cycle begun. Figure
7-8 illustrates the die cut vinyl preform (underneath) and the embossed shoe upper (superimposed) ready for incorporation into the
finished shoe.

Embossed rollers can be produced from RTV's for use by the
printing, plastic, and textile industries at a fraction of the cost of
steel rolls. A center shaft is primed and placed inside an outer casing.
The outer casing is lined with a thin flexible plastisol impression of
an original pattern. The butt joint of the plastisol must be carefully
notched. End plates are clamped on and the RTV pumped in via a
hose connection in the bottom end plate.[2]

The ways in which low viscosity silicone rubbers can be applied
to molding seems endless. One piece contour vacuum bags for the
molding of glass reinforced plastic laminates can be made by brush
coating or dipping a finished part or a master form with $\frac{1}{32}$ in. (.8
mm) or more of RTV.

Upon vulcanizing, a tough, seamless, silicone rubber bag is obtained which will not wrinkle when the vacuum or autoclave pressure
is applied and will not deteriorate with heat cycling.

Pressure pad molding[5] is a process in which the high thermal coefficient of expansion of silicone rubber, which is about 18 times that
of steel, is put to advantage. A master tool is placed in a rigid steel
box and RTV mix is poured over it just as in making the simple mold
described on p. 149. When the RTV has cured it is removed. The
layup of material to be heat and pressure cured is made on the master tool. The RTV form is placed back in the box and a heavy cover
is bolted on. If there is space between the cover and the RTV it
should be filled with a silicone rubber pad. The box is then heated
to molding temperature. The expansion of the silicone applies the
necessary pressure to produce a quality part. This method seems to
be ideal for the molding of very large, irregularly shaped parts.

Inhibition of the cure of liquid silicone rubbers, evidenced by a
gummy or uncured layer at the surface, can occur when the rubber
comes in contact with compounds containing sulphur or organome-
tallic salts during cure.

One-package liquid silicone rubber compounds are mainly based
on moisture dependent condensation curing systems. They must be
kept tightly sealed before use. On exposure to air, moisture in the
air acts on the curing agent. In the case of a polymer end-stopped

(a)

(b)

with an acetoxy group the reaction would proceed as follows:

$$-O-\underset{\underset{CH_3}{|}}{\overset{\overset{CH_3}{|}}{Si}}-O\cdot OCCH_3 + H_2O \rightarrow O-\underset{\underset{CH_3}{|}}{\overset{\overset{CH_3}{|}}{Si}}-OH + CH_3COOH$$

(Acetoxy)

$$-O-\underset{\underset{CH_3}{|}}{\overset{\overset{CH_3}{|}}{Si}}-OH + CH_3CO\cdot O-\underset{\underset{CH_3}{|}}{\overset{\overset{CH_3}{|}}{Si}}-O- \longrightarrow$$

$$O-\underset{\underset{CH_3}{|}}{\overset{\overset{CH_3}{|}}{O}}-\underset{\underset{CH_3}{|}}{\overset{\overset{CH_3}{|}}{Si}}-O-\underset{\underset{CH_3}{|}}{\overset{\overset{CH_3}{|}}{Si}}-O- + CH_3COOH$$

(Acetic acid)

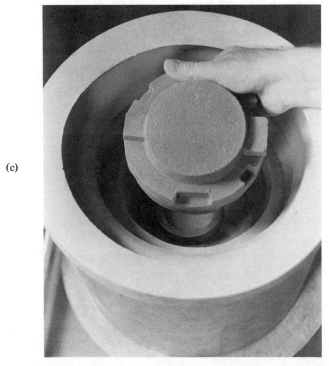

(c)

Figs. 7-5A, 5B, and 5C. The core for a motor clutch housing, cast from a "no bake" core sand mix, is shown being released from the flexible silicone rubber mold as a vacuum is applied. This intricate core would be difficult to mold in any other way. (*Photo by Paul Flagg. Courtesy Precision Flexmold, Inc. Racine, Wis.*)

Fig. 7-6. Compo-Fit Model "E" six station machine for the flow molding of vinyls. Equipped with a 20 KW R.F. unit. Four and eight station models are also available with ten and forty KW RF, respectively. Used for the production of shoes, handbags, luggage, golf bags, bowling bags, belts, and novelty items. The model "E" can turn out a pair of shoe uppers in 16 to 18 seconds. (*Courtesy Compo Industries, Inc., Waltham, Mass.*)

A comparison of the three types of RTV's, acetoxy, moisture dependent cure, silanol-alkoxy, condensation cure, and addition cure, is given in Table 7-1. In Table 7-2 additional properties of five different addition cure LVR's are presented.

The acetic acid by-product, which quickly dissipates into the air, is what causes the odor of vinegar one notices when using silicone household cement for bathtub caulking, etc. Vulcanization occurs first at the surface and then progresses inward as the moisture disperses through the silicone. Such an action proceeds slowly and is not practical for deep section curing. Alkoxy groups may be substituted for acetoxy groups in one package compounds. They are used where acetic acid by-products might be corrosive to certain metal components. The alkoxies, however, are slower curing compounds, consequently not as popular as the acetoxies. These products, because of their polar groups, make excellent adhesive sealants. Their outstanding weatherability in the hottest of climates and flex-

Fig. 7-7. Embossed vinyl sheet being removed from silicone rubber mold at flow molding station.

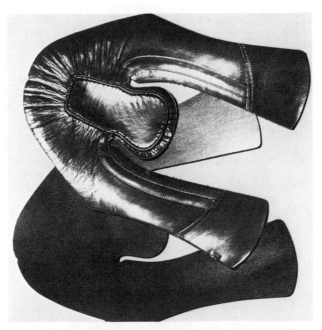

Fig. 7-8. Die cut vinyl shoe uppers before and after embossing with silicone rubber flow molds. On shallow parts such as this, 50,000 impressions may be successfully made from a single mold. (*Courtesy Compo Industries, Inc., Waltham, Mass.*)

TABLE 7-1.

	1 Part Acetoxy Cure RTV	2 Component Silanol Condensation RTV	2 Component Addition Cure RTV
Cure cycle	1–3 days RT @ 80% R.H.	4 hrs @ R.T.	8 hr–2 days R.T. or very fast cure at elevated temperature depending on part thickness
By products	Acetic acid	Alcohol	None
Linear shrinkage	0.6%	0.6%	0.1%
Adhesion	Excellent	Fair with primers	Poor
Deep section cure	No	Yes	Yes
Electrical properties	Excellent	Excellent	Excellent
Flame retardance	Poor	Poor	Excellent
Inhibition resistance	Good	Good	Poor
Hydrolytic stability (reversion resistance)	Poor	Poor	Excellent
High strength properties	Good	Fair	Good
Heat aging stability	Outstanding	Outstanding	Excellent
Weatherability	Excellent	Excellent	Excellent
Viscosity range	Non-pourable	Pourable	Pourable

E. M. Jeram

TABLE 7-2. ADDITION CURE RTV SYSTEMS OFFER CLEAR, TRANSPARENT PRODUCTS COVERING A WIDE RANGE OF VISCOSITIES AND PHYSICAL PROPERTIES.

Product	RTV 615*	RTV 670*	Custom Product	Custom Product	RTV 7100*
Application	Electronic encapsulant	Embossing roll compound	Electronic encapsulant	Laminating compound	Silicone membrane
Viscosity, cps	4,000	8,000	60,000	350,000	4,000,000
Tensile strength, psi	850	1,200	600	550	1,000
% Elongation	150	80	300	550	1,000
Shore A	45	75	45	40	25
Tear strength, psi	15	60	60	75	175
Consistency	Pourable	Pourable	Pourable	Pourable	Thixotropic paste

*Product designations of Silicone Products Dept., General Electric. (The commercial production of 7100 type material has been postponed for an indefinite period.)
    E. M. Jeram

ibility in the coldest of climates makes them ideal for the building industry. They can be used to caulk joints of masonry, metal, wood, or plastics and seal windows. Since they do not stiffen with cold, they can be applied out of doors in winter. Indoors they can be used on bathtubs, showers, sinks, tile, etc. As a protective coating for plywood, metal, or masonry building panels, they can be sprayed, brushed, or rolled on from a solvent dispersion. Even silicone rubber roofing is being applied in this manner. After spray coating the roof with a foam-in-place urethane coating used for its light weight and thermal insulation properties, the roof is then finished with a thin protective layer of silicone rubber which will repel water yet breath, and which ultra violet radiation will not deteriorate. Silicone roofing systems are particularly advantageous in the locations such as Florida and the Virgin Islands where asphalt roofing deteriorates so rapidly in the strong sunlight.

An application that is rapidly growing to be a multi-million dollar industry is the "formed-in-place gasket" (FIPG). A thin bead of a single component, rapid cure, silicone adhesive sealant is applied to one of the surfaces to be sealed. It may then be pressed immediately against the mating surface and in approximately 20 min. will have set a tight seal. The bead may also be allowed to cure before assembly, however never longer than 2 hr or it will be too stiff to flow. In either case, the silicone easily conforms to the surfaces, eliminating many of the drawbacks of the old type of cork, paper, and rubber-asbestos gaskets. The ideal characteristics of resistance to extremes of temperature and oils and washing solutions makes silicone adhesive sealant the choice for many automotive, appliance, and lighting seals.

For short run production or replacement gasketing, the RTV sealant may be applied with a caulking gun; however, automatic equipment has been developed which will apply the gasket bead at rates as high as 10 in./sec. Optical control allows the tracing of intricate patterns. Multiple nozzles expedite the handling of several parts at a time. Figure 7-9 illustrates an automatic machine for FIP gasketing of valve covers used on Oldsmobile V8 engines. Rates of well over 450 units[6] an hour are possible. Valley covers which fit between the cylinder banks at the top of V8 engines are considered the toughest of assembly line gasketing jobs. At the Pontiac Motor Division, General Motors' automated FIP gasketing is used on valley covers. Pontiac reports[7] that the silicone compound cost is only half as

Fig. 7-9. Automated equipment for the application of silicone rubber formed in place gaskets to valve covers for Oldsmobile V8 engines. Covers are loaded into the four magazines at right. They are cammed from the magazine, four at a time, and dropped into transfer nests. They are then transferred to the gasketing station, located approximately in the center of the machine, where four dispensing guns are mounted to a common X-Y axis table (see Fig. 7-10). The RTV is supplied to the guns from one of two 55 gal (209 liter) drum pumps. These are set for automatic change-over for constant operation. After the bead of RTV is applied, the covers are loaded onto four tracks which carry the parts to the engine assembly line where they are assembled to engines within 20 min. On the extreme left is the hydraulic power pack. A finished valve cover may be seen lying in front of the second station. (*Courtesy Wilson Machine Div., Wilson Engineering Saginaw, Mich.*)

much as the old pressure bonded cork gasket. There are only half the leaks experienced and any gap in the gasket bead can be repaired with hand applied material. Other savings lie in the elimination of costly inventories of many types of preformed gaskets and the reduction in replacements due to failures in the field caused by loosening of bolts with the gradual compression set of preformed gaskets. FIP equipment costs range from $20,000 for simple models to $75,000 to $1,000,000.00 for the big automatic models just described. Other automotive engine applications for FIP gasketing are the thermostat towers, water pump, oil pan, oil filter housing to block, transmission, and differential cover plates etc. An example of their use in the appliance field is seen in Fig. 7-12. The FIP gasket applied to the pump housing of a washing machine will not soften with heat or embrittle after repeated exposure to hot and rinsing cycles and contact with strong detergents (see references 8 and 9 for more data).

Silicone adhesive sealants are used in many other applications; boat windows, bulk heads, hulls, deck hardware, bolts, oven door

Fig. 7-10. The FIPG station.   Four dispensing guns can be seen mounted to a common X-Y axis table which is controlled by the photo trace head above.   Two valve covers can be seen lower left as they approach the FIPG station.   (*Courtesy Wilson Machine Div., Wilson Engineering Saginaw, Mich.*)

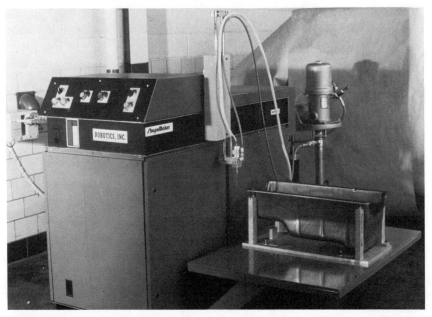

Fig. 7-11. A smaller single-station unit controlled by either a computer developed cam system or optical line tracing system. (*Courtesy Robotics, Inc.*)

Fig. 7-12. Molded plastic washing machine pump housing with formed in place gasket. (*Courtesy Silicone Products Dept., General Electric Co.*)

windows, refrigerator defrost mechanism gaskets, automobile windows and tail lights, aquariums, and other hobby cementing jobs. There is even a medical grade* for the bonding of implantable silicone assemblies or implantable silicone to other implantable synthetics, and the dip coating from dispersion of cardiac pacemakers and other electronic implantable devices.

FUTURE DEVELOPMENTS

All of the RTV rubbers can be injection molded,[10] including those listed in Table 7-2 (p. 160), but excepting the single package moisture dependent types. The General Electric addition reaction silicone rubber referred to as 7100 is particularly attractive—it has excellent physical properties, although it is a thixotropic paste rather than a liquid, it flows easily under very low pressure, and it cures quickly at low temperature—at 250°F (120°C), 6 in. $\times$ $\frac{1}{2}$ in. $\times$ $\frac{1}{4}$ in.

---

*Silastic medical adhesive, Type A, Dow Corning Corp.

(15 cm X 1.3 cm X .64 cm) test bars were cured in 10 sec.[10]   7100 has the potential to be cured quickly at even lower temperatures. Lower temperatures result in lower mold shrinkage and therefore greater part accuracy. The low molding pressures—no more than 250 to 300 psi (18 to 21 kg/cm^2)—allows greater flexibility in mold design. It also means that the standard type of heavy duty mixing and molding equipment is unnecessary. The high elongation and tear strength values for 7100 contribute to its easy removal from intricate

Fig. 7-13. Surgical "T" tube drain, molded in one piece from low viscosity, addition reaction, silicone rubber. There are no mold parting line marks along the length of any of of the legs of the tube. This is an example of the avenues opened up with these new materials. (*Photo by Paul Flagg. Courtesy Medical Engineering Corp.*)

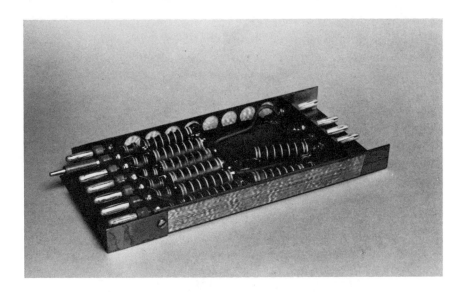

Fig. 7-14. SILGAN^{TM} potting agents cure without exotherm, protecting delicate, heat-sensitive components in electronic module.

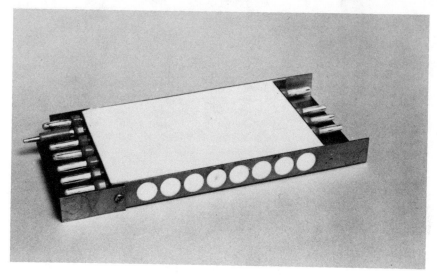

Fig. 7-14. (*Continued*)

molds with heavy undercuts or long straight draws. Figure 7-13 7100 has also been successfully extruded in very small diameters. Because of its low green strength it was extruded directly into a liquid vulcanizing bath of triethylene glycol at 260°F (125°C). The support of the liquid prevented flattening of the extrusion prior to its vulcanization.

At least three companies have programs designed to develop processes which can take full advantage of the unusual molding characteristics of the RTV's. They have the potential to be adapted to RIM* molding and there is little doubt that, like the liquid urethanes, they will contribute greatly to the future silicone molding scene.

A new family of proprietary, high strength composites that offers engineers design flexibility and cost savings in electrical, electronic and mechanical applications has been developed. Known as SILGAN** Elastomers, the new materials combine the excellent low viscosity and ease of handling properties of silicones with the superior high tensile and tear strengths associated with such organic polymers as epoxies and polyurethanes. They cure at room tempera-

---

*Reaction injection molding.
**Trade Mark of SWS Silicones Corp. a subsidiary of Stauffer Chemical Co.

TABLE 7-3.

Property	J-500*	H-622*
Tensile strength, psi	1,200	1,500
Tear strength, die-B	250	325
Dielectric constant, 100 Hz	2.9	3.0
Volume resistivity, ohm cm	1.6×10^{15}	1×10^{16}
Dielectric strength, volts/mil	500	590
Dissipation factor, 100 Hz	0.007	0.008
Thermal shock resistance	Excellent	Excellent
Brittle point, °C	Below −90	Below −90
Hydrolytic stability	Excellent	Excellent
Specific gravity	1.04	1.05
Durometer, shore A	85	90
Cure conditions	Room temperature	Room temperature
Uncured properties	Ready to use, self-leveling, liquid	Two-component, flowable, liquid

*SILGAN product numbers.

ture without exotherm and with low shrinkage. They also demonstrate superior low temperature flexibility and resistance to corrosion, moisture, and harsh environments. SILGAN Elastomers represent a technological breakthrough in which liquid composites are produced by the in-situ polymerization of an organic component in a support phase of silicone liquid polymer. The elastomers achieve their unusual high strength properties as a result of the dispersion of rod-like organic particles in a liquid silicone matrix. Using the new in-situ polymerization technology, an almost unlimited number of elastomers with a wide range of physical, chemical, and electrical properties can be produced. The first generation composite RTV materials are based on a styrene-acrylic ester copolymer and are commercially available as either one or two-component systems. Processing is similar to the regular RTV's. A list of properties is given in Table 7-3.

References

1. Bobear, W. J., in *Rubber Technology*, 2nd Ed. edited by Morton, New York, Van Nostrand Reinhold, 1973.
2. General Electric Silicones, Technical Data Book S-40.
3. U.S. Patent 3,776,683.

4. Henning, R., "QO[R] Flexmold, a New Pattern Concept," A.F.S. Regional Foundry Conference, Milwaukee, Wis., Feb. 6, 1975.
5. Beck, Earl W., "Silicone Rubber puts on Squeeze for High Quality Composite Layups." *Plastics World* (June 16, 1975).
6. *Automotive Industries*, June 1, 1974.
7. "Pontiac Scores with Silicone," *Production* (Sept., 1973).
8. "Formed-in-place Gaskets," Technical Data Book S-42A, Silicone Products Dept., General Electric.
9. *Formed-in-place Gaskets*, Bulletin 61-076, Dow Corning Corp.
10. Mellinger, G. A., "Processing of RTV Silicones," *Inter company report*, Synthesis and Characterization Branch, Chemical Laboratory, General Electric.

8 | SPECIALIZED FABRICATION METHODS

FABRIC REINFORCED SILICONE RUBBER SEALS*

General Requirements   The special requirements of seals for aircraft applications have led to the development of a variety of seals based on silicone rubber reinforced with textile fabrics. Such seals have subsequently found applications in other fields. In generalized terms the requirement is to seal the peripheries of large doors or other access panels or hatches subject to repeated opening and closing, without imposing high closing pressures on the door or frame structures. Large structures commonly call for proportionally high dimensional tolerances. Consequently, the gap to be sealed may exhibit considerable variation in width from point to point along its periphery; the mean gap may also vary from model to model of the same equipment. In aircraft applications gap dimensions may also be subject to changes due to varying 'g' forces or thermal expansion. Therefore, this type of seal must be capable of sealing a relatively wide and variable gap, and further be able to maintain efficient sealing at maximum gap after service at minimum separation of the adjacent metal structures.

SEALS

In aircraft doors the pressure differential across the seal is usually low, typically 5 to 10 psi (.35 to .7 kg/cm^2), but other uses may call

---

*This section contributed by R. N. Thomson, Technical Manager Precision Rubbers Division, Dunlop Ltd. All photos in the section courtesy of Precision Rubbers Division, Dunlop Ltd., England.

for much higher pressure differences. On the other hand requirements for very low leak rates at pressure differentials below 1 or 2 psi may also impose special problems. Other functional requirements include resistance to abrasion by relative movements of the door and frame either on closing or due to structural vibrations, flexibility over the required service temperature range, and resistance to environmental conditions, for example, ozone attack, surface contamination by lubricating and hydraulic oils, fuels and cleaning fluids.

Seal Types and Design Considerations Seals of the types under review are applicable to doors or orifices of peripheral length from a few feet to 50 ft. or more; for example, the cargo bay door on a large military aircraft may be at least 10 ft. X 15 ft. (3m X 4.5m) in size. The basic requirement of low, or in some cases zero, closing pressure prohibits the use of straightforward compression seals of circular or rectangular cross section. Very soft solid rubber extrusions or sponge sections fail to meet the "variable gap" requirement for the following reason. Significant compression is necessary at maximum gap to ensure sealing efficiency, and hence compression in the minimum gap condition is unacceptably high for good recovery unless the seal section is very large. Further, the mechanical strength sets a lower limit to rubber hardness or sponge density. Thus, lip seals or hollow section seals are preferred. Lip seals are largely self-explanatory; generally they comprise two portions, one for attachment to the structure and the other a deformable lip which contacts the moving panel. Conformations are usually simple, as illustrated by typical cross section examples in Fig. 8-1, although they may be complicated by molded-in metal strips for attachment or stiffening purposes; careful attention to design is necessary at sharp corners or small radius bends in order to avoid gaps at full deflection.

Hollow section seals may be classified as non-inflatable or inflatable types. The former are typified by simple 'O' and 'P' section seals, but special sectional shapes are frequently required in accordance with the door closure geometry of the particular application, as illustrated in Fig. 8-2. Orifices may be provided in the seal wall on the side exposed to the high pressure to ensure that the pressure differential supplements the initial sealing force due to compression; this "self-inflating" type is distinct from true inflatable seals provided

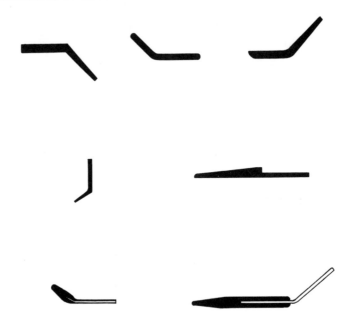

Fig. 8-1. Typical lip type seals, the two lower seals are illustrated with molded-in metal strips.

Fig. 8-2. Hollow section seals.

with a connection for inflation from a separate supply source at a pressure higher than the differential pressure across the seal face. Fig. 8-3 shows typical inflatable seal sections. Examples a, b, c, and d are normally installed in a groove or channel which prevents lateral expansion of the seal; the side lobes function as a rolling diaphragm, thus advancing the central sealing portion into contact with the opposing structure.   These seals are self-retracting on release of the internal pressure and hence impose zero door closing forces; since the "high-lift" designs (Figs. 8-3c and d) retract below the top of the grooves into which they are installed, they are ideal for sliding doors or canopies as they are not subjected to abrasion by operation of the door. Their ability to seal wide gaps also accommodates wide tolerances and wear in the door slide mechanism.

When space considerations do not permit inflatable seals housed in a groove or channel, a flat tubular type may be employed. This seals against a metal nib on the door or frame, as shown in Fig. 8-3e.

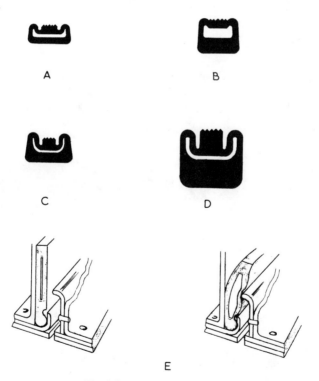

Fig. 8-3. Typical inflatable seals.

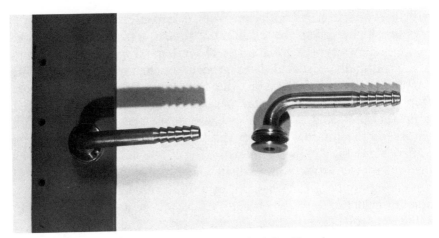

Fig. 8-4a. Air connections for inflatable seals.

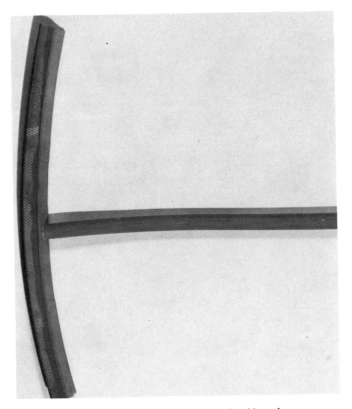

Fig. 8-4b. Air connections for inflatable seals.

Air connections have almost as many variations in detail as seal sections, but fall into three main types. The simplest (Fig. 8-4a) is analogous to the early type of flanged metal connector provided on automotive inner tubes secured by a collar and nut, but the fabric reinforcement reduces any tendency for the rubber to be displaced laterally; the low compression set of silicone rubber also reduces loss of sealing efficiency with time. This type of connector has the disadvantage of increased bulk and usually necessitates a recess for its accommodation. Flexible tail pipes molded as part of the seal structure, (Fig. 8–4b), overcome this problem, and may also simplify installation of the seal, as the actual connection to the air source can

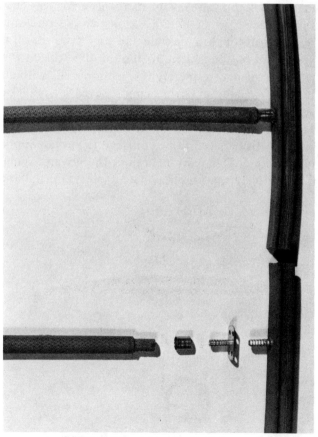

Fig. 8-4c. Air connections for inflatable seals.

conveniently be made at some distance from the seal. Careful attention must be paid to the joint, ensuring continuity of fabric reinforcement for mechanical strength, as considerable strain may be imposed when fitting in awkward situations. The third type of connector illustrated, (Fig. 8-4c), is therefore preferred where wall thickness of the seal permits its use. In this case, a metal insert is bonded in, and the fabric reinforced tail pipe attached after molding. If high inflation pressures are involved, a metal sleeve is swaged or crimped over the joint.

Means of attachment of seals to the door or frames are also varied, and generally dictated not only by the construction and materials of these components but by considerations of space and closure geometry. The housing of inflatable seals in machined grooves or fabricated channels has already been mentioned; the channel is usually in the frame to avoid complications of pressure supply to the movable door, although a flexible tail pipe connection may be employed if it is more convenient to mount the seal on the door. 'P' section seals are of course merely 'O' section seals with a tail for attachment, a metal clamping strip being secured by bolts or rivets passing through the tail. Many variations of groove or clamping strip methods have been used and call for no special comment, but one method of attachment believed to be confined to aircraft applications is worthy of mention. This is by adhesion, the novelty lying in the provision of a relatively rigid interlayer to facilitate installation and

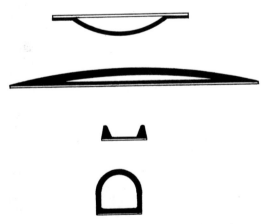

Fig. 8-5. Seals with molded-in-place bonding substrate.

ensure adequate joint strength.   Silicone rubbers may readily be bonded to a variety of materials during vulcanization, but the adhesive strength achievable between fully vulcanized silicone rubber and metal using, for instance, RTV silicone rubber, is insufficient for many applications.   A thin metal or glass reinforced plastic strip is therefore bonded to the base of the seal in the molding operation. This prevents distortion of the seal during installation and provides a suitable surface for adhering to the aircraft structure with a room temperature curing two-part epoxy resin adhesive.   Fig. 8-5 illustrates seals incorporating this feature, and Fig. 8-6 shows the method employed on the thrust reversal panels of the Rolls-Royce RB211 engine as installed in the Lockheed Tristar.

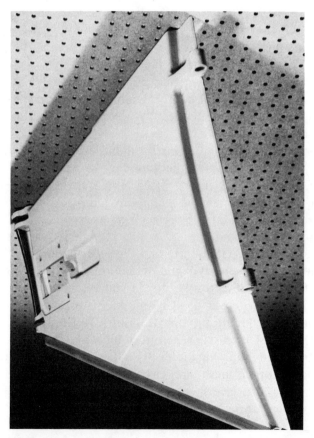

Fig. 8-6. Jet engine thrust reversal panels with bonded hollow section seal.

Construction and Materials   The combination of service conditions requiring immunity to ozone cracking, resistance to surface contamination by aircraft fluids, and a wide operating temperature range can best be met by appropriate grades of silicone rubber. These functional requirements suggest that an all-rubber construction would be satisfactory, but the relatively low strength of silicone rubbers renders these vulnerable to mechanical damage and abrasive wear. Mechanical strength is therefore augmented to acceptable levels by the incorporation of textile reinforcement. A composite construction of silicone rubber and textile fabric offers great versatility, freeing the designer from limitations imposed by strength and stiffness consideration for a single material. In many cases, a low compression set silicone rubber based on a methyl-vinyl polysiloxane polymer is suitable.   If the seal is to be subjected to severe contamination by aircraft fuels, fluorosilicone rubber may be used throughout, but resistance to intermittent surface contamination may be more economically provided by confining the fluorosilicone to the outer layer only.   Experience has shown that a rather soft rubber is preferable for good sealing as the seal conforms more readily to local discontinuities in the opposing surface.   A vulcanized hardness of 50–60 Shore A is typical.

Reinforcing fabrics vary in both the basic textile and fabric construction.   For operating temperatures up to 320°F (160°C), polyester (e.g., Dacron)* woven or knitted fabrics are normally employed, but a requirement for higher maximum temperatures may be met with more heat resistant fabrics such as glass or textiles based on aromatic polyamid fibres (e.g., Nomex)*.   Glass fabrics have the disadvantage of poor fatigue life and therefore should not be used in seals subjected to severe dynamic deflections.   Fabric weights in the range 1.5 to 8 ozs (35.6 to 190 g/m^2) and thickness 0.005 to 0.030 in. (.13 to .76 mm) cover most requirements, heavier reinforcement being obtained by multi-ply construction. Knitted fabric constructions of the tricot mesh type permit good strike-through of the silicone rubber, thus improving inter-ply adhesion; woven fabrics with a corresponding open mesh are easily distorted during processing. Knitted fabrics also give greater flexibility in the composite structure than woven fabrics of equal strength.

---

*E. I. du Pont.

For the reinforcement of thin-walled inflatable seals, fabric based on continuous filament yarns rather than staple yarns should be employed, to avoid the possibility of leakage due to penetration of the rubber by individual staples. Slow leaks can occur by penetration of the inner ply of rubber at one point, "wicking" along a yarn of the fabric and penetration of the outer rubber ply at a remote point. In addition to providing mechanical strength and stiffness to the seal structure, fabrics are also employed to provide an abrasion resistant outer surface. For this purpose, closely woven or knitted fabrics are required to minimize the strike-through of the silicone rubber. Surface friction is also reduced by this feature.

Manufacture   Large seals, as described above, cannot economically be molded in a single operation. Production quantities required are usually relatively small and consequently, tooling costs for molds 8 ft. X 4 ft. (2.5 X 1.25 m) and above would be prohibitive. Very large presses would also be required to accommodate such molds. The preferred production method is to mold straight lengths of the section required and to join these together by subsidiary molding operations; a seal of any dimensions with constant cross-section requires only a straight mold, typically 10 ft. (3 m) long, and a "jointing block" for its manufacture. This method also substantially reduces manufacturing plant costs as press platen size does not set an upper limit to product dimensions; seals of unlimited size can theoretically be produced from relatively short molds and corresponding presses. In practice, it has been found convenient to standardize on molds 10 to 11 ft. long, this giving a reasonable compromise between the number of joints required in a large seal and practical difficulties in the handling of larger molds. A typical hydraulic press used in the manufacture of aircraft seals is shown in Fig. 8-7; the 'C' frame or open-sided construction permits lateral loading of the long molds and contributes to flexibility of shop lay-out. Most large seals, however, incorporate some features or feature requiring additional manufacturing operations and tooling. An inflatable seal, for instance, requires a means of attaching the inflation connection, which in some designs is itself a flexible tube of reinforced silicone rubber (Fig. 8–4b). In this case a modified jointing mold is provided for the attachment of the inflation pipe. Other designs may call for sharp corners or even changes of section around the periphery

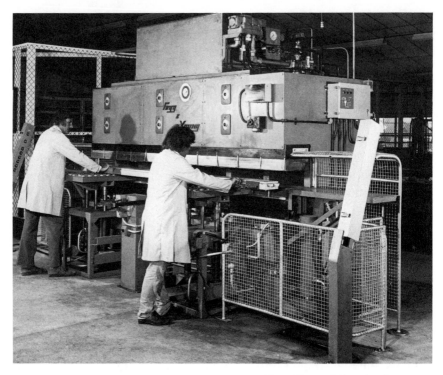

Fig. 8-7. Special open throat press for the molding of long reinforced seals.

of the seal which can only be accommodated by special molds. Examples of these two cases are illustrated in Figs. 8-8 and 8-9. The seal illustrated in Fig. 8-8 is of constant section, and the minimum bend radius 'R' in the installed configuration is large enough in relation to the cross section to permit the seal to be molded in a straight mold; the required length is produced by repeated "step molding" in the same tool as explained below. The final closure and attachment of the inflation tube is performed with a separate short "joint block" mold. Figure 8-9 shows a seal for which the above procedure is not applicable. The two right angled corners, each with a change of section, necessitate right- and left-handed corner molds. If the section were constant, a single tool would of course suffice for both corners.

A useful "rule of thumb" for determining the minimum bend radius which a seal can tolerate without significant distortion of the section is 8 times the seal section in the plane of the bend. Thus the

P section seal (Fig. 8-2) can be bent to a 4 in. (10 cm) inside radius in the plane perpendicular to the tail, but only to an 8 in. (20 cm) radius in the plane containing the tail. This rule must, nevertheless, be used with caution, as the effective height of the seal can some-

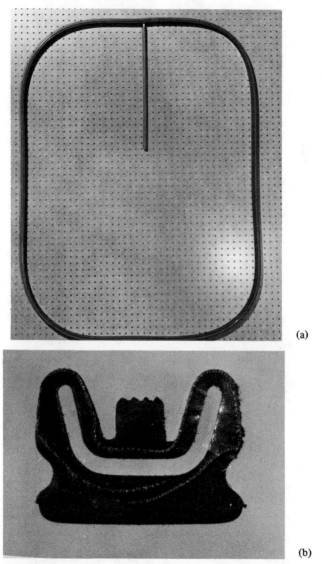

(a)

(b)

Fig. 8-8a and b. Inflatable seal with constant cross section (8-8b) and generous radii may be molded in a straight mold.

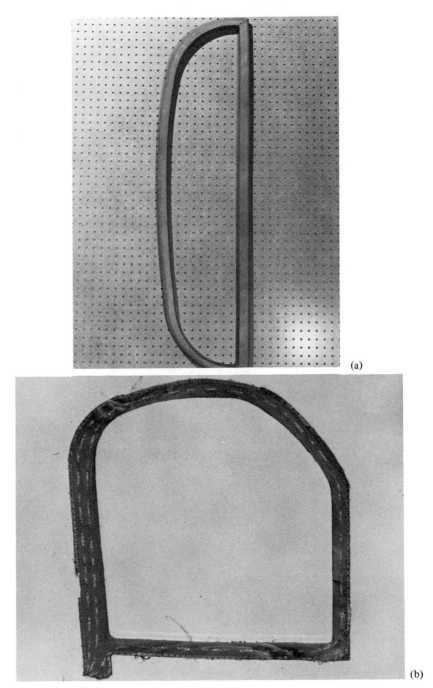

(a)

(b)

Fig. 8.9.

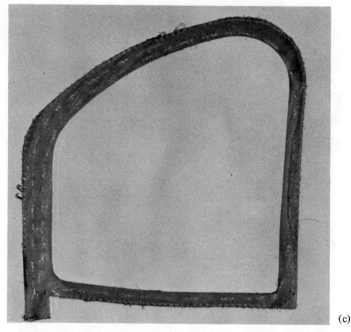

(c)

Fig. 8-9. (a) Inflatable seal with sharp corners having changing cross sections (b) and (c) in the curved and straight sides, respectively, requires both right- and left-hand corner molds.

times be reduced by bends of comparatively large radius, resulting in leakage at the bends. Inflatable seals may also suffer in this way, and the self-retracting feature of the sealing nib may also be impaired by too sharp a bend.

Many practical applications require curvature in more than one plane, for instance, in aircraft doors or hatches where the seal has to conform to a three-dimensional curve of the external contour. Large composite radii present no problems, but sharper curves in three dimensions would require large complicated tools to produce the desired shape by direct molding. Fortunately, silicone rubbers are amenable to "heat setting" and it is often possible to produce complex three-dimensional shapes from straight molds and simple subsidiary setting jigs or formers.

In its simplest form "heat setting" merely involves constraining the molded product to a desired configuration during the post-cure in an air-circulating oven (Fig. 8-10). Since rather less than 100% 'set' is obtained by this means, it is usually necessary to exaggerate

Fig. 8-10. Operator lays straight molded seals on trays in desired configuration before loading in oven for post curing.

the shape of the jig or form; a small degree of recovery on release from the form after "post-cure" then results in the required conformation. This procedure is only applicable to relatively minor modifications of the molded shape. More drastic alterations may be achieved if it is employed in conjunction with silicone rubber compounded to undergo a "two-stage cure".* This technique involves the use of two separate peroxides having significantly different initiation temperatures. The combination of 2,4-dichlorobenzoyl peroxide and dicumyl peroxide is generally preferred, with effective initiation threshholds of 230°F (110°C) and 300°F (150°C), respectively. A low level of 2,4-dichlorobenzoyl peroxide is employed, and the initial molding performed at the lower temperature. This provides an adequate degree of vulcanization to ensure the structural integrity of the seal on removal from the mold, but the

---

*British Patent 868,377.

product may be permanently set to any required configuration as described above, the oven temperature being set at a temperature high enough to initiate the reaction of the dicumyl peroxide. This process is illustrated in Fig. 8-11a and b. The large hollow section as produced by the straight mold is distorted to the required shape of the corner by insertion of a short bent core; since the change of shape is severe, creases are removed and the accuracy of the seal section preserved by over-wrapping with woven glass tape.

The sequence of manufacturing operations for a typical seal is as follows:

Material preparation—coating of fabric by calendering.
Hand building, molding, joining, trimming, postcuring, inspection, and testing.

Calendering and fabric coating follow normal practice and rolls of materials are prepared for cutting to sizes required for the building operation. Considerable economies in waste off-cuts of coated fabric may be made by cutting the fabric to the required widths before calendering, the narrow strips being hand-fed individually into the lower nip of a three-roll calender. The coated fabric strips are then separated from the wider rubber sheet, and the excess rubber reprocessed. The low strength of the soft silicone rubber permits this to be performed "on the run" by a skilled operator. The mold itself is employed as a building form. In the case of hollow sections, coated fabric or calendered rubber sheet is first wrapped round the mold core and the core then positioned in the lower mold plate for completion of the build. This is a skilled operation, the critical requirement being to produce a void-free mold blank with the various fabric layers correctly positioned and a minimum of cavity over-fill. This minimizes mold flow and consequent distortion of the fabric; very little rubber should be displaced into the flash grooves. Thus molding is essentially a consolidation rather than a shaping process. Figure 8-12 shows building in progress, and illustrates a typical 11 ft. mold.

To enable fully vulcanized joins to be made between molded lengths, the ends of each molded length are left unvulcanized. This is achieved by cooling each end of the mold during the press cure. The vulcanized length of seal is then removed from the mold, and the uncured ends separated by hand to expose the various fabric layers.

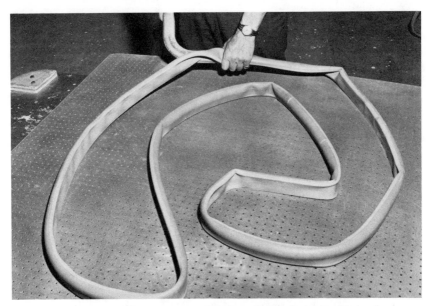

Fig. 11a. Operator places corner forming core into straight molded seal.

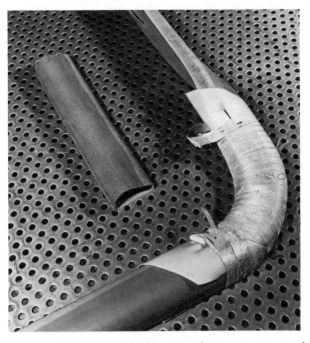

Fig. 11b. The corner is then wrapped with woven glass tape to prevent wrinkling of the reinforced silicone rubber. After post curing, the core is removed and the opening in the seal wall is patched.

Fig. 8-12. 11-foot straight section mold being loaded by skilled operators.

A second length is then built on, with very short overlaps in each fabric ply. Joints between different plies are staggered. This process is repeated until the required length is produced; the two uncured ends are then joined in the same way using a short "jointing block". With hollow sections, the core employed when making the final joint must be removed by cutting the seal for 2 or 3 in. (5 or 8 cm) along its length, the cut being positioned away from the sealing face. This slit is subsequently repaired using room temperature vulcanizing silicone rubber. Special techniques are required in this connection for inflatable seals. One method is to build strips of PTFE film between the fabric plies at the point where the slit required for final core removal is to be made. Small pieces of closely woven fabric coated with RTV silicone rubber are then inserted in place of the

PTFE strips to reinforce the repair. The completely molded seal is finally hand trimmed where necessary and postcured in a large air-circulating oven. If required, heat setting of bends or corners is carried out at the same time, as described previously.

Visual and dimensional inspection completes the process. Inflatable seals are also pressure tested under water to check for leaks, usually at twice the working pressure. Some 10 to 20 pressure cycles are performed, as a single pressurization may fail to reveal a leak. Very slow leaks are revealed by recording pressure loss against time, allowance being made for the high permeability of silicone rubber.

Sterilizer Seals   Fabric reinforced silicone rubber seals were initially developed for the aviation industry, but have also found applications in other fields. Noteworthy among these are door seals for hospital sterilizer units, where resistance to steam at 35 psi (2.5 kg/cm^2) gauge pressure is required (281°F, 138°C). A typical sterilization cycle is as follows:

1. Close door
2. Inflate seal to 50 psi (3.5 kg/cm^2)
3. Apply vacuum for 2½ min.
4. Admit steam at 35 psi (2.5 kg/cm^2) for 2½ min.
5. Exhaust steam
   Repeat 3 to 5
6. Apply vacuum
7. Admit steam for full sterilization time (30–60 min.)
8. Exhaust
9. Admit air
10. Deflate seal
11. Open door

Reinforced silicone rubber inflatable seals have a life capability of 3000 cycles in this demanding application.

REINFORCED HOSE AND DUCT

Silicone rubber coated fabric is used to build extreme service automotive radiator hose and flexible heater ducts for aircraft, missile, and industrial use. While some fabric reinforced hose is extruded on a continuous basis, p. 108, heavy duty hose and flexible duct are usually built up by wrapping the materials around a mandrel and vulcanizing in a steam autoclave or in a circulating hot-air oven.

Silicone rubber is applied to the fabric by the methods described in Chapter 5. Straight sections of hose may be made by wrapping the mandrel with sheet material until the desired thickness is reached. Tricot weave is often used because it allows "strike through" of the rubber, leading to a more homogeneous wall section, which is less subject to ply separation.

Another method is to spiral wrap with tape. Some tapes are square cut but others are bias cut. Bias cut tapes (cut at a 45° angle to the selvage edge), are stretchier, give a more flexible hose, and can be used to tape curved sections without wrinkling. Some hose have spiral reinforcing wire wound between fabric layers. Still others have no fabric but have spiral wound cord applied in opposite directions between layers of unsupported rubber sheet. Again, a spiral wound wire layer may be placed between the fibre cord layers for added strength.

The construction of duct is very similar to that of hose. Often, more flexibility is required however, in which case the walls may consist of one layer of thinly coated fabric. Spiral wire reinforcement is required on the thinnest wall duct to prevent collapsing. The edge of the tape may be rolled over the wire prior to taping in order to firmly retain it when a single overlap construction is used. Mandrels should be hollow to obtain the best heat transfer to the I.D. of the hose and they should be made of non-corroding metal—aluminum or stainless steel tubing with a polished O.D. will do. The O.D. should be tapered from one end to the other in order to facilitate removal of the hose or duct.

Bends in heavy walled stiff hoses may be formed through the application of the two stage cure system described on p. 184, or through the use of either curved or flexible mandrels. Before wrapping the mandrel, apply a release coating of 3% aqueous solution of sodium phosphate containing water softeners* or Dupanol WAQ**. Taping of the mandrel should be performed on a lathe in order to obtain a tight, even lap. When the build-up is complete, cotton or nylon tape, wet with release, is applied or, if a smooth finish is desired,

---

* Such as Rain Drops, A. E. Staley Mfg. Co.
** E. I. du Pont.

polyester film tape. The taped mandrel is then placed in an autoclave on brackets, which prevents mandrels from touching one another or the oven sides, and cured at the temperature recommended for the particular catalyst used. A rule of thumb for the required vulcanizing time is 7 min for the first $\frac{1}{8}$ in. (3 mm) of wall thickness plus 3 min for each additional $\frac{1}{8}$ in. (3 mm). Naturally, the cure time will vary with the weight of the mandrel and the materials which have been used as reinforcement of the rubber. HAV's may be used to vulcanize high temperature, thin walled duct. Post curing of these bulky products can be time consuming and expensive, consequently "no postcure" compounds, which are available from the silicone compound suppliers, are popular. The highest temperature applications will have glass or Nomex* as the reinforcing material. Automotive will generally have polyester fabric or cord which will perform satisfactorily up to 350°F (175°C). Some glass reinforced ducting with a metallic reflective coating will handle air as high as 700°F (370°C).

Silicone rolls which are too large to be molded by the process described on p. 133, may be fabricated in the same manner as hose. The shaft in this case would act as the mandrel. It would be cleaned and primed for maximum adhesion of the rubber. Freshly prepared sheet $\frac{1}{8}$ in. (3 mm) to $\frac{1}{4}$ in. (6 mm) thick is wrapped around the shaft until approximately 10% greater thickness than the finished roll diameter is built up. The cotton or nylon cover tape, wet with release, is then applied from the center out, in order to squeeze as much air as possible out the ends. Since the rubber on the roll is generally much thicker than hose wall, also usually softer and containing no reinforcement, end plates should be attached to the core to prevent the rubber from squeezing out during cover taping and vulcanizing. Vulcanizing is carried out identically to hose and duct.

SILICONE RUBBER SPONGE

Silicone rubber sponge is made by incorporating a chemical blowing agent when mixing the rubber compound. The ideal condition exists when the blowing agent decomposes, producing bubbles of gas which form the cells of the sponge just prior to vulcanization of the rubber.

---

* Trade Name E. I. du Pont.

The removal from the market of a chemical blowing agent called Nitrosan* has created considerable difficulty in the manufacture of certain types of sponge, principally HAV extrusion. The decomposition range of Nitrosan, 175 to 212°F (80 to 100°C), was ideal for use in conjunction with 2,4-dichlorobenzoyl peroxide as the vulcanizing agent. At the time of publication, an adequate substitute for Nitrosan was not on the market. In some applications, it has been possible to substitute a very soft solid compound of 20 durometer A or lower.

The alternative chemical blowing agent, Unicel N.D.** must be used in conjunction with high temperature vulcanizing agents such as tert.-butyl perbenzoate, which has a general cure temperature range of 290 to 310°F (145 to 155°C). Press blown slabs or simple molded shapes may be produced with this combination. One to three % by weight of Unicel N.D. is usually milled into the rubber

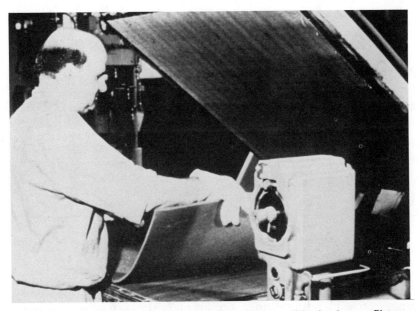

Fig. 8-13. Molding of silicone rubber sponge sheet using a tilting head press. Platens are steam heated. Note that they are fabric covered to allow the escape of gases. Timer can be seen in foreground. (*Courtesy. The Conneticut Hard Rubber Company, An ARMCO company*).

---

* Formerly made by E. I. du Pont.
** Made by E. I. du Pont.

TABLE 8-1

Properties	Grade		Continuous Length Med.
	Firm	Med.	
Density, lb/cu in. (max.)	.030	.020	.020
Compression deflection, compressed to 75% of original thickness.			
Room temperature, psi	12–20	6–14	6–14
Compression set %, compressed to 50% of original thickness.			
22 hr @ +212°F, % max.	60	60	60
Water absorption, immersion,			
24 hr @ +75°F, % max.	5	5	5
Corrosion of steel, 24 hr @ 158°F	None		
Low temperature, brittleness,			
5 hr @ –100°F bend, flat	No cracking		
Temperature range	–100 to +500°F		
Color	Orange/tan		

AVAILABILITY: SHEET SIZE AVAILABLE FROM STOCK: 24″ × 24″
–36″ × 36″

Thickness, In.	Grade		Tolerance In.
	Firm	Med.	
$\frac{1}{16}$	√		$\pm\frac{1}{64}$
$\frac{1}{8}$	√	√	$\pm\frac{1}{32}$
$\frac{3}{16}$	*	√	$\pm\frac{1}{32}$
$\frac{1}{4}$	*	√	$+\frac{3}{64} - \frac{1}{32}$
$\frac{3}{8}$	X	√	$\pm\frac{3}{64}$
$\frac{1}{2}$	X	√	$\pm\frac{3}{64}$

Special order: Thickness up to 1 in. are available.
*$\frac{3}{16}$ in. & $\frac{1}{4}$ in. sheet available in firm grade.

compound after it is softened. The Unicel disperses easily and with proper cross blending should produce a fairly even cellular structure. The density of the sponge will vary with the amount of blowing agent added, the molding temperature and time, and the degree of confinement applied while between the press platens or in a mold. A typical press for molding sponge is seen in Fig. 8-13. Note that the platens are covered with a heavy fabric, which may be dusted

TABLE 8-2. LOW COMPRESSION SET SILICONE SPONGE RUBBER.

Properties	Grade	
	Soft	Med.
Density, lb/cu in (max.)	0.13	0.20
Compression deflection, compressed to 75% of original thickness. Room temperature, psi	2-7	6-14
Compression set %, compressed to 50% of original thickness. 22 hr @ +212°F	15	15
Water absorption, immersion, 24 hr @ + 75°F, % max.	5	5
Corrosion of steel 24 hr @ 158°F	None	
Low temperature, brittleness, 5 hr @ −100°F bend, flat	No cracking	
Temperature range	−100 to +500°F	
Color	Red	Gray

AVAILABILITY: SHEET SIZE AVAILABLE FROM STOCK: 36 in. × 36 in.

Thickness, in.	Grade		Tolerance, in.
	Soft	Med.	
$\frac{1}{16}$	×	✓	$\pm\frac{1}{64}$
$\frac{1}{8}$	✓	✓	$\pm\frac{1}{32}$
$\frac{3}{16}$	✓	✓	$\pm\frac{1}{32}$
$\frac{1}{4}$	✓	✓	$\pm\frac{3}{64} -\frac{1}{32}$
$\frac{3}{8}$	✓	✓	$\pm\frac{3}{64}$
$\frac{1}{2}$	✓	✓	$\pm\frac{3}{64}$

with mica or treated with a release agent such as Duponol WAQ*. The fabric allows gas to escape, preventing the formation of surface holes or sinks. Rigid Teflon glass laminate may be used instead of fabric. It improves both release and heat transfer.

All silicone rubber heat vulcanizing compounds, including the fluorosilicones, can be sponged. To obtain the desired properties, some experimenting is usually required to get the proper balance of density with the durometer or stiffness of the base stock.

In molding sponge slab, the material is blown to finished size and completely vulcanized in the press. The press temperature will

---

*Made by E. I. DuPont.

TABLE 8-3. FLAME RETARDANT, LOW COMPRESSION SET, SILICONE SPONGE RUBBER.

Properties	Med. Grade
Density, lb/cu in. (max.)	.020
Compression deflection, compressed to 75% of original thickness. Room temperature, psi	6–14
Compression set %, compressed to 50% of original thickness. 22 hr @ +212°F	15
Water absorption, immersion, 24 hr @ +75°F, % max.	5
Corrosion of steel 24 hr @ 158°F	None
Low temperature, brittleness, 5 hr @ –100°F bend, flat	No cracking
Temperature range	–100 to +500°F
Color	Blue/gray

With the specimen supported in a vertical position, a 2,000 degree (approximate) flame $1\frac{1}{2}$ in. high is applied for 12 sec. When the ignition source is removed, there is no residual flame and less than a ten second afterglow.

AVAILABILITY: SHEET SIZE AVAILABLE FROM STOCK: 36 in. × 36 in.—MEDIUM GRADE.

Thickness in In.	Tolerance in In.
$\frac{1}{16}$	$\pm\frac{1}{64}$
$\frac{1}{8}$	$\pm\frac{1}{32}$
$\frac{3}{16}$	$\pm\frac{1}{32}$
$\frac{1}{4}$	$+\frac{3}{64} \ -\frac{1}{32}$
$\frac{3}{8}$	$\pm\frac{3}{64}$
$\frac{1}{2}$	$\pm\frac{3}{64}$

range from 310 to 340°F (155 to 170°C) the press time 10 min or more.

Properties of silicone sponge material available commercially* are given in Tables 8-1 through 8-3.

Silicone rubber sponge is widely used as a gasket and lightweight economical vibration damping material where extremes of temperature are experienced or non-corrosion characteristics are required. It is often supplied with pressure sensitive adhesive applied to one or

*Cohrlastic. Made by the Connecticut Hard Rubber Co.

both sides and as tapes. An interesting RTV foam* has been developed in which the foaming gas is a by-product of the vulcanization reaction. It is a two package system. The standard density is 15 to 18 lb/cu ft (.2 kg/cu m). Used as an encapsulant for electronics equipment, it has also been used as a sealant in firewall openings where services or structural elements pass through. In tests, it has proven to be an effective fire and smoke barrier. Heavy metals can be added where radiation shielding is desired or conductive fillers where some conductivity or bleeding off of static charges is required.

---

*3-6548, Dow Corning Corp.

9 | APPLICATIONS OF SILICONE RUBBER

The great versatility of silicone rubber, coupled with its long service life, has led to applications in practically the full spectrum of industry.

In this period of public demand for longer maintenance free performance of their products, manufacturers are realizing that the small additional cost of a seal or electrical insulator made from silicone rubber is very minor compared to the cost of having to replace a cheaper part, made of an inferior material, which could not last out the life of the warranty. Nowhere is this any more apparent than in the automotive industry.

AUTOMOTIVE

Probably the first automotive silicone rubber application was the automatic transmission shaft seal, one type of which is diagramatically illustrated in Fig. 9-1. A seal which retails at about $4.00 but which has an average labor replacement cost of about fifteen times that amount, dictates the use of the highest possible performance materials. Not only does the silicone rubber resist the action of the hot transmission fluid and the frictional heat of the shaft on the seal lip, but the neutral nature of the silicone prevents the corrosive pitting of the shaft during long periods of engine idleness which can occur with sulphur containing rubbers. Electronic ignition systems which eliminate the need for ignition tune-ups use a silicone dielectric gel as a filler in the electronic ignition module. The gel protects the semiconductor elements by acting as a vibration damper for the wirebonds and weld wires and preventing moisture condensation inside the ignition module. The higher ignition voltages necessitated

196

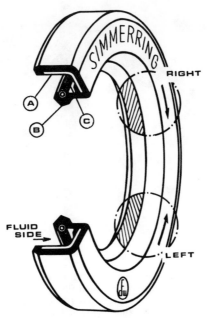

Fig. 9-1. Silicone rubber, bonded to metal, automatic transmission seal with molded in "pump" grooves. (A) steel shell, (B) seal lip, (C) garter spring. Arrows show the direction of shaft rotation in relation to the direction of the grooves. As the shaft rotates fluid seepage is pumped back to the fluid side. Some seals have an additional outer dirt lip which prevents dirt from coming in contact with the seal lip and being pumped into the fluid. Maximum operating temperature of the silicone seals in contact with engine or transmission oils is 325°F (163°C). (*Courtesy Carl Freudenberg, West Germany*)

by the need to fire the engine unfailingly despite worn spark plugs or poor fuel mixtures, in order to assure cleaner exhaust, coupled with the higher under-the-hood temperatures of today's autos, dictates the use of extruded silicone rubber ignition wire insulation (Fig. 9-2) and molded silicone rubber spark plug boots. Coolant and heater hoses have long been a source of automotive maintenance problems, sometimes as expensive as a burned out engine. Silicone rubber hoses are being used initially on the big freight hauling trucks and by municipal transit buses, where even the downtime and labor related to the periodic replacement of regular hoses is quite costly. The changing of hoses on a big rig can take as long as 12 hr. Silicone rubber hoses have superior resistance to hot ethylene glycol, diesel fumes, and engine cleaning solvents and are expected to last as long as the engine. The low compression set of the silicone rubber under the retaining clamps prevents loosening of the clamps with subsequent leakage of

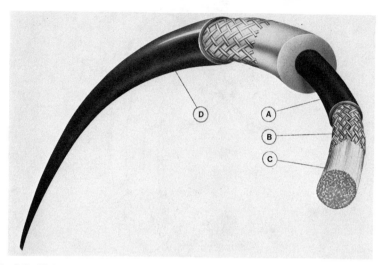

Fig. 9-2. High performance, suppressor-type ignition wire has a conductive silicone rubber sheath (A) encasing a graphite impregnated fiber glass core (C). Fiberglass braid (B) provides added strength. The conductive silicone rubber doubles circuit reliability at the same time sealing out moisture and being unaffected by under the hood temperature extremes. Electronic interference with radio and other communications equipment is eliminated. The conductive silicone is sheathed with an insulating layer, braided glass reinforcement, and finally, a protective silicone rubber jacket (D). (*Courtesy Carol Cable Company*)

engine coolant. Molded fluorosilicone rubber check seals are used in carburetors to replace metal components.

RTV sealants, in addition to being used for formed-in-place engine gaskets (p. 161), are used in the repair and installation of windshields, light covers, and trim. It has been estimated that approximately $2\frac{1}{2}$ lb (1.1 kg) of silicone rubber is used per car today and that this will increase to from 5 to 7 lb (2.3 to 3.2 kg) by 1980.[1]

AEROSPACE

Silicone rubber, since its early development, has played a key role in the aerospace industry, mainly because of its resistance to temperature extremes. Apart from the airframe opening seals discussed in Chapter 8, there are electrical connectors (Fig 9-3), cable insulation, environmentally sealed switches (Fig. 9-4), dust and ice boots, gaskets, "O" ring seals in jet engines and hydraulic assemblies, hot air duct, oxygen masks, control diaphrams, and vibration control pads for oxygen systems. The ablation characteristics of silicone rubber

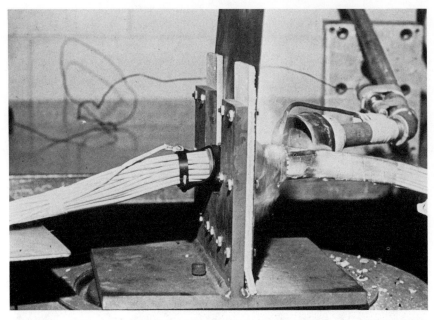

Fig. 9-3. AN type electrical connectors with silicone and fluorosilicone rubber grommets and seals (see p. 90) are manufactured to the most exacting specifications. They must be held to very close tolerances, be fuel and reversion resistant, and must maintain their electrical integrity through such severe testing as MIL C5015 firewall test pictured above. (*Courtesy Amphenol Connector Division*)

dictate its use in the coating of rocket fuel valves, supply cables, and silo doors for protection from rocket blast. The high performance standards of the aerospace industry contributed a great deal to the early growth of silicone rubber applications. The automotive field, however, is where by far the greatest growth is presently taking place.

APPLIANCE

The combination of excellent electrical properties and the retention of sealing characteristics at high temperatures has been a great boon to the designers of coffee pots, electric frying pans, steam irons, and other appliances where the silicone gaskets play a dual role of electrical insulator and steam or hot water seal as well as allowing the appliance to be immersable in wash water. Extruded door gasketing reduces heat loss and staining of exterior stove surfaces. The resis-

Fig. 9-4. The complex control panel of a Boeing 747 displays many micro switch "TL" type environment proof toggle switches (arrows). These switches have an operating temperature range from $-85°F$ ($-65°C$) to $160°F$ ($70°C$) due to the molded/bonded silicone rubber seal. They are completely protected from moisture and dirt. They meet military specification MIL-S-3950. (*Courtesy Boeing Commercial Airplane Co.*)

tance of the silicone rubber to hot detergent solutions has led to its widespread use in dishwashers and washing machines.

ELECTRICAL

By far the largest volume of silicone rubber consumed by the electrical industry, is used for the manufacture of wire and cable. Figure 9-5 a–g includes the diagrams and specifications of seven popular constructions of wire and cable, including an automotive ignition wire of more simple construction than shown in Fig. 9-2.

In some special cases, involving short sections or delicate conductors, the silicone rubber is not extruded directly over the conductor. It is applied instead as extruded tubing. One method involves expanding the tubing by immersing in a solvent such as toluol for a minute or two, sliding over the conductor and allowing it to shrink

APPARATUS LEAD WIRE—BRAIDLESS

RATING: 300 and 600 volts
TEMPERATURE: 150 and 200°C
APPLICATION: For high temperature use in motors, transformers, generators, fixtures, appliances and electronic devices.
CONSTRUCTION: Stranded tinned copper conductor, silicone rubber insulation.
FEATURES: Mechanical toughness without the nuisance of braids, temperature and flame resistance flexibility.
SPECIFICATIONS: UL-various style numbers.

(a)

APPARATUS LEAD WIRE—BRAIDED

RATING: 300 and 600 volts
TEMPERATURE: 150, 155, 180, and 200°C
APPLICATION: For high temperature use in motors, transformers, generators, etc.
CONSTRUCTION: Stranded tinned copper conductor, silicone rubber insulation, asbestos or glass braids.
FEATURES: Heat resistance, flame resistance, flexibility.
SPECIFICATIONS:

	UL	CSA	IEEE
Styles	Various	SEW-2,	Class F and
		SEWF-2	Class H

(b)

FIXTURE AND APPLIANCE WIRE

RATING: 300 and 600 volts
TEMPERATURE: 150, 200, and 230°C
APPLICATION: Wire for installation in lighting fixtures and similar equipment. This wire is also used for connecting lighting fixtures to the conductors of the circuit which supplies the fixture. Certain silicone rubbers have UL recognition for use at temperatures not exceeding 230°C.
CONSTRUCTION: Stranded tinned copper conductor, silicone rubber insulation, glass braid.
FEATURES: Heat resistance, flame resistance, flexibility.
SPECIFICATIONS:

	UL	CSA
Types	SF-1, SF-2, SFF-1, SFF-2	CEW-1, SEW-2, SEWF-1, SEWF-2

(c)

Fig. 9-5a-g. Wire and cable diagrams and specifications.

COMMERCIAL SHIPBOARD CABLE

RATING: 300 volts to 5 kV
TEMPERATURE: 95°C
APPLICATION: General shipboard power and control cable usage and particularly where ambient temperatures exceed 50°C. Preferred construction where moisture resistance is required in addition to flame and heat-resistance.
CONSTRUCTION: Stranded tinned copper conductor, silicone rubber insulation, glass braid, conductors cabled together (if more than single conductor), fillers, tape, PVC jacket, aluminum or bronze armor.
FEATURES: Heat resistance, moisture resistance, non-conducting ash.
SPECIFICATION: IEEE-45.
TYPES: SS1A, SS1B, DS1A, DS1B, TS1A, TS1B, FS1A, FS1B, MS1A, MS1B.

(d)

SHIPBOARD TELEPHONE CABLE

RATING: 300 volts
APPLICATION: Telephone circuits on Naval vessels.
CONSTRUCTION: Bare copper conductor, silicone rubber insulation, nylon sheath, two conductors cabled to form a pair, specified number of pairs cabled together, binder, PVC jacket.
FEATURES: Non-conducting ash.
SPECIFICATION: MIL-C-915
TYPE: TTSU

(e)

POWER AND CONTROL CABLE—COMMERCIAL

RATING: 600V and 5 kV
TEMPERATURE: 125°C
APPLICATION: Power, control and signal circuits subjected to high temperature ambients, wet or dry locations, exposed or in conduit, radioactive environments.
CONSTRUCTION: Power Cable, Stranded tinned copper conductor, silicone rubber insulation tape, asbestos braid, (or extruded sheath). **Control Cable.** Stranded tin-ed copper conductor, silicone rubber insulation, glass braid, two or more conductors cabled together, tape asbestos braid (or extruded sheath or interlocked steel armor).
FEATURES: Heat, moisture and ozone resistance, flexibility at room and low temperatures, increased current-carrying capacity, radiation resistance, flame resistance, non-conducting ash, non-corrosive fumes.
SPECIFICATIONS: IPCEA S-19-81, UL 44, and utility specifications.
TYPES: IPCEA "Ozone resisting silicone rubber," UL—"Type SA."

(f)

Fig. 9-5 a–g. (*Continued*)

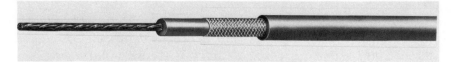

IGNITION CABLE—COMMERCIAL AUTOMOTIVE

RATING: 35 kVac

TEMPERATURE: 177°C (350°F) to 232°C (450°F)

APPLICATION: Ignition cable for use on engines for passenger cars, trucks, etc.

CONSTRUCTION: Semi-conductive glass fiber core, ethylene propylene rubber insulation, open-weave glass braid, silicone rubber sheath.

FEATURES: Resistance to high temperatures ozone resistance, high dielectric strength, service reliability.

SPECIFICATIONS: Automotive industry

TYPE: 7MM

(g)

Fig. 9-5 a–g. (*Continued*)

back to a tight fit as the toluol evaporates. Since toluol is highly flammable, fire prevention precautions must be taken. Another method involves expanding the tubing with compressed air while the conductor is being drawn into it.

Silicone rubber tapes are used for the insulation of large cables, irregular shaped conductors such as form wound motor coils, and on splices and terminals. They may be supported with fabric for added mechanical strength or unsupported for use as primary insulation in high voltage applications. The tapes may be fabricated by extrusion (p. 105) or slit from calendered sheet (p. 126). It has been reported[2] that a comparison of extruded and calendered tapes, made from the same batch of silicone rubber and to the same thickness, showed the extruded product to have 25% better dielectric strength than the calendered. The most economical method of producing flat tapes, however, is by the calendering process.

In order to bond and thus establish a sealed system, tapes fabricated from standard silicone rubber stocks must be applied in an uncured condition, or, if fully cured, be applied along with a silicone adhesive paste. Self adhering silicone rubber tapes can be produced which greatly simplify their application. Boric acid added to silicone gums, along with the reinforcing fillers, upon vulcanization (using dicumyl peroxide as the catalyst) will produce a rubber which will weld to itself at room temperature, although tack-free to the touch. During the vulcanization process, the boric acid, through a condensation reaction, cleaves the Si—O—Si linkage to form Si—O—B compounds. Optimum properties are achieved when there are 300 to 400 silicon atoms to one boron atom[3] (less than .5% by weight of B). At greater concentrations of boron it becomes difficult to achieve vulcanization and the product is sticky.* Above a 400/1 ratio the welding characteristics drop off.

The self-adhering stocks process well. After freshening on a two roll rubber mill, tapes are usually produced continuously by the extrusion process. The HAV may be operated between 650 and 750°F (345 to 405°C) depending on the speed of the extruder. The time-temperature relationship is very important in controlling the adhesion or weldability of the finished tape. An interleave is necessary when rolling the vulcanized tape to prevent adhesion between plies. Polyester film interleaving has proven the most satisfactory–it withstands the temperature of the hot tape as it comes out of the HAV. It does not contain plasticizers which would migrate and there is just enough adhesion to the tape to prevent unraveling of the roll while in use. Standard flat, self-adhering tapes are produced in various widths, thicknesses, and colors. They are specified as the outer anti-tracking wrap on high voltage cable splices and terminations by the Electro-Products Division of 3M (3M No. 70 tape). They are used on large motor and generator connections because of the ease of handling. In winter, when other tapes get stiff and lose their tack, silicone rubber tapes are used for all types of outdoor splice and termination insulation jobs. On military jet aircraft the self-adhering tape is used on connections, splices, and wire bundles, retaining its resiliency and electrical characteristics at the high temperatures experienced at Mach 1–2 speeds. Because self-adhering stocks do not bond to anything other than themselves, it is easy to cut through the insulation and bare a wire or connection for testing or repair, then retape the section of insulation removed and have it seal over again. Self-adhering tape has been produced in a triangular cross section using an extrusion die of the design described on p. 104. When half lapped, triangular tape will produce an even thickness of insulation on a conductor. The voids at lap joints are also reduced to a minimum. A colored guide line is usually provided to facilitate accurate lapping— different guideline colors are used to identify different thicknesses of

---

*At a concentration of about 100 Si to one B "bouncing putty" is obtained. This material, which exhibits plastic flow or acts as a solid depending on the rate it is stressed, will not crosslink. As a toy it is reputed to have sales of millions of dollars a year.

Fig. 9-6. Stretch tape. (*Courtesy Moxness Products*)

tape. The self-adhering triangular tapes are ideal for the insulation of form wound coils used in motors destined for hot, humid installations such as deep mines, the tropics—anywhere that moisture seepage, abrasive dust, or fungus deterioration could cause standard insulation systems to fail.

Reinforced stretch tape, the fabrication and construction of which is described on p. 105, is produced as a self-adhering tape (Fig. 9-6). Supplied in 25% stretch, identified as SA, and 15% stretch, identified as SB, this self-adhering stretch tape may be applied around corners or over irregularly shaped conductors without the wrinkling that occurs with non-stretch tapes. If it is applied over an unsupported self-adhering layer of insulation, it will fuse to it adding to dielectric as well as mechanical strength.

Following are the properties of both SA and SB type tapes:

PHYSICAL PROPERTIES

Limiting stretch to a predetermined value serves as a design and process control, assuring:

Uniform insulation thickness even around sharp edges.
Uniform breakdown voltage.
Conformability (not usually found in a reinforced tape).

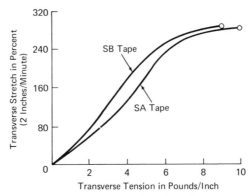

Fig. 9-7. Transverse stretch of reinforced stretch tape.

Both types of Stretch-Tape have considerable transverse stretch, as is illustrated in Fig. 9-7. Combined with linear stretch, this property provides a high degree of conformability to irregular surfaces.

The change in width at the optimum tension range, as indicated in Fig. 9-8, provides a guide to initial spacing and tape length requirement.

Although minor thickness variations will occur as a result of the surface pattern developed at normal stretch, the change in tape thickness is negligible at any elongation.

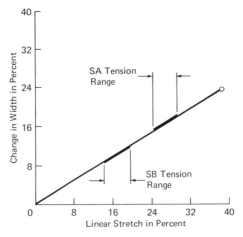

Fig. 9-8. Change in width with linear stretch of RST.

In practice, when coils, bus bars, and other conductors are wound, the decrease in wall thickness over sharp edges does not exceed 10% of the original tape thickness. An edge radius on the bus bar or coil decreases this variation.

ELECTRICAL PROPERTIES

Dielectric Strength   Dielectric strength was measured on 1 in. X .020 in. tape stretched to a nominal elongation on a tubular electrode. Voltage rise, 500 vps, 5 sq in. electrode area:

1. Measured at each temperature after a 2-hr soak at that temperature:

   70°F
   100°F
   200°F   400 to 500 vpm rms
   300°F
   400°F

2. Measured at room temperature after heat aging:

24 hr @ 480°F	400 vpm rms
168 hr @ 480°F	300 vpm rms
24 hr @ 600°F	225 vpm rms

Dielectric strength was measured with $\frac{1}{4}$ in. electrodes (ASTM-D-149):

   70°F   750 vpm rms

Moisture Absorption   Moisture absorption, based on dry weight (96 hr over $CaCl_2$):

96 hr @ 96% R.H.	0.9%
96 hr in H_2O at room temperature	0.9%

Volume Resistivity   Volume resistivity shown graphically in Fig. 9-9, was measured using 60 sq in. electrodes at an applied voltage of 500 volts, employing the method described in ASTM-D-257.

Dielectric Constant   Dielectric constant and power factor as a function of temperature are illustrated in Fig. 9-10. Tests were made as specified in ASTM-D-150.

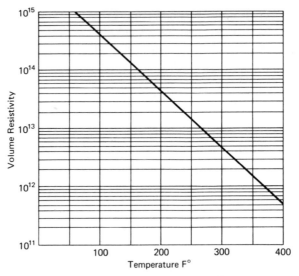

Fig. 9-9. Volume resistivity of RST.

An excellent example of a complete silicone rubber insulation system is to be found in diesel-electric traction equipment manufactured by the Electro-Motive Division of General Motors. The huge locomotives which are the life line of today's fast, heavy, freight

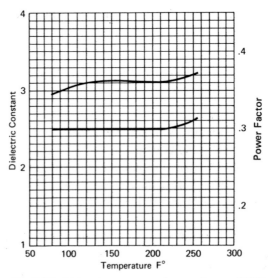

Fig. 9-10. Dielectric constant and power factor of RST.

throughout the world, achieve around the clock dependability through an all-silicone insulation system which includes extruded and calendered tapes, coated wire, moldings, and RTV adhesive sealants.

Silicone rubber "R" (woven glass reinforced) tapes manufactured from coated glass fabric produced on a three-roll calender (p. 125) are used to insulate the form wound coils (Fig. 9-11) of the big diesel driven alternators Fig. 9-12 and the field and interpole coils of the traction motors. The "R" tape is used because it gives a good bond, sealing the coil against moisture and dirt. It conforms well, eliminating all air spaces. In addition to reducing corona, this improves the heat conductivity of the insulation layer which reduces the temperature rise of the equipment. It remains resilient even at below zero

Fig. 9-11. Operator is hand taping a form wound coil at the bends. The straight sections have already been taped with "R" tape the full width of the section. The "R" tape is then bonded to the coil in a vacuum chamber. A steel lined snap-on jacket is positioned on the coil first. The coil, with the jacket in place, is inserted in a rubber boot and a vacuum is drawn to apply even pressure over the total surface of the coil including the bends. Vulcanizing heat is obtained by the application of a high amperage current to the conductor. The coils are then cured for 16 hours in conveyor ovens with the temperature starting at 338°F (170°C) and increasing gradually to 455°F (235°C). Insulated form wound coils ready for post curing may be seen in the background hanging from the moving conveyor. (*Courtesy Electro-Motive Div., GMC*)

Fig. 9-12. Stator of 4200 amp, 1200-volt alternator with silicone "R" tape insulated, form wound coils in position. Molded nylon bracing blocks are used. They are bonded in place with G.E. 106 red RTV adhesive. Molded silicone rubber caps may be seen on each stub connection. Other connections are made with self-adhering silicone rubber tape which is protected with a cover layer of glass tape. The whole assembly is then dip coated with silicone-alkyd varnish for further protection. (*Courtesy Electro-Motive Div., GMC*)

temperatures. Figs. 9-13 to 9-16 illustrate silicone applications in the commutator and contactors of the locomotive traction motors.

Cable harness on the generating sets and the wiring in the high voltage control cabinets of the locomotives are all silicone rubber insulated.

Capacitor bushings are fabricated from extruded silicone rub-

Fig. 9-13. Cables carrying ac current from the alternator are hooked into rectifier banks where the current is converted to dc for driving the dc traction motors. The connections are insulated with the long silicone rubber boots seen transfer molded on p. 59. (*Courtesy Electro-Motive Div., GMC*)

ber tubing. A tough, low compression set VMQ type of compound is used. Where a very precise outside diameter is required, the tubing is usually centerless ground. It is then cut to precise lengths. The capacitor bushing acts as a seal for the liquid dielectric of the capacitor and also as a terminal insulator. Where transformers, filters, or other electronic components must be assembled in a metal case, feed through terminals can be sealed in the same manner. Figure 9-17 shows an extruded bushing being substantially compressed between two rigid insulators. A long life insulating seal is formed at

Fig. 9-14. A bead of silicone paste sealant being applied accurately with a special fixture to a Nomex "V" ring prior to assembly into the commutator. (*Courtesy Electro-Motive Div., GMC*)

a very low cost. Although normally an excellent insulating material, silicone rubber may be made electrically conductive by the use of specific grades of carbon black as fillers. Heat resistance, weather resistance, and low temperature flexibility are retained, but physical properties are relatively low. Silicone rubber with volume resistivity in the range of 5 to 15 ohm-cm can be manufactured reproducibly. Fine silver powders have also been used as fillers to produce electrically conductive silicone rubber. Carbon black can interfere with peroxide curing systems, especially when an extruded product is to be HAV'd. Consequently, an addition reaction curing system will result in more satisfactory processing. A recently developed electrically conductive silicone rubber based on an addition reaction system* has the typical properties, listed in Table 9-1.

Conductive silicone rubber contact pads for calculators and adding machine keyboards, when compared with metal, practically eliminate corrosion and make "bounceless" contact, which minimizes electrical noise and double signals. The conductivity increases with the appli-

---

*SE 7600 C & K, Silicone Products Dept., General Electric.

Fig. 9-15. The assembly of the commutator for the traction motor is a very delicate operation. Two of the insulating "V" rings seen in Fig. 9-14 are used, one at each end. The neat bead of silicone rubber sealant may be seen at the junction of the "V" ring and the commutator sections. Silicone sealants are ideal for the bonding of disimilar materials having different coefficients of expansion. (*Courtesy Electro-Motive Div., GMC*)

cation of pressure and decreases when the material is stretched, which would indicate that it could be used for certain types of switching or control functions. An example of the change in electrical resistance with applied pressure of a particular formulation of conductive silicone rubber is shown in Fig. 9-18.

Effective microwave oven gasketing can be made from conductive silicone rubber. Reduction of R.F. interference and oven sealing is accomplished with the same product. Conductive silicone rubber

Fig. 9-16. Traction motor contactors are subjected to heavy electrical and mechanical stresses. The brusholder boot, seen compression molded on p. 49, has been cemented in place with RTV sealant. Aluminum hydrate has been added as a filler to the silicone rubber compound to improve the electrical track resistance. (*Courtesy Electro-Motive Div., GMC*)

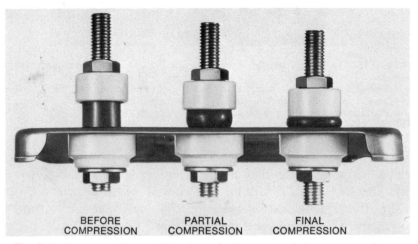

Fig. 9-17. An extruded cut off insulator bushing shown being compressed between porcelain insulators and metal can cover to form an effective seal. (*Courtesy Sphere Inc.*)

TABLE 9-1 TYPICAL PROPERTIES.

ASTM Method	Conditions, Tests or Properties	Blend Ratio	
		SE7600C 50 Parts	SE7600K 50 Parts
	Press Cure Conditions	10 min at 280°F (140°C)	
D-676	Durometer, shore "A"	75 ± 5	
D-412	Tensile strength, psi	600	
D-412	Elongation, %	150	
D-624	Tear resistance, lb/in.	60	
D-991	Volume resistivity, ohm-cm	7.0	
	Linear shrinkage, %	4.0	
D-395	Compression set, %		
	70 hr at 300°F	35	
	22 hr at 350°F	45	
	Heat Aging (200 hrs at 500°F) (260°C)		
	Durometer "A"	77	
	Tensile, psi	625	
	Elongation, %	100	
	Volume resistivity	4.0	

coatings may be applied where it is desirable to bleed off electrostatic charges or eliminate corona between high voltage insulation and ground contacts.   A unique application for conductive silicone rubber is the molded electrodes illustrated in Fig. 9-19 for percutaneous electronic nerve stimulation to deaden pain.   The soft flexible surface conforms easily to the patient's limb contour and is comfortable.   Electrodes used in the electronic stimulation of bone growth are also made in this manner.   Special silicone rubber compounds* with proprietary fillers are high loss dielectrics.   They are used where flexibility is an advantage in microwave transmission lines such as terminations, loads, and attenuators.   The largest growth area in the electrical field in the next 10 years will likely be in wire and cable with the emphasis on fire safety in nuclear plants.   Silicone rubber insulated cable gives the only real protection.

*ECCOSORB®, Emerson & Cuming, Inc.

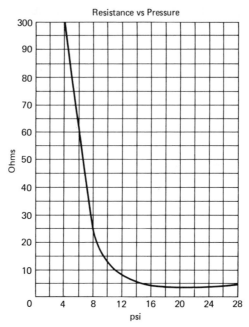

Fig. 9-18. Conductive silicone rubber; electrical resistance decreases as applied pressure is increased. (*Courtesy Dynacon Industries Inc.*)

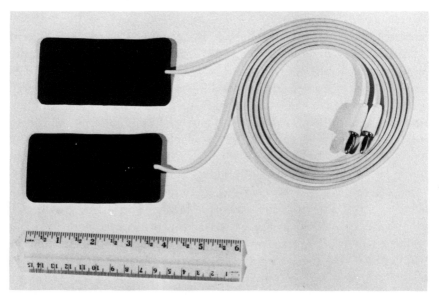

Fig. 9-19. Electrodes molded of conductive silicone rubber used for percutaneous electronic nerve stimulation to deaden pain. (*Courtesy Stimulation Technology, Inc.*)

MEDICAL

It was inevitable that silicones—with their characteristic inertness and resistance to aging under severe environmental conditions—would be investigated for medical applications. The observation about 1945 that water would not cling to the surface of glass after coating with a microscopically thin layer of silicone fluid was used to ensure complete drainage of penicillin and blood storage bottles.[4] It was also found that blood stored in the silicone treated bottles did not clot as quickly as that stored in untreated bottles.[5] In 1954 McDougall[6] reported "Cultures* of various tissues of warm blooded animals, which are known to be extraordinarily sensitive to foreign influences, show no deviations from the usual growth picture on contact with liquid, semi-solid, and rubber-like silicone products." Also during the 1950s, many researchers[7, 8, 9, 10, 11] reported on the use of silicone rubber as an implantable material. (Later studies[12] indicate that the silicones are not likely to be carcinogens.) Today, silicone rubber is by far the most widely used soft material for human implants and this usage is rapidly increasing in both volume and variety of devices where flexibility, softness, dependability, sterilizability, etc. are required.

The engineering, manufacturing, and marketing of medical devices from silicone rubber, while applying the same basic principles described in previous chapters, is a considerably more difficult and complicated endeavor. All basic materials which are to be used in the fabrication of implantable devices, or devices which will be in contact with mucous membrane for extended periods, must undergo long term implant tests in animals. In the course of these tests it must be demonstrated that there is no toxicity to the host, no undue inflamation of the tissues with which it has been in contact, and no migration of by-products to vital organs. The material itself must not show signs of deterioration. When a material has cleared this first hurdle, every new lot, even when manufactured under the most stringent of good manufacturing practices, should be run through a short series of tests to determine that the lot is free of heavy metals, pyrogens, is non-toxic and during an animal implant period of 7 days will not cause an inflamatory tissue reaction.

*Fig. 9-33 on p. 233 illustrates comparative tissue reaction to catheters fabricated from three different materials, including silicone.

Such a series of tests is referred to as an "acute series". It is important that suppliers of raw materials be monitored. They may make changes in their processing details which, although seemingly minor, may have far reaching effects on biocompatibility. Traveler cards and record keeping must make it possible to trace every manufacturing step and lot of material used in each device. In addition, the devices must be handled all through manufacturing and packaging in such a way that they cannot become contaminated or changed chemically to produce undesirable by-products. Fixturing, tooling, and machine operations must all be engineered to eliminate potential contamination. Such careful manufacturing practices are further complicated by the fact that they must be performed under clean room conditions. This is important mainly because any organic impurity (hair, dry skin scales, lint, etc.) accidentally incorporated into a silicone rubber product will carbonize and discolor the silicone rubber product at post-curing temperatures. Even though the contaminant may be completely imbedded in the product and would not create a health hazard, the discolored product would be considered unsalable. Since the post-curing occurs after fabrication, contamination usually is not apparent until most of the manufacturing cost is already invested. Therefore, rigid clean room controls can pay for themselves. The installation of an effective clean room is very expensive and should be well planned. Assembly areas will generally have laminar flow (unidirectional) finely filtered air. However, where machine operations produce contaminants often, in the case of silicones, accompanied by high heat loss, the flow of clean air must be altered. If exhaust fans are used, auxiliary clean air supply louvres must be located near the equipment. They must provide a greater volume of air than that being exhausted in order to maintain a positive pressure in the clean room. The clean air inlet and exhaust outlet should be located so the movement of air occurs up, down or horizontally across the work place, whichever will keep contamination to a minimum. Because of the large volume of air being moved, the heating and cooling plant must be adequate. It is also advisable to control humidity; extremes of humidity are quickly reflected in poor quality in the silicone rubber product. Because of the characteristic of silicone rubber to quickly pick up and hold an electrostatic charge attracting flash and other particulate matter, many operations should be performed in the presence of a destaticizer or ionized air stream. A clean room arrangement for the molding of implantable silicone rubber parts is

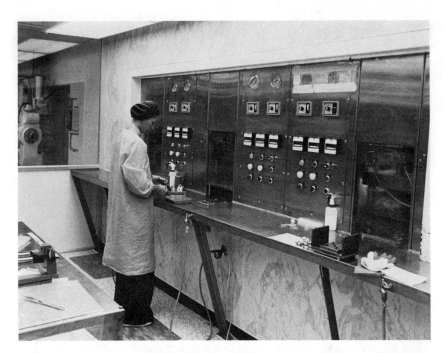

Fig. 9-20. Clean room molding operation. Hydraulic press equipment can be seen behind the lift window on the right. Hand molds are used and are open only while in the clean room. When the lift window is open to allow the operator to move the mold in or out of the press, pressurized clean air blows horizontally from front to back across the press platens keeping them free of loose dirt. The molds and breaker stands are stainless steel to prevent rust smudging of parts. Chromium plating of molds is unsatisfactory for this purpose. The work bench is also stainless steel rather than laminated plastic to prevent contamination from wear and chipping. Although presses and pumps are outside of the clean room, press controls are easily accessible to the clean room operator. A dual set of controls is available on the machine side for the use of setup and maintenance personnel. Air in the compressed air lines passes through micro filters. Molders wear lint free clothing and gloves. In the left background, part of a two roll mixing mill can be seen through the partition window. The large mill drive is outside of the mill clean room. The drive shaft passes through the wall. The rolls on clean room mills should be surfaced with hard stainless steel for best performance. The mill operator may be seen compounding a batch of medical grade silicone rubber (Fig. 9-21). (Photo by Paul Flagg, *Courtesy Medical Engineering Corp.*)

shown in Fig. 9-20. Generally, implants and blood handling products are manufactured in a class 100 clean room. Various tubes and products used in life support but not for implanting are often produced in a class 10,000 clean room.*

---

*Class 100 clean room; pressurized room supplied with air through a bank of high efficiency particulate air filters (HEPA) that remove 99.97% of all particles larger than .3 microns. Should have no more than 100 particles per cu ft. of air.

Class 10,000: Does not use as efficient a filter bank, should have no more than 10,000 particles per cu ft.

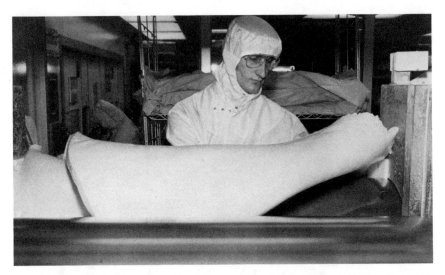

Fig. 9-21. A batch of silicone rubber being compounded for use in medical product application. The two roll mill is easier to clean than other types of mixing equipment and is very versatile. Mill roll packings must be designed to keep lubricants away from the edge of the rolls. When the materials being compounded are for food or medical applications the lubricants used must not contain heavy metal soaps or other toxic additives. Mills which are used for silicone rubber, even in industrial plants, should be isolated from the mixing of other materials because the contamination of silicone rubber with organic materials can result in poor appearance and a deterioration of electrical insulation characteristics when the organic materials char during the post curing of the silicone rubber at elevated temperatures.

The use of silicones in implantable life-saving devices, such as electronic heart pacers, is a dramatic development. Many thousands of people are alive today or live more comfortably due to artificial pacemakers (Fig. 9-22) which use electrical impulses to make the heart operate. Silicone rubber insulates and protects their components from the corrosive effects of body fluids. The pulse generator, which has a volume of about 4–5 in.^{3} (75 cc) and will weigh 6 to 7 oz (185g) is often implanted in a subcutaneous pocket just below the clavicle (collar bone) Fig. 9-23. The pulse generator contains the complete electronic circuitry but most of its weight and volume is due to the batteries which are expected to supply energy to pace the heart over a period of several years. It is usually potted in epoxy plastic and sealed with a thin dip coating of silicone rubber.* The

*The commonly used material is a 15% solids dispersion of Medical silicone adhesive A, Dow Corning Corp.

Fig. 9-22. Cardiac pacemaker.

pacing signal is conveyed to the heart via a flexible, spiral coiled, stainless steel or Elgiloy® wire lead. Extruded silicone rubber tubing is shrunk over the lead.*   A connector is attached to one end of the conductor, an electrode, usually of platinum to the other. The ends of the tubing are then sealed at the terminations with silicone rubber moldings which are either molded in place or molded separately then bonded in place with adhesive. The flexible lead is threaded through one of several blood vessels until the electrode is in the proper position in the heart. In Fig. 9-23 the lead is shown introduced into the cephalic vein close to its junction with the brachial vein. The external jugular could also be easily used. The lead may be guided with a stainless steel stylet which would temporarily be placed in its hollow center providing it with the necessary stiffness. Figure 9-24 illustrates unipolar and bipolar leads with molded in place terminations and Fig. 9-25 illustrates the severe, destructive, flex testing to which randomly selected leads are subjected.

There are many other life saving applications of silicone rubber. It is used in heart valves, for which replace badly disease damaged or congenitally defective heart valves.   Hydrocephalus shunts for

---

®—Elgiloy Co. Div. of American Gage & Machine Co., Elgin, Ill. 60120.
*This may be accomplished by either of the methods described on p. 200.

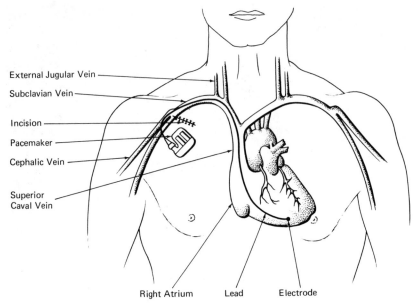

External Jugular Vein
Subclavian Vein
Incision
Pacemaker
Cephalic Vein
Superior Caval Vein

Right Atrium   Lead   Electrode

Fig. 9-23. Implantation of cardiac pacemaker.

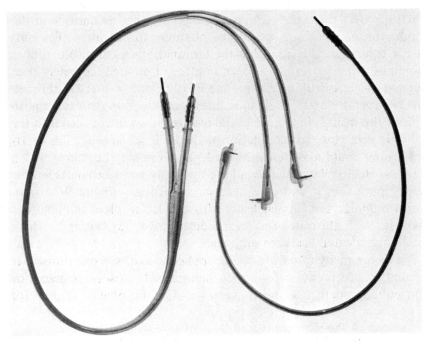

Fig. 9-24. Myocardial electrodes—Bipolar lead left, Unipolar lead right. (*Courtesy Medtronic, Inc.*)

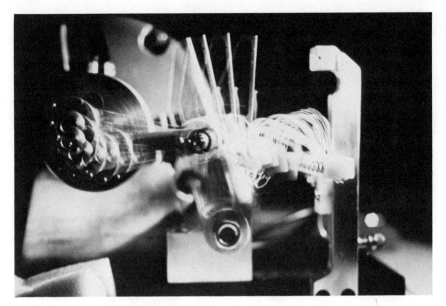

Fig. 9-25. Pacemaker leads on flex life test. (*Courtesy Medtronic, Inc.*)

persons afflicted with hydrocephalus (water-on-the-brain) utilize silicone rubber tubing. Excessive spinal fluid accumulated in the brain is drained through the silicone rubber tube which is equipped with a special valve-pump mechanism. One end of the tube is inserted through a small hole in the skull and the other end is run subcutaneously into the abdominal cavity from where the fluid absorbed and eventually eliminated. This shunt was probably the first implantable silicone rubber device to be developed and marketed. It was the brainchild of John Holter, founder of the Holter Company*. Arteriovenous shunts are a method of permanently cannulating persons with kidney failure who must be dialyzed (connected to an artificial kidney machine, two or three times a week). The implanted A-V shunts provide a permanent means of connecting the patient quickly to the machine. An artificial ureter, Fig. 9-26, of silicone rubber features a molded anti-reflux valve at the lower end where it enters the bladder. Bands of polyester velour are bonded to the outside diameter near each end of the tube. Tissue ingrowth into the velour from the vestigial ends of the excised ureter assure permanent attachment of the prosthesis. The inside of the tube is coated with a proprietary high

*Extracorporeal Medical Specialties, Inc., King of Prussia, Pa., 19406.

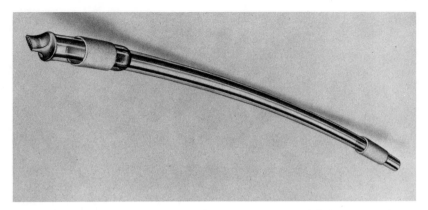

Fig. 9-26. Silicone rubber artificial Ureter. (*Courtesy Société des Usines Chimiques Rhone–Poulenc Départment Génie Médical*)

luster silicone coating to facilitate easy flow of urine from the kidneys to the bladder and to resist encrustation.

Some of the most dramatic results with silicone implants are found in the field of plastics and reconstructive surgery. Psychological problems often result from congenital or traumatic deformities and from underdeveloped external organs. When the physical condition is corrected surgically, one result can be a noticeable improvement in personality. Before silicone implant materials became available, the plastics surgeons used tissue from other parts of the body to augment the area they were correcting. This caused scars and disfiguration where the tissue was removed and the transplant tissue often did not survive in the new location. Because silicone implant materials are impervious to the action of the human organism and their consistency can be varied from the softness of the female breast through the consistency of various tones of muscle to the hardness of cartilage, the plastics surgeon today is able to solve almost any augmentation problem with silicones. Silicone rubber is available in preformed shapes, or in blocks which can be carved to the desired shape, for the reconstruction or augmentation of ears, noses, chins, and cheeks. Silicone orbital plates are available for repair of blowout fractures of the orbital floor—this is a fracture of the very thin section of the bone of the eye socket between the base of the socket and the sinus cavity, which can occur when the eye receives a direct blow, such as from a ball. The eyeball transmits pressure hydraulically around the socket, shattering it at its weakest point. As the affected eye sinks

toward the break, double vision (diplopia) results. Insertion of the
silicone rubber orbital floor corrects this condition in a relatively
quick and uncomplicated way. Silicone rubber finger joints reinforced with polyester fabric (Fig. 9-27) are responsible for the restor-
ation (Fig. 9-28) of many thousands of hands disfigured and made
practically useless by the crippling of arthritis. The polyester mesh
fabric reinforcement is incorporated into the one piece silicone rub-

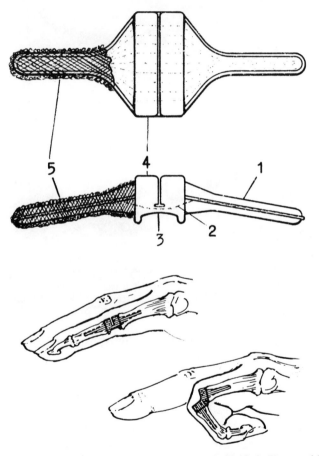

Fig. 9-27. Design features of Niebauer finger joint: 1. Molded silicone rubber integral
unit. 2. Polyester reinforcement molded in place. 3. Thin hinge section for easy flexing
and long flex life. 4. Buttress to prevent buckling of hinge when finger is in extension. 5.
Both stems are covered with polyester fabric to gain attachment to the bone through the in-
vasion of fibrous tissue. The sketch below shows the position of the prosthesis with the
finger extended and with it flexed. Artificial finger joints come in various sizes.

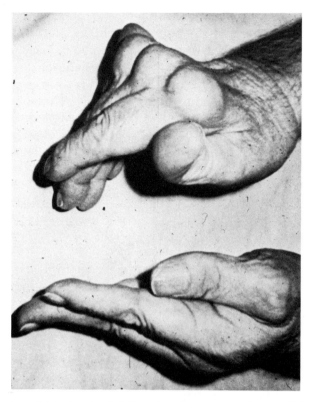

Fig. 9-28. An arthritic right hand deformed at the metacarpophalangeal joints. The left hand has been restored to normal appearance and near normal function by removal of the diseased joints and their replacement with Niebauer(TM) Cutter silicone rubber finger joint prostheses. (*Courtesy J. Leonard Goldner, M.D. Duke University Medical Center, and Cutter Laboratories, Inc., Berkeley, Calif.*)

ber joint at the time it is molded. This substantially increases the flex life of the thin hinge section and it also improves the tensile strength by over ten times. After molding, the stems of the joint have a double layer of polyester mesh fabric sewn to them. The silicone rubber alone would cause no appreciable reaction when placed into the intramedulary canal of the bone. Fibrous tissue infiltrates rapidly into polyester mesh, however, and in less than a month the prosthesis will be attached firmly to the bone.[13]

Other polyester reinforced silicone rubber prostheses include replacements for:

The trapesium joint of the thumb.
The humeral head at the shoulder.

The distal radius at the wrist.

The proximal radial head at the elbow.

The ulnar head at the wrist.

The metetarsophalangeal joint of the great toe.

The flexor tendons of the hand.

Probably the most popular of silicone implants is the mammary implant. It consists of a strong, thin, but very stretchy silicone rubber envelope filled with a clear silicone gel of the same general weight and texture as breast tissue. These implants come in many sizes and shapes, allowing the surgeon to achieve optimum cosmetic results. The surgical techniques used for inserting the implant under the breast tissue are relatively simple and are often performed under local anesthetic as an office procedure. The implant envelopes are usually fabricated by dip forming, a process much like the dip forming of latex products. In this case a solvent dispersion of approximately 15% catalyzed silicone rubber by weight is used. Several dips of the former are made until the desired thickness is obtained. Some envelopes are made as thin as .004 to .006 in. (.13 mm) in order to achieve exceptional softness in the finished prosthesis. Air drying is performed between each coat. After the final coat, the formers are placed in an oven to cure the envelope. The envelope is then stripped off the former, the opening made by the former mandrel is sealed, using a patch and adhesive of the same silicone rubber formulation as the envelope. The envelope is then ready to be filled with silicone gel. The proper volume of unvulcanized gel is introduced into the envelope under high pressure via a hypodermic needle. The hole made by the needle is then sealed with adhesive and the gel vulcanized by oven heating the implant.

The gel used is an addition reaction liquid silicone similar to that described on p. 148. The molecular end stoppers are controlled closely to allow just enough cross-linking on vulcanization to result in a very soft consistency but with enough cohesion that if the envelope were to be pierced in an automobile accident or in any other way, the gel would stay in position. The gel materials used, like all other medical-grade silicones, are ultra clean and subjected to an exhaustive series of biotests before they are released for this application.

Shapes other than the tear drop shown in Fig. 9-29, include plain rounds having various combinations of diameters and projections and

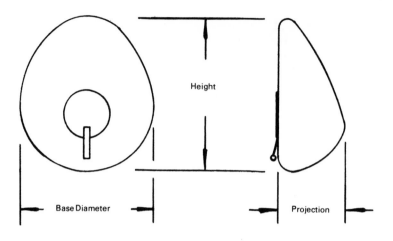

Volume*	Base Diameter	Height	Projection
180 cc	9.0 cm.	10.5 cm.	6.0 cm.
230 cc	9.5 cm.	11.2 cm.	6.5 cm.
265 cc	10.0 cm.	12.0 cm.	6.6 cm.
290 cc	10.5 cm.	12.5 cm.	7.0 cm.
325 cc	11.0 cm.	12.8 cm.	7.3 cm.

Fig. 9-29. Illustrates a popular style of prosthesis designed by Gilbert Snyder, M.D. The standard sizes available are given. (*Courtesy Medical Engineering Corp. Racine, Wis.*)

also devices with various degrees of auxillary prolongation, especially designed for use after subcutaneous (nonradical) mastectomy.

One type, the Surgitek-Dahl Adjustable Volume mammary implant* is designed so the gel is injected into the envelope after the envelope is inserted into the pocket created by the surgeon for the implant, consequently a much smaller incision need be made. This device is particularly advantageous where the patient has noticeable asymetry and different volumes are needed on each side. Some mammary implants are provided with patches attached to the back surface. The patches, made of open weave polyester fabric,** polyester felt, or perforated silicone sheet, allow fibrous tissue infiltration, thus affixing the device to the chest wall.

Silicone mammary implants which require a surgical procedure should not be confused with early injections of industrial grade silicone oils which led to many undesirable results and has been pro-

---

*U.S. Patent No. 3,883,902.
**Patent No. 3, 293,663

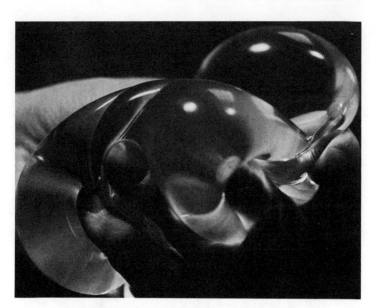

Fig. 9-30. A Surgitek® mammary implant is squeezed strenuously. The photo illustrates the soft, stretchy nature of the silicone materials, combined with their toughness and clarity. Their resistance to high temperatures allows for quick, simple steam sterilization techniques. Surgitek is a registered TM of Medical Engineering Corp. Racine, Wis. (*Photo by Paul Flagg*)

hibited by the Federal Food and Drug Administration since 1966.* Over 10 years of satisfactory experience with the implants, involving several hundred thousand cases, point to their efficacy. Not all silicone mammary prosthesis envelopes are filled with gel. A substantial number are filled with sterile saline solution, popularly referred to as inflatables. Although slightly heavier than the gel filled devices, they do have a livelier feel. They also have the advantage of being filled after the envelope is positioned in the surgically produced pocket, consequently the incision can be smaller and the volume adjusted until just the right aesthetic effect is achieved. On the other hand, if a break occurs in the envelope, the saline fill is rapidly absorbed by the body and the patient is faced with asymmetry until additional surgery and a replacement can be arranged. A Surgitek® self-sealing inflatable mammary implant contains a radio opaque self-sealing valve, which allows the addition or withdrawal of saline solution,

*FDA Consumer, May 1975

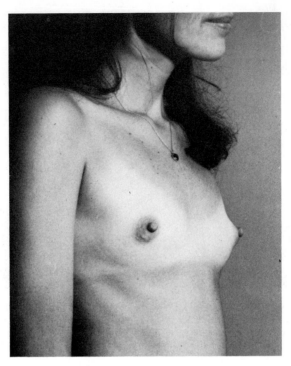

Fig. 9-31a. Pre-operation photo of a woman with mammary aplasia (underdeveloped breasts).

even after the device has been implanted, simply by inserting a sterile hypodermic needle through the skin and the valve and injecting or aspirating sterile saline with a syringe.

Other gel or liquid filled silicone rubber devices include testicular implants for cosmetic replacement of testicles removed because of disease, congenital conditions, or trauma, vaginal stents (forms) for the surgical reconstruction of the vagina, and penile implants for males who have erectile incompetence through disease, trauma, or psychological block.

Silicone rubber is being used to solve problems in the broad field of cannulae, catheters, and various other tubes for human and animal life support. An example is the Foley Catheter.* (Fig. 9-32.) Primarily used as a urinary drain, it incorporates a retention balloon near

*Fabrication methods of the Foley Catheter are described on pages 141 and 143.

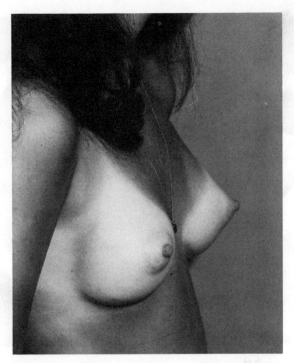

Fig. 9-31b. Post-operation photo showing augmentaion with the use of a pair of Surgitek-G. B. Snyder Mammary Implants. (Courtesy of the Williams & Wilkins Co., Baltimore, Md) Gilbert Snyder, "Planning and Augmentation Mamma Plasty," *Plastic and Reconstructive Surgery* **54**, (2), 133, Aug 1974)

the tip.   The balloon can be inflated or deflated with a syringe by inserting the tip of the syringe into a valve opening on the "Y" of the catheter.   Silicone rubber Foley Catheters minimize the inflamation of the urethral and bladder lining tissues, particularly where the drainage must continue for an extended period of time.   There is also a substantial reduction in the encrustation of the balloon wall and the inner drain wall by salts which precipitate from the urine and adhere tenaciously to non-silicone materials.   Encrustations on the balloon wall are particularly traumatic when a catheter is removed. The results of a tissue culture study, pictured in Fig. 9-33 are impressive proof of the negligible human tissue reactivity to silicone rubber.

Other silicone rubber drains include supra pubic catheters to drain the bladder through the abdominal wall instead of the urethra, T tubes used in conjunction with operations for gall stones (see p. 165),

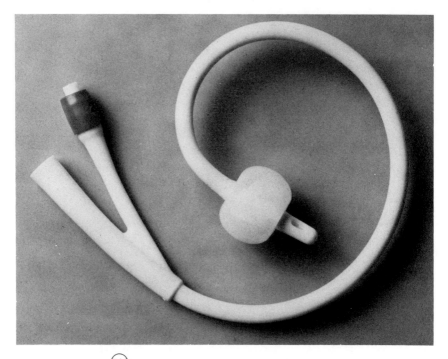

Fig. 9-32. Silicath⟨TM⟩ 100% silicone elastomer Foley catheter. SILICATH is a trademark of Trav. Labs. Inc. (*Courtesy of Travenol Laboratories, Inc.*)

chest drains, and many other special types for various patient conditions. All of these offer improved performance, increased patient comfort, easier removal, and lower long term costs because they can be resterilized in a matter of minutes by steam.

Anesthesiologists and ear, nose, and throat specialists, through the use of silicone rubber endotracheal tubes and tracheostomy tubes, are able to avoid much of the trauma to the delicate linings of the nasal cavity and trachea caused by the older types of stiff rubber and plastics tubes. Silicone tubes can be made extra soft and flexible and therefore are especially advantageous for nasal intubation. Such soft tubes may be reinforced with spiral wound stainless steel wire to prevent kinking when they are bent or flexed through sharp curves. Figure 9-34 illustrates a wire reinforced endotrachial tube. Serious nosebleeds (Epistaxis) can be stopped with a silicone rubber epistaxis catheter (Fig. 9-35). The silicone rubber balloons, which may be inflated separately, apply gentle pressure against the nasopharynx tissues. The open end tube allows for normal breathing through the nose while the catheter is in place. After the bleeding has been controlled, the balloons are deflated and the catheter easily withdrawn because of the non-stick characteristics of silicones.

Heart lung machines are applied as a temporary device to supply circulation and oxygenation of the blood in an extracorporeal circuit, chiefly during open heart surgery. The "heart" of the heart lung machine is a positive displacement roller-type pump of which there are two types; single roller and double roller. Special precision walled silicone rubber tubing is used in these pumps in order to get total occlusion without excessive pressure being applied to the blood cells. The most commonly used blood oxygenator is described as a bubble oxygenator. Oxygen is bubbled directly through the blood. The oxygenated blood is then run through a debubbling chamber in

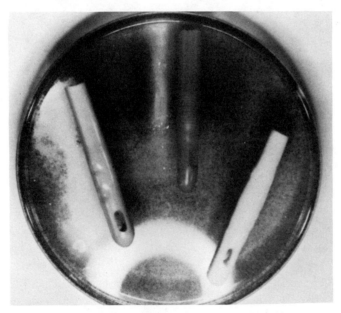

Fig. 9-33. Tissue culture study provides a sensitive indicator of biocompatibility. Foley catheters were placed in contact with a culture of living cells and, following a period of exposure, were rolled over to expose the area of contact. The large white area alongside the catheter at left is a zone of cell death; a narrower zone is also present alongside the rubber catheter (center). The white, 100% silicone catheter shows no deleterious effect on cell growth. (Courtesy of John T. Kimbell, Vice Chairman of the Board Baxter Laboratories, Inc. "Industrial considerations of biomaterials," *Medical Instrumentation*, 7: 150, 1973. Reprinted with permission.)

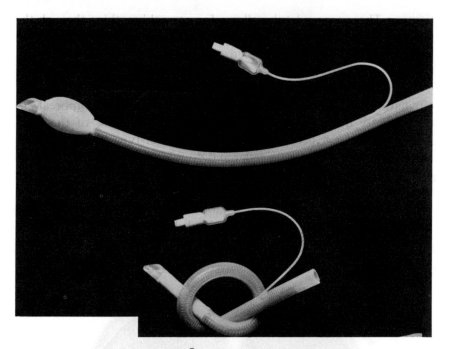

Fig. 9-34. Surgitek® wire reinforced endotrachial tube.

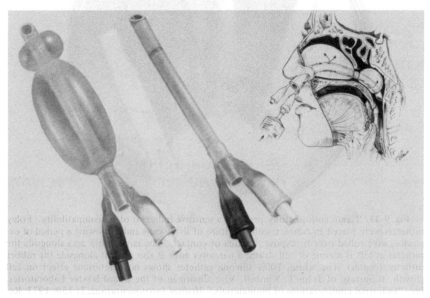

Fig. 9-35. Epistaxis catheter. (*Courtesy Medical Engineering Corporation*)

which the surface area has been treated with silicone defoaming fluid. Bubble type oxygenators are good for short term, extracorporial support only. They have been shown to damage blood elements and cause microaggregation as well as gas embolization, which cause various degrees of harm to vital organs.[14]

Silicone rubber can be fabricated into very thin, highly gas permeable,* membranes; consequently, it is an ideal blood-oxygen interface and when used in a membrane oxygenator, it prevents foaming of the blood and the denaturation of its protein fractions. Therefore, silicone membrane oxygenators may be used for long term support of patients with acute failure of pulmonary function and when used during open heart surgery, will diminish the need for adding homologous blood to the system, thereby decreasing the threat of infection or reaction. Silicone membrane may be produced in either capillary or sheet form. Membrane oxygenators presently in use incorporate the sheet form. Membrane sheet may be fabricated either by the extrusion or casting process. The extrusion of membrane sheet involves production of large diameter thin-walled tubing, which can be used either in the "lay flat" condition or can be slit to form a continuous sheet. The practical limitation on the thickness of membrane produced in this manner from currently available medical grade silicone rubbers is .003 to .004 in. (about $90 \mu m$). Much thinner membranes may be obtained by the casting process. Dr. T. Kolobow (Chief, Pulmonary and Cardiac Assist Devices, the Laboratory of Technical Development, National Heart and Lung Institute, N.I.H.) has reported the successful casting of membranes from silicone rubber dispersions as thin as .0004 in. ($9 \mu m$)![15] Kolobow used 10 to 20% dispersions of silicone rubber in toluol. The dispersion was centrifuged to eliminate undispersed silica filler aggregates which are the chief source of pinholes in the finished product. Such thin membranes must be reinforced with open weave or knitted fabric. The addition of the fabric leads to an uneven surface which can increase mixing of the blood phase as it flows over the membrane and thereby improve the gas transfer rate of the oxygenator.

The catalyst 2% by weight of 50% 2,4-dichlorobenzoyl peroxide in silicone oil is first dissolved in toluene and centrifuged to remove sediment before adding to the silicone rubber dispersion. The cata-

---

*See Table 9-2 for Gas Permeability Values.

TABLE 9-2. TYPICAL GAS PERMEABILITIES FOR DIMETHYL SILICONE MEMBRANE

$$1 \times 10^{-9} \frac{\text{cc's gas (RTP) cm thick}}{\text{sec.} \cdot \text{cm}^2 \cdot \text{cm Hg} \cdot \Delta^P}$$

Gas	Dimethyl Silicone	Gas	Dimethyl Silicone
H_2	55	$n-C_5H_{12}$	1670
He	30	$n-C_6H_{14}$	785
NH_3	500	$n-C_8H_{18}$	715
H_2O	3000	$n-C_{10}H_{22}$	360
CO	30	HCHO	925
N_2	25	CH_3OH	1160
NO	50	$COCl_2$	1250
O_2	50 to 60	Acetone	490
H_2S	840	Pyridine	1595
Ar	50	Benzene	900
CO_2	270 to 320	Phenol	1750
N_2O	365	Toluene	760
NO_2	635	Xe	171
SO_2	1250	CCl_4	5835
CS_2	7500	CH_2O	925
CH_4	80	C_2H_2	2200
C_2H_6	210	Freon 11	1290
C_2H_4	115	Freon 12	107
C_2H_2	2200	Freon 22	382
C_3H_8	340	Freon 114	211
$n-C_4H_{10}$	750	Freon 115	51

A handy "rule of thumb" for converting the above data to easily understood values, accurate within 10% follows:

$$1 \times 10^{-9} \frac{\text{cc's gas (RTP), cm thick}}{\text{sec, sq cm, cm Hg } \Delta^P}$$

is equal to

$$1 \frac{\text{liter, mil thick}}{\text{hr, sq yd, atm } \Delta^P} \quad \text{(actually 0.91)}$$

Thus an oxygen permeation of

$$50 \times 10^{-9} \frac{\text{cc's cm}}{\text{sec, sq cm, cm Hg } \Delta^P}$$

is approximately equal to 50 liters of oxygen per hour permeating through one square yard of 1-mil dimethyl silicone membrane with a 1 atm pressure difference across the membrane. Considering that a man at rest consumes only 300 cc O_2/min, one can see how devices separating useful amounts of gas can be constructed with 1-mil dimethyl silicone rubber film.

Adapted from General Electric Permaselective Membrane Bulletin GEA-8685A

lyzed dispersion is then cast on virgin aluminum foil and conveyed through an oven much like an HAV but having separate drying and curing sections. Because oxygen inhibits the surface cure of such a catalyst system, physical properties can be achieved only by curing in a nitrogen atmosphere. It is expected that the application of the new addition reaction type of silicone rubber compounds will overcome this difficulty.

The membrane oxygenator shown in Fig. 9-36 features a flat reinforced silicone rubber membrane envelope wound in a spiral coil

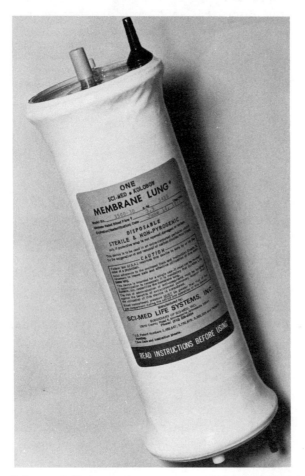

Fig. 9-36. Coil type of silicone membrane oxygenator. (*Courtesy Sci-Med Life Systems, Inc.*)

upon a polycarbonate spool, the entire unit is encased by a tight-fitting silicone rubber sleeve. The interior of the envelope is the gas compartment. A spacer screen inside this envelope permits gas flow.

Blood flows between turns of the envelope in a thin film. Oxygen from the gas compartment diffuses through the membrane into the blood stream. Carbon dioxide diffuses through the membrane into the gas compartment and is flushed from the lung.

A single pump is employed to establish blood flow through the lung and to the patient.

While silicone rubber has good antithrombogenic properties, there are applications for elastomeric devices in medicine where it lacks sufficient toughness. An artificial heart, for example, would require an extremely tough elastomer able to withstand millions upon millions of flexings without failure. There has been some interesting work done with block co-polymers of silicone with other tougher polymers in an attempt to bridge this gap. By reacting polyurethanes with polyorganosiloxanes having reactive end groups, scientists at AVCO Everett Research Laboratory have developed a whole family of materials which have a range of desirable physical properties as well as a significant degree of blood compatability.

One of these materials* is used in a temporary circulatory assist device called an Intra-Aortic Balloon pump. These pumps have been used successfully since late 1968. By 1974 about 8000 cardiac patients had been treated. The balloon is carried up to the aorta on the tip of a catheter, it is inflated and deflated in rhythm with the heart, improving the circulatory process until patients suffering from cardiogenic shock are past the critical stage, which may take as long as 7 to 12 days in some cases. At the 21st Annual Meeting of the American Society for Artificial Internal Organs, it was reported** that a calf had been kept alive for 78 days with an implanted, totally artificial heart, made essentially of silicone-polyurethane elastomer. During this period, the calf grew by about 66 lb (30 kg). A block co-polymer of silicone and polycarbonate developed by General Electric scientists looked promising. It was strong, perfectly clear, required no strengthening fillers, had good thrombogenic properties, and it was a thermoplastic. It could be extruded like a thermoplastic

---

*Avcothane—51.
**William J. Kolff, Division of Artificial Organs, College of Medicine, The University of Utah, Salt Lake City, Utah.

and was used to make membrane capillary. It could be heat or solvent sealed, not only to itself but to other materials such as polycarbonate and acrylic. Unfortunately, the immediate market has not been able to support it during its development stage. Such developments, however, help point the way to improved silicone materials for application to the health field. The market for medical silicones in 1977 is expected to reach a total of close to $35,000,000. world wide and should grow at an average annual rate of at least 20%.

MISCELLANEOUS

There are numerous other applications of silicone rubber which are dependant on its unique properties. The non-stick characteristic leads to its use in rolls for handling hot plastics in the production of film, embossing, laminating (see Figs. 9-37 and 9-38) or even the spreading and smoothing of hot tin over tin plate steel. Although there are elastomers with better damping properties than silicone

Fig. 9-37. Film laminator equipped with silicone rubber laminating rolls. Operation of lamination is diagrammatically illustrated in Fig. 9-38. (*Courtesy General Binding Corporation*)

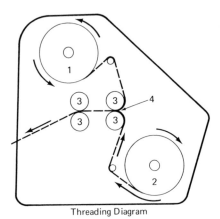

Threading Diagram

Fig. 9-38. Operating diagram of laminator shown in Fig. 9-37. 1. Upper feed roll of plastic laminating sheet. 2. Lower feed roll of plastic laminating sheet. 3. Silicone rubber laminating rolls (these may be seen being compression molded in Fig. 6-5). 4. Point of introduction of documents, drawings or photos. The laminators can be used to permanently protect pressed flowers.

rubber, wherever extremes of temperature are encountered, silicone rubber is the preferred choice for vibration and noise isolation. It exhibits little change in transmissibility or resonant frequency over the temperature range $-65°$ to $+300°F$ ($-55°C$ to $+150°C$). From large bonded to metal missile shock mounts to silicone rubber foam protected delicate electronic assemblies or even noise dampers on motorcycle mufflers, silicone gives the most dependable service.

For an extreme service mechanical application, it would be hard to beat the use of a molded silicone rubber collapsible core for the injection molding of thermoplastic parts having internal undercuts.[16] A mandrel which stretches the rubber core to full diameter during the molding cycle drops back during ejection, allowing the core to retract away from the inside walls of the plastics molding.

Silicone rubber-tetrafluorethylene composite films have been used as self-sealing diaphrams in the packaging of analytical chemical standards for gas chromatography.[17] Purity of the standard is assured because a sample can be withdrawn using a syringe equipped with a hypodermic needle to penetrate the self-sealing diaphragm without exposing the standard to either evaporation or contamination.

In foundry practice, permanent metal patterns for the production of shell molds have had molded-bonded in place silicone rubber undercut sections, such as thin fins, which flex, allowing the set shell mold to be removed from the pattern.

Fig. 9-39. Vibration absorption pad for liquid oxygen converter. A description of this pad and its performance was included on the original artwork (*Courtesy Bendix Corp.*) The Bendix Corporation* improves performance of liquid oxygen converters, and saves 53% through the use of Moxness Dimpled Vibration Absorption Pads. Vibration absorption was previously performed by a sponge rubber pad. The characteristics of sponge rubber vary greatly. Moxness dimpled pads have very exact vibration absorption characteristics and are lower in cost than sponge. Silicone Rubber exhibits very little change in transmissibility or resonant frequency over the temperature range –65° to +300°F. Coupled with its unparalleled resistance to ageing in this same temperature range–you are assured continuous high reliability. (*Courtesy Bendix Corp.*)

*Pioneer Central Division.

CONCLUSION

The phenomenal growth of silicone rubber applications and their surprising diversity is related to the complex of properties of the silicones–it is this complex of properties (including chemical) which will, with continued research and development effort, maintain the growth.

The rubber fabricator selects from an ever expanding variety of basic materials, allowing him more opportunity to achieve the distinct physical characteristic necessary for the optimum function of the rubber part or device he is manufacturing. Along with this, he will have greater flexibility as far as the process he uses is concerned. A case in point is the new addition reaction rubbers.* They eliminate the use of organic peroxides. They have a better extrusion and vulcanization rate and, in most applications, oven post cure is unnecessary. The new high strength addition reaction RTV rubbers should lead to even more revolutionary processing methods. The

*e.g., SE 4552 C & K 50 duro, SE 7 SE4772 C & K, 70 Duro Silicone Products Dept., General Electric.

chemical technology is available to make a hydrophylic silicone rubber. This could open up new areas in medicine and commercial applications. Contributing to the improved reliability, safety, and economy of appliances, autos, locomotives, planes, will increase the total value of finished silicone rubber goods over the 2 billion dollar mark by 1980.

References

1. *Rubber World*, April, 1976, p. 12.
2. Lynch, H. W. "Considerations in the Production of Silicone Rubber Insulation for Form Wound Coils," Annual Conference on the Application of Electrical Insulation, Washington, D.C., 1959.
3. Wick, Dr. M., "Boron Siloxane Elastomers," *Kunststoffe*, No. 8 (Aug. 1960).
4. Braley, Silas A., "The Use of Silicones in Plastic Surgery," *Plastic & Reconst. Surgery*, 51, No. 3 (Mar., 1973).
5. Jaques, L. B., Fidlar, E., Feldsted, E. T., and MacDonald, A. G., "Silicones and Blood Coagulation," *Canad. M.A.S.*, 55, 26–31 (1946).
6. McDougall, J. D. B., *Nature* (London), pp. 172, 174 (1953).
7. DeNicola, R. R., "Permanent Artificial Urethra," *J. Urology*, 63, 168 (1950).
8. Brown, J. B., Freyer, M. P., Randall, P., and Lu, M., "Silicones in Plastic Surgery," Laboratory and Clinical Investigations, A Preliminary Report. Plastic and Reconst. Surgery, 12, 374–376 (1953).
9. DiMant, S., "Silicone Rubber in Surgery," *Lancet*, 267, 533 (1954).
10. Marzoni, F. A., Upchurch, S. E., and Lambert, C. J., "An Experimental Study of Silicone as a Soft Tissue Substitute," *Plast. & Reconstr. Surg.*, 24, 600–608 (1959).
11. Speirs, A. C. and Blocksma, R., "New Implantable Silicone Rubbers," *Plastic & Reconst. Surgery*, 31, 166 (Feb. 1963).
12. Cholnoky, Tibor de, "Augmentation Mammaplasty, *Plastic & Reconst. Surg*," p. 577 (June 1970).
13. Niebauer, John J. and Landry, Richard M. Daron. "Silicone Prosthesis for the Metacarpalphalangeal and Interphalangeal Joints," The Hand (Journal of the British Society for Surgery of the Hand), 3, No. 1 (1971).
14. Lee, H. and Neville, K., "Handbook of Biomedical Plastics, Pasadena Technology Press, pp. 6–14.
15. Kolobow, T., Hayano, F., and Weathersby, P. K., "Dispersion-Casting Thin and Ultrathin Fabric-reinforced Silicone Rubber Membrane for Use in the Membrane Lung, *Medical Instrumentation*, 9, No. 3 (May–June, 1975).
16. *British Plastics* (Sept., 1971).
17. *Rubber World*, p. 33 (Aug., 1975).

APPENDIX TABLES

The Rubber Division of the American Chemical Society has officially adopted the International System of Units generally known as SI. English or cgs units are not permissible for oral presentations or for papers published in *Rubber Chemistry and Technology*. Detailed instructions for the use of SI are given by Conant (*Rubber Chem. Technol.* **48**,1(1975)) and in "Standard Metric Practice Guide" (ASTM desig. E380-72).

The SI system is a simplified one; for instance, 38 names are sufficient to quantify all physical properties (vs. 3½ pages of units listed in the *Encyclopedia Britannica*). There is no doubt that units currently in use in certain specialties, but not adequately provided for in the new system, will probably, be retained for sometime. Also, because of their convenience, units which SI prefers to avoid, but which lie close to the range of sizes of the properties we intend to measure, will be dropped with reluctance, slowly.

There are new units: A *newton* (N) is the force required to accelerate a mass of one kilogram by one metre per second per second. It is to be used for *all* expressions of force including weight. A *pascal* (Pa) is a pressure of one newton per square metre. It has a much smaller value than that used in most practical situations, kPa or MPa will be more commonly used. However in this text we have preferred to express pressure equivalents as kg/cm^2.

Following are the SI units with their symbols:

BASE UNITS IN THE SI SYSTEM

Quantity	Name	Symbol
Length	metre	m
Time	second	s
Mass	kilogram	kg
Electric current	ampere	A
Thermodynamic temperature	kelvin	K
Other temperature usages	degrees Celsius	°C
Luminous intensity	candela	cd
Amount of substance	mole	mol

Note that the symbol K for kelvin is used without a degree symbol.

243

DERIVED UNITS WITH SPECIAL NAMES

Quantity	Name	Symbol	Equivalent to
Electric conductance	siemens	S	A/V
Electric capacitance	farad	F	C/V
Electric potential	volt	V	W/A
Electric resistance	ohm	Ω	V/A
Energy, work, quantity of heat	joule	J	$N \cdot m$
Force	newton	N	$m \cdot kg/s^2$
Frequency	hertz	Hz	1/s
Illuminance	lux	lx	$cd \cdot sr/m^2$
Inductance	henry	H	Wb/A
Luminous flux	lumen	lm	$cd \cdot sr$
Magnetic flux	weber	Wb	$V \cdot s$
Magnetic flux density	tesla	T	Wb/m^2
Power, energy flux	watt	W	J/s
Pressure, stress	pascal	Pa	N/m^2
Quantity of electricity, electric charge	coulomb	C	$A \cdot s$

METRIC PREFIXES WHICH MAY BE USED
WITH ALL BASE SI UNITS

Symbol	Prefix	Equivalent to
T	tera	10^{12}
G	giga	10^9
M	mega	10^6
k	kilo	10^3
*h	hecto	10^2
*da	deka	10^1
*d	deci	10^{-1}
*c	centi	10^{-2}
m	milli	10^{-3}
μ	micro	10^{-6}
n	nano	10^{-9}
p	pico	10^{-12}
f	femto	10^{-15}
a	atto	10^{-18}

The prefixes are preferred to the powers of 10 to indicate orders of magnitude. The prefixes representing multiples of 1000 are also preferred. Those marked with an * should be avoided wherever possible. Double prefixes should not be used (pF not $\mu\mu$F).

TEMPERATURE CONVERSION TABLE

°C	°F	°C	°F	°C	°F	°C	°F
−115	−175	−5	+23.0	+35	+95.0	+175	+347
−110	−166	−4	24.8	36	96.8	180	356
−105	−157	−3	26.6	37	98.6	185	365
−100	−148	−2	28.4	38	100.4	190	374
−95	−139	−1	30.2	39	102.2	195	383
−90	−130	0	32.0	40	104.0	200	392
−85	−121	1	33.8	41	105.8	205	401
−80	−112	2	35.6	42	107.6	210	410
−75	−103	3	37.4	43	109.4	215	419
−70	−94	4	39.2	44	111.2	220	428
−65	−85	5	41.0	45	113.0	225	437
−60	−76	6	42.8	46	114.8	230	446
−55	−67	7	44.6	47	116.6	235	455
−50	−58	8	46.4	48	118.4	240	464
−45	−49	9	48.2	49	120.2	245	473
−40	−40.0	10	50.0	50	122.0	250	482
−38	−36.4	11	51.8	55	131.0	255	491
−36	−32.8	12	53.6	60	140.0	260	500
−34	−29.2	13	55.4	65	149.0	265	509
−32	−25.6	14	57.2	70	158.0	270	518
−30	−22.0	15	59.0	75	167.0	275	527
−28	−18.4	16	60.8	80	176.0	280	536
−26	−14.8	17	62.6	85	185.0	285	545
−24	−11.2	18	64.4	90	194.0	290	554
−22	−7.6	19	66.2	95	203.0	295	563
−20	−4.0	20	68.0	100	212.0	300	572
−19	−2.2	21	69.8	105	221.0	305	581
−18	−0.4	22	71.6	110	230.0	310	590
−17	+1.4	23	73.4	115	239.0	315	599
−16	3.2	24	75.2	120	248.0	320	608
−15	5.0	25	77.0	125	257.0	325	617
−14	6.8	26	78.8	130	266.0	330	626
−13	8.6	27	80.6	135	275.0	335	635
−12	10.4	28	82.4	140	284.0	340	644
−11	12.2	29	84.2	145	293.0	345	653
−10	14.0	30	86.0	150	302.0	350	662
−9	15.8	31	87.8	155	311.0	355	671
−8	17.6	32	89.6	160	320.0	360	680
−7	19.4	33	91.4	165	329.0	365	689
−6	21.2	34	92.2	170	338.0	370	698

Interpolation Values

°F	1.8	3.6	5.4	7.2	9.0	10.8	12.6	14.4	16.2
Diff	1	2	3	4	5	6	7	8	9
°C	.6	1.1	1.6	2.2	2.7	3.3	3.8	4.4	5

Note: For degrees kelvin (K) add 273.16 to °C.

(DENSITY) TO WEIGHT VOLUME RELATIONSHIP

Density $\times 10^{-3}$ = (g/cc) or (kg/1000 cc)	oz. (Avoir) per in.^{3}	g per in.^{3}	Pounds per 1000 in.^{3}
.90	.52	14.75	32.52
.95	.55	15.57	34.33
1.00	.58 (.57808)	16.39	36.14
1.05	.61	17.21	37.95
1.10	.64	18.03	39.76
1.15	.67	18.85	41.56
1.20	.69	19.67	43.37
1.25	.72	20.49	45.18
1.30	.75	21.31	46.99
1.35	.78	22.13	48.80
1.40	.81	22.95	50.61
1.45	.84	23.77	52.41
1.50	.87	24.59	54.22
1.55	.90	25.40	56.01
1.60	.93	26.22	57.82
1.65	.95	27.04	59.62
1.70	.98	27.86	61.43
1.75	1.01	28.68	63.24
1.80	1.04	29.50	65.05
1.85	1.07	30.32	66.86
1.90	1.10	31.14	68.66
1.95	1.13	31.96	70.47
2.00	1.16	32.78	72.28
2.05	1.19	33.60	74.09
2.10	1.21	34.42	75.90
2.15	1.24	35.24	77.70
2.20	1.27	36.06	79.51
2.25	1.30	36.88	81.32
2.30	1.33	37.70	83.13
2.35	1.36	38.52	84.94
2.40	1.39	39.34	86.75
2.45	1.42	40.16	88.55
2.50	1.45	40.98	90.36

[a]Identical for practical purposes.

CONVERSION TABLE FOR COMMONLY USED UNITS
ENGLISH–METRIC, METRIC–ENGLISH

Length

inch	X	25.4	= millimetre	X	.039 = inch
foot	X	.3	= metre	X	3.3 = foot
yard	X	.9	= metre	X	1.09 = yard

Area

$inch^2$	X	645.2	= $millimetre^2$	X	.002 = $inch^2$
$foot^2$	X	.09	= $metre^2$	X	10.76 = $foot^2$
$yard^2$	X	.84	= $metre^2$	X	1.2 = $yard^2$

Volume, Capacity

$inch^3$	X	16.39	= $centimetre^3$	X	.06 = $inch^3$
$foot^3$	X	.03	= $metre^3$	X	35.3 = $foot^3$
$yard^3$	X	.77	= $metre^3$	X	1.31 = $yard^3$
quart (U.S.)	X	.95	= litre	X	1.06 = quart (U.S.)
gallon (U.S.)	X	3.79	= litre	X	.26 = gallon (U.S.)
gallon (U.S.)	X	.004	= $metre^3$	X	264.17 = gallon (U.S.)

Mass

ounce (avoir.)	X	28.35	= gram	X	.035 = ounce (avoir.)
pound	X	.454	= kilogram	X	2.2 = pound
ton (U.S. short)	X	.907	= metric ton	X	1.1 = ton (U.S. short)

Density

lbs/ft^3	X	.016	= g/cm^3	X	62.43 = lbs/ft^3
lbs/ft^3	X	16.02	= kg/m^3	X	.06 = lbs/ft^3

Pressure

psi	X	.07	= kg/cm^2	X	14.22 = psi
psi	X	6.9	= kPa	X	.15 = psi

Energy and Power

ft-lb	X	1.36	= joule	X	.74 = ft-lb
horsepower (U.S.)	X	.746	= kW	X	1.34 = horsepower
Btu (Int.)	X	1055.1	= joule	X	.001 = Btu (Int.)
Btu/lb	X	2.33	= kJ/kg	X	.43 = Btu/lb
$Btu \cdot in/h \cdot ft^2 \cdot {}°F$	X	.144	= W/m-K	X	6.94 = $Btu \cdot in/h \cdot ft^2 \cdot {}°F$

Velocity

in/min	X	.42	= mm/s	X	2.36 = in/min
ft/sec	X	.305	= m/s	X	3.28 = ft/sec

TIME SAVING METRIC CONVERSION CHART

Inches to mm 1" = 25.4 mm

Inches	0	1	2	3	4	5	6	7	8	9	Inches
	mm	25.400	50.800	76.200	101.600	127.000	152.400	177.800	203.200	228.600	
0.015625	0.397	25.797	51.197	76.597	101.997	127.397	152.797	178.197	203.597	228.997	1/64
0.03125	0.794	26.194	51.594	76.994	102.394	127.794	153.194	178.594	203.994	229.394	1/32
0.046875	1.191	26.591	51.991	77.391	102.791	128.191	153.591	178.991	204.391	229.791	3/64
0.0625	1.588	26.988	52.388	77.788	103.188	128.588	153.988	179.388	204.788	230.188	1/16
0.078125	1.984	27.384	52.784	78.184	103.584	128.984	154.384	179.784	205.184	230.584	5/64
0.09375	2.381	27.781	53.181	78.581	103.981	129.381	154.781	180.181	205.581	230.981	3/32
0.109375	2.778	28.178	53.578	78.978	104.378	129.778	155.178	180.578	205.978	231.378	7/64
0.125	3.175	28.575	53.975	79.375	104.775	130.175	155.575	180.975	206.375	231.775	1/8
0.140625	3.572	28.972	54.372	79.772	105.172	130.572	155.972	181.372	206.772	232.172	9/64
0.15625	3.969	29.369	54.769	80.169	105.569	130.969	156.369	181.769	207.169	232.569	5/32
0.171875	4.366	29.766	55.166	80.566	105.966	131.366	156.766	182.166	207.566	232.966	11/64
0.1875	4.763	30.163	55.563	80.963	106.363	131.763	157.163	182.563	207.963	233.363	3/16
0.203125	5.159	30.559	55.959	81.359	106.759	132.159	157.559	182.959	208.359	233.759	13/64
0.21875	5.556	30.956	56.356	81.756	107.156	132.556	157.956	183.356	208.756	234.156	7/32
0.234375	5.953	31.353	56.753	82.153	107.553	132.953	158.353	183.753	209.153	234.553	15/64
0.25	6.350	31.750	57.150	82.550	107.950	133.350	158.750	184.150	209.550	234.950	1/4
0.265625	6.747	32.147	57.547	82.947	108.347	133.747	159.147	184.547	209.947	235.347	17/64
0.28125	7.144	32.544	57.944	83.344	108.744	134.144	159.544	184.944	210.344	235.744	9/32
0.296875	7.541	32.941	58.341	83.741	109.141	134.541	159.941	185.341	210.741	236.141	19/64
0.3125	7.938	33.338	58.738	84.138	109.538	134.938	160.338	185.738	211.138	236.538	5/16
0.328125	8.334	33.734	59.134	84.534	109.934	135.334	160.734	186.134	211.534	236.934	21/64
0.34375	8.731	34.131	59.531	84.931	110.331	135.731	161.131	186.531	211.931	237.331	11/32
0.359375	9.128	34.528	59.928	85.328	110.728	136.128	161.528	186.928	212.328	237.728	23/64
0.375	9.525	34.925	60.325	85.725	111.125	136.525	161.925	187.325	212.725	238.125	3/8
0.390625	9.922	35.322	60.722	86.122	111.522	136.922	162.322	187.722	213.122	238.522	25/64
0.40625	10.319	35.719	61.119	86.519	111.919	137.319	162.719	188.119	213.519	238.919	13/32
0.421875	10.716	36.116	61.516	86.916	112.316	137.716	163.116	188.516	213.916	239.316	27/64
0.4375	11.113	36.513	61.913	87.313	112.713	138.113	163.513	188.913	214.313	239.713	7/16
0.453125	11.509	36.909	62.309	87.709	113.109	138.509	163.909	189.309	214.709	240.109	29/64
0.46875	11.906	37.306	62.706	88.106	113.506	138.906	164.306	189.706	215.106	240.506	15/32

Fraction	Decimal	0	1	2	3	4	5	6	7	8	9
31/64	0.484375	12.303	37.703	63.103	88.503	113.903	139.303	164.703	190.103	215.503	240.903
1/2	0.5	12.700	38.100	63.500	88.900	114.300	139.700	165.100	190.500	215.900	241.300
33/64	0.515625	13.097	38.497	63.897	89.297	114.697	140.097	165.497	190.897	216.297	241.697
17/32	0.53125	13.494	38.894	64.294	89.694	115.094	140.494	165.894	191.294	216.694	242.094
35/64	0.546875	13.891	39.291	64.691	90.091	115.491	140.891	166.291	191.691	217.091	242.491
9/16	0.5625	14.288	39.688	65.088	90.488	115.888	141.288	166.688	192.088	217.488	242.888
37/64	0.578125	14.684	40.084	65.484	90.884	116.284	141.684	167.084	192.484	217.884	243.284
19/32	0.59375	15.081	40.481	65.881	91.281	116.681	142.081	167.481	192.881	218.281	243.681
39/64	0.609375	15.478	40.878	66.278	91.678	117.078	142.478	167.878	193.278	218.678	244.078
5/8	0.625	15.875	41.275	66.675	92.075	117.475	142.875	168.275	193.675	219.075	244.475
41/64	0.640625	16.272	41.672	67.072	92.472	117.872	143.272	168.672	194.072	219.472	244.872
21/32	0.65625	16.669	42.069	67.469	92.869	118.269	143.669	169.069	194.469	219.869	245.269
43/64	0.671875	17.066	42.466	67.866	93.266	118.666	144.066	169.466	194.866	220.266	245.666
11/16	0.6875	17.463	42.863	68.263	93.663	119.063	144.463	169.863	195.263	220.663	246.063
45/64	0.703125	17.859	43.259	68.659	94.059	119.459	144.859	170.259	195.659	221.059	246.459
23/32	0.71875	18.256	43.656	69.056	94.456	119.856	145.256	170.656	196.056	221.456	246.856
47/64	0.734375	18.653	44.053	69.453	94.853	120.253	145.653	171.053	196.453	221.853	247.253
3/4	0.75	19.050	44.450	69.850	95.250	120.650	146.050	171.450	196.850	222.250	247.650
49/64	0.765625	19.447	44.847	70.247	95.647	121.047	146.447	171.847	197.247	222.647	248.047
25/32	0.78125	19.844	45.244	70.644	96.044	121.444	146.844	172.244	197.644	223.044	248.444
51/64	0.796875	20.241	45.641	71.041	96.441	121.841	147.241	172.641	198.041	223.441	248.841
13/16	0.8125	20.638	46.038	71.438	96.838	122.238	147.638	173.038	198.438	223.838	249.238
53/64	0.828125	21.034	46.434	71.834	97.234	122.634	148.034	173.434	198.834	224.234	249.634
27/32	0.84375	21.431	46.831	72.231	97.631	123.031	148.431	173.831	199.231	224.631	250.031
55/64	0.859375	21.828	47.228	72.628	98.028	123.428	148.828	174.228	199.628	225.028	250.428
7/8	0.875	22.225	47.625	73.025	98.425	123.825	149.225	174.625	200.025	225.425	250.825
57/64	0.890625	22.622	48.022	73.422	98.822	124.222	149.622	175.022	200.422	225.822	251.222
29/32	0.90625	23.019	48.419	73.819	99.219	124.619	150.019	175.419	200.819	226.219	251.619
59/64	0.921875	23.416	48.816	74.216	99.616	125.016	150.416	175.816	201.216	226.616	252.016
15/16	0.9375	23.813	49.213	74.613	100.013	125.413	150.813	176.213	201.613	227.013	252.413
61/64	0.953125	24.206	49.609	75.009	100.409	125.809	151.209	176.609	202.009	227.409	252.809
31/32	0.96875	24.606	50.006	75.406	100.806	126.206	151.606	177.006	202.406	227.806	253.206
63/64	0.984375	25.003	50.403	75.803	101.203	126.603	152.003	177.403	202.803	228.203	253.603

INDEX

INDEX